Dreams of Peace and Freedom

Dreams of Peace and Freedom
Utopian Moments in the Twentieth Century

Jay Winter

Yale University Press   New Haven & London

Set in Adobe Minion type by Duke & Company, Devon, Pennsylvania.
Printed in the United States of America by Vail-Ballou Press, Binghamton, New York.

Library of Congress Cataloging-in-Publication Data
Winter, J. M.
Dreams of peace and freedom : utopian moments in the twentieth century / Jay Winter.
p.   cm.
Includes bibliographical references and index.
ISBN-13: 978-0-300-10665-7 (hardcover : alk. paper)
ISBN-10: 0-300-10665-3 (hardcover : alk. paper)
1. Utopias—History—20th century. 2. Utopian socialism—History—20th century.
I. Title.
HX806.W56 2006
335'.020904—dc22

                                                                    2006009254

A catalogue record for this book is available from the British Library.

The paper in this book meets the guidelines for permanence and durability of the Committee on
Production Guidelines for Book Longevity of the Council on Library Resources.

10   9   8   7   6   5   4   3   2   1

For Diana

On a day like today, my master William Faulkner said, "I decline to accept the end of man." I would fall unworthy of standing in this place that was his, if I were not fully aware that the colossal tragedy he refused to recognize thirty-two years ago is now, for the first time since the beginning of humanity, nothing more than a simple scientific possibility. Faced with this awesome reality that must have seemed a mere utopia through all of human time, we, the inventors of tales, who will believe anything, feel entitled to believe that it is not yet too late to engage in the creation of the opposite utopia. A new and sweeping utopia of life, where no one will be able to decide for others how they die, where love will prove true and happiness be possible, and where the races condemned to one hundred years of solitude will have, at last and forever, a second opportunity on earth.

—GABRIEL GARCÍA MÁRQUEZ, "The Solitude of Latin America," Nobel Prize Lecture, 8 December 1982

Contents

Acknowledgments

I owe a debt of no small magnitude to friends and colleagues who have taken the time to advise me about matters small and large related to this book. Antoine Prost has been a sure and steady friend and critic over decades. He told me what this book was about, and saved me from innumerable errors. So have Joanna Bourke, Emmanuel Sivan, Karin Tilmans, Ken Inglis, Don Lamm, Dov Jacobs, and Harvey Mendelsohn. All read the entire manuscript in its different manifestations, and all have saved me from many infelicities of style and interpretation. Diana Sorensen was a scrupulous and judicious commentator, always prepared to give generously of her time to help me refine a phrase or an idea or to avoid some Eurocentric trap. I know the book is better for their efforts, and I thank them all.

I have had the benefit too of the hospitality of many academic institutions. Yale is an ideal environment for scholars and teachers; it is hard to imagine a more congenial place for an historian to work. Colleagues and students in a number of university seminars helped me develop my ruminations over many years. The Huizinga Institute in Amsterdam provided me with a home to try out some of these ideas in a delightful master class. Thanks are due to Karin Tilmans and Frank van Vree for their warm hospitality.

The John Simon Guggenheim Foundation provided me with a Fellowship which enabled me to begin this project. The new *conservateur* of the Fondation Albert Kahn in Boulogne-Billancourt, M. Gilles Baud-Berthier, helped me finish it. Grants from the Griswold and Hilles funds at Yale were also of great assistance.

I have always written history by teaching it. To the multitude of students at Cambridge and Yale who unwittingly have contributed to this book, I offer my heartfelt thanks. Responsibility for any errors that remain is mine and mine alone.

Introduction
Minor Utopias and the Visionary Temperament

The history of the twentieth century is almost always written as the story of a series of catastrophes. Over four decades, I too have contributed to this apocalyptic vision of the recent past. Yet for many years I have felt that this dominant historical narrative is incomplete. This book is an attempt to fill in some of what has been left out. In particular, I want to tell the story of moments in the twentieth century when a very disparate group of people tried in their separate ways to imagine a radically better world. I term these people "minor utopians," to differentiate them from others whose "major utopias" wound up producing mountains of victims on a scale the world had rarely seen. "Major utopians" like Stalin and Hitler murdered millions of people in their efforts to transform the world.

No one can claim that historians of the twentieth century have spent too little time on Stalin and Hitler. Interest in their lives and crimes is perennial and, at times, alarmingly voyeuristic. Evil fascinates. Instead, I want to suggest that while attending to the shadow of the Holocaust and the Gulag, it is worthwhile to turn to more obscure facets of recent history of a very different character. Alongside the major utopians, there have been minor utopians, people who configured limited and much less sanguinary plans for partial transformations of the world. This book attempts to tell their story. It is not a continuous one, but a series of moments of possibility, of openings, of hopes and dreams rarely realized, but rarely forgotten as well. The contrast between major and minor utopias and utopians forms the core of this book. Let us consider what this distinction can yield.

The Utopian Tradition

"Utopia" is a term coined by Thomas More, the sixteenth-century English divine and statesman. The term means "no-place," not to be found on the map. It exists; we just haven't found it yet. The term is easily (and intentionally confused) with "Eutopia," the place of happiness. This homonym suggests something about what utopia is, and also the playfulness of its inventors.[1] By speculating on the empty spaces on the map, we are in a position to define better the ones we know, or think we know.

Since the time of Thomas More, hundreds of literary utopias have been conjured up.[2] In the twentieth century, there have been many of them, and of their mirror image, "dystopias," nightmares about a place or a time where absolute evil has triumphed.[3] Through George Orwell's *1984* (1948) or Margaret Atwood's *A Handmaid's Tale* (1985), to take two well-known examples, millions of readers have come to know about utopia and its perversions. Science fiction has utopian elements, though it sometimes substitutes the ambiance of the exotic for social thought.

Utopia is more than a literary phenomenon. It has been the core, the driving force, of many political and social movements. Many people in this century have believed that fundamental elements of conflict and misery can be eliminated once and for all through social action. They imagine not only piecemeal reform, but root and branch transformations. The founders of the kibbutz movement in Israel were utopians; their achievements are matters of dispute. Vast projects of urban development have emerged from utopian visions; the results have been mixed at best.[4] There is no doubt, though, about the outcome of other utopian projects. Under communism and under fascism, gigantic plans for the transformation of society through murderous social engineering and the elimination of internal enemies produced massive suffering and injustice on a scale which beggars description.

It would be a mistake, though, to see the utopian temperament as a form of derangement, a mild or severe mental disorder leading inevitably to ruin. Religious movements have always harbored utopian elements, though only occasionally have they dominated the mainstream, as in Iran after the fall of the Shah in 1978.[5] Ecological groups believe in saving the world in another way, just as the nuclear disarmament movement believed in the 1960s and 1980s. Their hopes are directed toward averting catastrophe rather than toward constructing an ideal society. But the first is, of course, a precondition for the second.

Utopia is a discourse in two contradictory parts. First, it is a narrative about discontinuity. It is a story through which men and women imagine a radical act of disjunction, enabling people, acting freely and in concert with others, to realize the creative potential imprisoned by the way we live now. But secondly, since the narrative is written by men and women rooted in contemporary conditions and language, it inevitably shows where they are, even as it describes where they want to be. Utopias force us to face the fact that we do not live there; we live here, and we cannot but use the language of the here and now in all our imaginings.[6] That is why the work of the imagination is such a powerful entry point into the historical contradictions of this (or any other) period.

Utopia, in sum, is a fantasy about the limits of the possible, a staging of what we take for granted, what is left unsaid about our current social conventions and political cultures. Those who expose these silences, often playfully, begin to disturb the contradictions in the way we live.[7] As Paul Ricoeur has argued, "from this 'no place' an exterior glance is cast on our reality, which suddenly looks strange, nothing more being taken for granted."[8] What is made strange is made contingent, and what is contingent need not last forever.

Minor Utopias

This book is not a history of twentieth-century utopias, though it is important to recognize the enduring character of the utopian tradition. As I have noted, the term "utopia" is now thoroughly discredited by contamination through association with the crimes of the great killers of the twentieth century. Major utopias of that kind have indeed been constructed by politicians turned gardeners, in Bauman's phrase, "weeders" of the undesirable elements in our world. Major utopians uproot, cleanse, transform, exterminate.[9] Their totalitarian visions, and their commitment to the ruthless removal from the world of those malevolent elements blocking the path to a beneficent future, are at the heart of what I term "major utopias."

In this book, I want to explore a different cultural and political space, one sketched out in 1982 by Gabriel García Márquez in his speech accepting the Nobel Prize for Literature. In Stockholm, standing in the place of his master William Faulkner, who had received the prize three decades before, García Márquez reflected on Faulkner's refusal to accept annihilation as man's inevitable fate: "Faced with this awesome reality that must have seemed a mere utopia through all of human time, we, the inventors of tales, who will believe anything, feel entitled to believe that it is not yet too late to engage in the creation of the opposite utopia. A new and sweeping utopia of life, where no one will be able to decide for others how they die, where love will prove true and happiness be possible, and where the races condemned to one hundred years of solitude will have, at last and forever, a second opportunity on earth."[10]

In light of García Márquez's plea, I will tell the story of what may be termed "minor utopias," imaginings of liberation usually on a smaller scale, without the grandiose pretensions or the almost unimaginable hubris and cruelties of the "major" utopian projects. In each chapter, I analyze visions of partial transformations, of pathways out of the ravages of war, or away from the indignities of the abuse of human rights. Such imaginings are powerful and sketch out a world very different from the one we live in, but from which not all social conflict or all oppression has been eliminated.

This notion of minor utopias is illustrated in Tom Stoppard's recent theatrical trilogy presenting the ideas of the nineteenth-century Russian thinker Alexander Herzen. The central character, Herzen urges his son (and the rest of us) to sail toward the "coast of utopia," but never to imagine that there is some holy grail to be found inland.[11] Herzen, in this sense, was indeed a minor utopian; a visionary without a blueprint of a future society in which social conflict no longer existed.

What distinguishes nineteenth-century from twentieth-century visions is the social context in which each unfolded. Many utopian projects of the nineteenth century were constructed against the backdrop of the upheavals associated with the French and the industrial revolutions, and the social movements spawned by each. In the twentieth century, some visionaries followed in this tradition, but others took as their point of departure a different set of upheavals arising from collective violence. It is the emergence of total war which has set the twentieth century apart and which has given to many twentieth-century visions their particular coloration and urgency. The complex and subtle dialectic between minor utopian visions and massive collective violence is at the core of this book.

Languages of Social Transformation

In the early part of the twentieth century, projects of social transformation centered around nation or social class as the carriers of a better future. In the second half of the century, such visions had different inflections and emphases. From the 1940s, and increasingly after 1968, minor utopians have focused less on nation and social class and more on civil society and human rights.

This contrast must be qualified. To be sure, since the 1960s the struggle for civil rights has been central to the history of the United States, Northern Ireland, and South Africa from the 1960s. But alongside this well-known trajectory was another one. The dream of a new human rights regime announced by René Cassin in 1948 (see chapter 4) was about the individual, not as a member of a social class or nation, but as the common denominator of humanity. Cassin spoke for human rights, not for civil rights. The notion of *Autogestion,* or local autonomy, central to the events of 1968 (see chapter 5), originated within the Marxist tradition, but quickly moved outside of it, to privilege ecological, feminist, and transnational perspectives developed on the local and urban, rather than exclusively on the national level. The quest for what is termed "global citizenship," so evident in the 1990s and after (see chapter 6), emerges directly out of the struggle for human rights and humanitarian action.

While social thinking in the early and in the later twentieth century overlap, the discourse of social transformation has shifted. At the end of the century, the quest for world peace had lost its mobilizing force. So had the Marxist tradition. Ebullient capitalism still had its advocates, but the gap between "north" and "south," and between rich and poor within the "north" has made capitalist triumphalism look threadbare at best. The early years of the twenty-first century seem light years away from the optimism of the Paris expo of 1900. Too much blood and too much suffering separate the two. In the space vacated by these earlier projects, late-twentieth-century visionaries adopted a more limited, decentered, eclectic, transnational approach, which paradoxically aims at the construction of "global civil society."

Critical Distance

This is not a book of advocacy. One danger of this kind of cultural history is the adoption of an uncritical stance towards thinkers and their projects. Hagiography serves no useful purpose, even though some of the figures whose ideas are surveyed in this book lived admirable lives. In exploring these visions of possible futures, I draw on two perspectives.

The first is a variation of Marx's dictum that men make history but not in the way they think they do, not under the conditions of their choosing. Visionaries imagine alternative forms of social life, but not in the way they think they do. They frequently carry within their thinking the very contradictions they seek to supersede. Thus Woodrow Wilson's notion of self-determination never escaped from the imperialist setting which he both decried and embodied. The 1937 Paris expo was a paean to the creative power of science. But this vision collided with the manifestly destructive power of science in the Spanish Civil War. The Basque city of Guernica was obliterated by bombing in the weeks preceding the opening of the expo, and this inspired Picasso's contribution to the Spanish pavilion. The world's fair of 1937 contained both imaginings of peace and depictions of war. This book explores the ways in which the visions of minor utopians are grounded in the here and now. This precludes detaching these visions from the prejudices, assumptions, and contradictory behavior of the individuals and social groups which produce them. Envisioning the future is frequently a way of trying to break with the past while unwittingly revealing the hold of the present on the way we think and live.

The second critical standpoint derives from the work of the historian Reinhard Koselleck. His interpretation of historical thinking creates a useful framework for the study of social visions in a time of collective violence. He posits a binary and asymmetrical relationship between what he terms the space of experience, or what appears to be the momentum of past events, and the horizon of expectations, or how we project that experience into the future. Experience is finite; expectations are infinite. There is an asymmetry, therefore, between what he terms the "past in the present" and the differently configured "future in the present"; the tension between the two generates our understanding of historical time.[12]

It may be useful to adapt this framework for our purposes. At certain moments, the link between past and future is fractured. War and other forms of collective violence destroy even the semblance of a link between the two. The space of experience is radically altered, and no one can predict the trajectory of future events. We can no longer see the antebellum horizon of expectations. The two world wars were among these radical disruptions; so were wars of decolonization, such as those in Algeria and Vietnam. So were civil wars and internal convulsions such as the ones which destroyed Yugoslavia in the early 1990s. So, it seems, was 9/11. Not all such events radically destabilize our sense of historical continuity. The resilience of some social groups or religious communities shields them at times from these ruptures. Others are not so fortunate. In some places and at some times of social turbulence or disturbance, a gap opens up between experience and expectations. In this domain, minor utopias emerge.

Many visionary projects arise in a period of collective violence. This pattern is evident throughout this book. The First World War led directly to the assertion of self-determination as a principle of what was intended to be a new international order, one that held the promise of outlawing war. The rise of fascism and the convulsions of the Spanish Civil War precipitated reflections whose traces are evident in the 1937 Paris expo. The Second World War and its crimes against humanity form the backdrop for the drafting of the Universal Declaration of Human Rights. It is impossible to separate the events of 1968 from the convulsions surrounding the war in Algeria, which ended in 1964, and the war in Vietnam, about to enter its most deadly phase. And the viciousness of the civil war in the Balkans, genocide in Cambodia and Rwanda, and domestic repression in Latin America were at the center of many of the issues elaborated in the 1990s and after regarding crimes against humanity. The following chapters tell very different stories, but violence casts a shadow on each of them.[13]

Principles of Selection

Why have I chosen the years 1900, 1919, 1937, 1948, 1968, and 1992 to bracket the chapters of this book? Some dates are unavoidable: 1919 and 1968 are determined by political events of the first magnitude. But others are more arbitrary: 1937 was the eve of the Second World War, but the nations presenting displays of their national achievements in the Exposition Internationale des Arts et Métiers de la Vie Moderne in Paris in that year had other agendas. Their visions of the future contrasted bleakly with the harsh realities of the time. Similarly, the framing of the Universal Declaration of Human Rights in 1948 was so close to the liberation of the death camps of the Second World War that the document may appear to be an act of defiance more than an advance in international affairs. But the contradictory or counterintuitive character of these visions is part of their intrinsic interest. I have chosen 1992 rather than 1989 in part because the visions of global citizenship which emerged at the beginning of the 1990s so clearly echoed and transformed elements present in the celebration of globalization in the Paris expo of 1900 which we survey in the first chapter. In addition, the literature on the fall of the Soviet empire and the communist era is still too marked by Western triumphalism to permit a judicious account of that critical moment in twentieth-century history. Perhaps it would be wise to approach 1989 with the same hesitancy as Chou En-lai did when, in 1970, Henry Kissinger asked him what he thought of the French Revolution. Too soon to tell, was the response.

The six episodes I explore here tell neither an exclusive nor a comprehensive story. But together they deserve to be part of any considered history of the twentieth century. The first three chapters deal with visions of peace, based on the centrality of nation and social class; the latter three describe visions of liberation, some collective, some individual, based on the centrality of civil society and human rights. It is only by placing these visions alongside the history of catastrophe that we can get a fuller sense of the turbulence and the tragedy of the historical period—what Eric Hobsbawm has felicitously termed "the age of extremes"—in which we live.[14] If Oscar Wilde were alive today, perhaps he would have offered a slight variation on one of his aphorisms: "A map of the world that does not include [minor] utopias is not worth even glancing at, for it leaves out the one country at which Humanity is always landing. And when Humanity lands there, it looks out, and, seeing a better country, sets sail."[15]

1 1900

The Face of Humanity and Visions of Peace

In 1900, the most compelling question writers, artists, politicians, and other thoughtful people addressed was, what would the new century bring? We, in our more cynical times, might be surprised at how positive such conjectures were.[1] To be sure, there were prophets of doom, like H. G. Wells, who conjured up a technological nightmare of a *War of the Worlds* in 1898.[2] The Polish-born novelist Joseph Conrad also brought a pessimist's gaze to the future of the European project in his *Heart of Darkness,* published first in serialized form in 1899. But these voices were in the minority. In many public displays and private meditations, most imaginings of the twentieth century celebrated progress on the global scale and projected it optimistically into the foreseeable future. The key to their varied futures was peace.

I will consider three such visions of peace in this chapter. The first was the project of the Parisian banker, Albert Kahn, to photograph the whole world, and to preserve it in Paris for all to see as an Archive of the Planet. This initiative was more than one man's crusade. Kahn was one of many who mobilized photography in order to show the overwhelming affinities between countries and cultures ostensibly hostile to each other. War from this point of view was an unnecessary and damaging family quarrel. The second is the cornucopia presented in the great world's fair of 1900 in Paris, a glittering visual encomium to European ingenuity and its spread through education and commerce to every corner of the globe. The liberal nineteenth-century message was clear: out of trade came a peaceful and beneficent future. War was bad for commerce, as generations of bankers and businessmen tirelessly affirmed. The third vision is that of the socialist Second International, and in particular that of its leader, Jean Jaurès. His quest for social justice and peace described a very different perspective from that of the organizers of the Paris expo or of Kahn's *Archives de la planète.* To Jaurès, peace would emerge when the voice of working people entered the conversation about international conflict. When they would gain the right to speak, they would expose war as a capitalist cabal, and force politicians to defend the well-being of the many rather than the interests of the few.

All three of these visions of the twentieth century were global in scale. Those who live at the beginning of the twenty-first century should pause before claiming globalization as a recent or unprecedented phenomenon. Who in 1900 could miss the framing of the world by imperial powers, armed with the latest technology?[3] The decade from 1895 to 1905 was marked by armed conflict in every continent. In 1895, Japan defeated China. Following her defeat, China was powerless to stop the informal dismemberment of the empire by Western interests representing Austria, France, Germany, Britain, Japan, and Russia. Then the United States joined in following the suppression of a violent nationalist revolt known as the Boxer Rebellion. It was put down with a special ferocity. "Bear yourselves like the Huns of Attila," was the instruction

Kaiser Wilhelm II gave his troops en route to China. They did so, killing, according to some estimates, over 100,000 Chinese in reprisals.

In 1896, perhaps 300,000 Armenians were massacred in the Ottoman Empire, as a result of the direct orders of Sultan Abdul Hamid, whose troops were engaged in war with Greece a year later. Between 1898 and 1903, as many as 100,000 people were killed in civil war in Colombia. In 1898, American forces seized the Philippines, Cuba, Puerto Rico, and Guam during hostilities with Spain. The United States then annexed Hawaii. Between 1899 and 1902 the British army fought a difficult guerrilla war to overcome a smaller band of Boer settlers in South Africa. The British ultimately succeeded but did so in part by attacking civilians; Boer families were incarcerated in what were termed "concentration camps," rife with disease. An uprising known as the Herero revolt by several Bantu-speaking tribes in German West Africa was quelled by German troops in 1904–6. Estimates vary, but it is possible that 80 percent of the Herero population was killed in the conflict. In February 1904, the Japanese attacked the Russian navy at Port Arthur in China; the Japanese forces prevailed in subsequent fighting, establishing Japan as a world power.

It is against the backdrop of worldwide violence that the dreams of peace and of a harmonious new century we examine in this chapter must be set. All three of the visions prophesied peace; all three underestimated the extent to which imperial competition and conflict confounded their prophesies and made war and mass violence, not peace, the dominant feature of twentieth-century history.

Albert Kahn and the Face of Humanity

Before 1914 transformed both the landscape of the planet and the language we use to understand it, pacifism was an international force. On 4 September 1900, the first Hague Convention on the peaceful resolution of international conflicts entered into force. Throughout the world, many groups declared their wholehearted commitment to the idea that war could be done away with, that it could be made into an anachronism. One man who shared this dream, this hypothesis about the possibility of limiting recourse to violence in international affairs, was the French banker Albert Kahn.

Kahn was a self-made man. He was an Alsatian Jew, born in 1860, when the two eastern provinces of France were under German rule. At age 16 he decided to seek his fortune in Paris. He was a shy man, something of a recluse, who remained a bachelor throughout his life. In the French capital he found employment as an apprentice in the banking house of a family friend. His work for the private bank of Eduard Goudchaux occupied him by day; by night, he studied philosophy. His tutor, Henri Bergson, was Jewish, too, and just a year older. Their friendship lasted long after both became famous, Kahn in the world of international finance, and Bergson in the field of philosophy. Bergson was the first Jew elected to the Académie Française. Both had a vision of the transformative power of knowledge. Their common interests and aspirations, shared in conversation over 60 years, marked a profound friendship.[4]

The two facets of his interest—finance and philosophy—fused in the field of international banking. His breakthrough came when he went to South Africa to help secure options for gold and diamond mining. Financing the De Beers and Rhodes operations was a gamble that paid off and handsomely. In 1897, at the age of 37, he became a partner in the bank.

South African interests were only the beginning of Kahn's work in international banking. After the turn of the century his attention turned to Japan. There he found a second home, and worked both as financier and as economic adviser in the Imperial Court. Here, too, he made friendships that lasted throughout the following turbulent decades.

It is in this period of phenomenally successful business activity, and the accumulation of a fortune in its wake, that Kahn apparently conceived of his life's work. His aim was to stay in the shadows, discreetly but firmly acting as the éminence grise behind a host of initiatives in the cause of world peace.[5] Was it the vision of economic growth in South Africa and Japan that led him to see the need to link prosperity to perpetual peace? (For without peace, Kahn believed, economic development was meaningless.) Was it the racial exploitation behind the hugely profitable extractive industries in the Cape, or the bloodshed of the Russo-Japanese war, that led him to fear for the future if productive forces were not harnessed to peaceful ends? Or, perhaps, did he suffer a crise de conscience in the 1890s, which led him to reconsider his beliefs and his mission in life?[6] We will never know for sure, since this intensely private man left little correspondence to posterity. But his fleeting comments, dictated after his economic ruin in the stock market crash of 1929, disclose a man with a mystical turn of mind. "I am convinced there is a pattern to history, a pathway leading from narrow particularism to universality," he wrote in one of his reveries.[7] He had a metaphysician's temperament, a taste for philosophical speculation about the quest for peace to which he returned throughout his later life. Kahn committed his fortune to educating people who lived in confined national frameworks to see the challenges and dangers of a world much more unified than ever before.[8]

From a small town in Alsace to Paris to Capetown to Tokyo: the trajectory Albert Kahn followed at the turn of the century was truly global. Once established in the world of international banking, Kahn saw the need to break down the insularity of European attitudes about the non-European world. To this end he began to sponsor a number of ventures to send young men and women on voyages of discovery. In 1898 he set up a scholarship program titled "Bourses de voyage autour du monde" (Scholarships for Trips Around the World). This was intended to widen the horizons of young men (and, later, young women) who had passed the *Agrégation,* the entrance exam into the field of university teaching, and who were *professeurs* at *lycées,* elite high schools, throughout France. Many would go on to careers in scholarship, politics, or public administration.

This benefaction, given to the University of Paris, and administered by the Ecole normale supérieure, came four years before the establishment of Cecil Rhodes's scholarships at Oxford. Both are the gifts of men whose fortunes came out of South African mining; both had a sense that great wealth carried the responsibility of using it to benefit the world. Both had a mystical element in their outlook. And both funded elite programs, aimed at the creation of an internationally minded group of future leaders. But consider the central difference. Rhodes wanted to bring young men from areas of white settlement (and from Germany) to what he saw as the "seat" of civilization, Oxford, whereas Kahn wanted to send his *boursiers* away from Paris. They were to be citizens of the world, not future proconsuls of an empire.[9]

Kahn made his views clear in the note he sent to the rector of the University of Paris setting up the scheme. Kahn believed firmly in meritocratic democracy; those who passed the Agrégation were selected not on social criteria but solely on intellectual merit. And yet, what Kahn feared was that those trained to teach the next generation would do so "without contact with life." This personal, direct engagement was the aim of the scholarships, funding those who

> would see that their interests should be directed towards the benefit of humanity as a whole. For this they need more than abstract knowledge, but contact with the world. This contact will show the variety of experience and contradict simple formulae about the world.
>
> We have to find a way to take note of the exact role the diverse nations play on the face of the globe, we need to determine their diverse aspirations, see where they lead, if they tend towards violent shocks or if they can be reconciled. Abstract discussion can only provide possibilities and probabilities, a contact with the world provides firm, vibrant, and communicable impressions.

Thus a small group of highly talented and well-educated people—the future "intellectual and moral elite of the nation," but who were "not old enough to have fixed ideas"—would come "to see with their eyes the different faces of the world over 15 months." They would thereby learn "something about social life in diverse parts of the world, how governments form public spirit, the means used to develop the genius of each nation, and how in particular domains, particular groups realize their potential."[10]

In its first two years, this program provided 15 scholarships of 15,000 francs each. The candidates had to have a clean bill of health and a working knowledge of English. They could choose different itineraries, but the preferred one was the following: Paris, London, Liverpool, Marseilles, Athens, Constantinople, Beirut, Damascus, Cairo, Ceylon, India, Burma, Singapore, Indonesia, Vietnam, Hong Kong, China, Japan, United States, Germany, Russia—Saint Petersburg, Moscow, Odessa—then Budapest, Vienna, and back to Paris, all in 15 months. They had to travel alone or in groups of two, and keep in contact with both French consulates and the Ecole normale supérieure.[11]

Eight years later, the program yielded a society—the "Cercle autour du monde," in which young people, fresh from their exploration of what Henri Bergson termed "the great book of the world," and distinguished older men and women would meet for conversation and, for the young, inspiration.[12] "I have antennae," Kahn noted, "I study events and then find personalities called to higher destinies."[13] Among the notables addressing this society of internationalists were the sculptor Auguste Rodin, the Indian philosopher Rabindranath Tagore, the Spanish man of letters Miguel de Unamuno, the British imperial writer Rudyard Kipling, the French socialist leader Jean Jaurès, and the future president of the French Republic Raymond Poincaré. A second center for such cosmopolitan encounters was opened in Tokyo in 1906.[14]

Kahn's belief in meritocracy did not diminish the inherent elitism of this project, which fitted perfectly into both the Third Republic and the velvet-gloved world of pre-1914 international diplomacy. To find those who mattered, and to convince them to see the world beyond the confines of their national and intellectual boundaries, Kahn sponsored a range of initiatives. Perhaps the most daring of them all was photographic and cinematographic in character. He called it "Les Archives de la planète" (Archives of the Planet).[15]

Kahn's archive was a collection of photographic and cinematographic images of many parts of the world. It is enormous, encompassing 75,000 still photographs and over 450 kilometers of film. In its entirety it provided a way of visualizing the world as a whole. It is important to highlight the Victorian pacifist core of this project, and its affinities with other liberal visions. Here I speak of a European variant of British liberalism, the liberalism of Victorian parliamentarians like Richard Cobden and John Bright, men who were persuaded that free trade was the fundamental source of the amity of nations. The more trade, the less likelihood that an increasingly interdependent world would destroy itself: such was the faith of several generations of free trade pacifists.

Kahn was one of them, but he added a darker note of skepticism and anxiety. Kahn was in Paris during the great expo of 1900, which I shall describe later in this chapter. Along with millions of others, he saw the new and varied machinery of progress which were on spectacular display. But Kahn knew as well that these engines of construction and creativity could all too easily become engines of destruction and disaster. Kahn was firmly convinced that knowledge of the world would place constraints on the exercise of power in it. To this end, he was prepared to devote his fortune to a unique kind of *Exposition universelle*.

This one would be fixed—in his estate on the outskirts of Paris. His collection of images would have a permanent home. In the mansion and gardens Kahn created and occupied in Boulogne-Billancourt, a suburb of Paris, from 1894, they would be displayed to all comers. There anyone could make a visual journey around the world.

Kahn believed that the collection and analysis of images was a matter of great importance for philosophy and for the emerging social sciences, in particular for geography. To see is to know, he believed, and to know is to better predict the future. This essentially positivist creed took on many different forms, but one was through the study of geography. This was an entirely Republican choice. Fashion had it that the political right in France sent its sons to study the classics; the left preferred geography, and through the study of the environment and of everyday life this led to an appreciation, a celebration of the people of France, the citizens of *la France profonde*.

The origins of the project lie in discussions between Kahn and his erstwhile tutor, Henri Bergson.[16] From 1900, he held a chair in the prestigious Collège de France, and in 1907 he published his most widely read book in moral philosophy, *Creative Evolution*. He would go on to win a Nobel Prize for Literature. At the time the Archives de la planète were launched, he was already a public figure, a symbol of the way the study of philosophy and the search for tolerance were one. Here Bergson and Kahn were entirely in agreement. There is a mixture of the very particular and the completely universal in their vision, and the Archives de la planète became a kind of visualization of the assimilated Jewish outlook both men shared. No longer shackled by the constraints of orthodox belief, they still held firmly to the ethical core of the message of the prophets. On one occasion Kahn stated firmly, "Je suis juif, profondément juif" (I am Jewish, profoundly Jewish).[17] His beliefs were probably closer to Theism than to Judaism, conventionally conceived, but such distinctions were of no interest to Kahn. What mattered was the cause. The activity of promoting peace was essential to this prophetic mission.[18]

Kahn, the active banker, could not possibly oversee the project himself. Instead he wanted to find a scholar to direct the project, a man who would share his vision and create "a sort of photographic inventory of the surface of the globe occupied and domesticated by man, as it was at the beginning of the twentieth century."[19] The director would have all the photographic tools and expertise he required "to fix once and for all, those aspects, practices and modes of human activity, the fatal disappearance of which is only a matter of time." A house in Boulogne-Billancourt would be at his disposal, as would a professorship at the Collège de France, where Henri Bergson taught. Kahn donated the princely sum of 300 million francs to endow the chair (equivalent to approximately 800 million euros today [2006]).[20]

Who could resist such an offer? The man Kahn found was Jean Brunhes, a young geographer teaching at the University of Fribourg in Switzerland. Brunhes was a native of Toulouse in the south of France. He was nine years younger than Kahn. A follower of the great French geographer Vidal de la Blache, Brunhes developed a humanistic approach to geography and later held the chair of geography at his university. His approach blended a religious vision, Christian ethics, and scientific methodology.[21] His aim was to trace systematically and scientifically what he termed the "physiognomy" of the world. This human metaphor was intentional. It was his view that the relationship between human society and the environment was reciprocal and dialectical: each transformed the other. To describe and analyze that process of adaptation and change was the work of the human geographer.

By the end of the nineteenth century, this task took on a new dimension. As a direct result of the revolution in transportation, the world was now enclosed. Men had reached, in Brunhes's phrase, "the limits of their cage." Interdependency was now unavoidable.[22] Photography was an essential tool of this kind of geographical study. Film and color photography could "fix" some semblance of accuracy in our image of ordinary life. Of special interest were those isolated communities even then being sucked into the globalized world; their features had to be captured before they were gone forever. Through these means, the human geographer could trace what Brunhes called the "general physiognomy of the town and house," and move from these forms of "natural vegetation" to the street, the town, the city, and the metropolis. This bird's-eye view of the human ecology was to be complemented by snapshots of individual inhabitants.[23]

Here the visions of Brunhes and Kahn merged. The impulse to present the face of humanity was essential both to the scientific study of geography and to the humanitarian quest for world peace. Here was a kind of proto-ecological consciousness, one in which a belief in universality came down to a notion that we are all inhabitants of one planet and share its bounty and its hazards, whatever ideologists may say about national differences. Out of this mélange of nineteenth-century positivism and pacifism Les archives de la planète was born.

Over the next 18 years, until his death in 1930, Brunhes directed a complex team of photographers and cinematographers. Working closely with the French film pioneer Léon Gaumont, they amassed thousands of color plates taken in 50 countries.[24] The amount of film footage that these pioneering cameramen generated was immense. These films were shown to invited audiences at Boulogne-Billancourt and annually in the Grand Amphitheater of the Sorbonne, with the President of the Republic in the audience. In 1914, Kaiser Wilhelm II had a private viewing.[25] The range of these images is stunning; no corner of the world is ignored. What they show is a traditional world on the edge of modernization, a world about to disappear but one in which men and women live lives not particularly different from the ones Kahn's countrymen led in France.

This mobilization of the image bore the unmistakable imprint of the pacifist's message. Kahn's view was that the encounter between the photographer and the subject was a human one, establishing a silent dialogue between the two. The person or group photographed were not objectified, or treated as species or oddities; instead they were imprinted with the same humanity as those who would come to see their image in future years. There is no indication he doubted these naive assumptions or modified them in light of the extensive correspondence sent back by photographers to Brunhes and Kahn during these photographic expeditions. These letters were full of the daily business of photography, its difficulties and conflicts and, occasionally, its pleasures.[26]

"The aim of the Archives of the Planet," Brunhes wrote in 1913, "is to establish a dossier of humanity seen in the midst of life, and at a unique moment, when we are witnessing a kind of 'moulting,' an economic, geographic and historic transformation of unprecedented proportions."[27] Here was the urgency of the task: a world of disparate social practices was being transformed. In the process much would be irretrievably lost. A vanishing world needed its chroniclers, and Kahn and Brunhes intended to ensure that at least a record would remain.

We can see clearly the mixed character of the project. There was a sadness, a wistful hurry to make a record of a world coming apart. In 1912 Kahn wrote that the Archives would record "aspects, practices, and modes of human activity the fatal disappearance of which is but a question of time." But there was also a conviction that the young needed to appreciate the very diversity and complexity of that world, dying and being born again, in order to avoid succumbing to forces tearing it apart. Only through facing humanity could war be averted. Kahn the banker knew all about the need to foresee the future in the financial world; his archive was an attempt to enable the coming generations to do so in the field of human affairs tout court.

Kahn's project stood at the intersection of ethnography, cinematography, and international affairs at a moment when the term "globalization" began to take on the form we know today. The world was beginning to share a common market in labor, in capital, and in the exchange of goods. The reach of the market was worldwide; that is why the photographers had to reach Mongolia and Japan.

Kahn's agenda was twofold: to capture what was new in the world, and to record what was in the process of vanishing. Industrialized sites jostle in the Kahn collection with images of Mongolian steppe life. The very new and the very old are both vividly captured. So are facets of the history of decolonization. In the interwar years, Kahn's photographers reached Africa. Some of his photographers, particularly in Dahomey, handed their cameras to the locals; others stayed resolutely behind the lens. Kahn's was a kind of League of Nations mandate of *l'imaginaire,* pointing toward the end of Western rule and the end of the time when Europeans photographed Africans and Asians as we photograph animals in a zoo today.

Once again the dialectic of new and old is apparent. Motion picture technology became an agent of nostalgia by documenting the disappearance of old ways as much as the emergence of new nations. What Kahn sponsored was a world's fair of images and sounds, not celebrated in the imperial heartland, but captured where they were, in Asia, Africa, the Middle East.

In these varied projects, Kahn aimed to promote international understanding among the young who would some day play central roles in world affairs. In the Kahn estate in Boulogne-Billancourt, his photographs and films would be preserved. Adjacent to the Archives de la planète, the young scholars who had benefited from the Bourse autour du monde would gather and tell of their encounters with the farthest reaches of the globe. There they would meet other prominent intellectuals, writers, scientists. Before 1914 the poet Charles Péguy, Catholic and socialist, was one of the people who made the pilgrimage to Boulogne-Billancourt. Kahn would take an active interest in promoting his work. Albert Einstein and Marie Curie were there, too. All shared a vision of the potential for a peaceful future and the fear that such a future would be torn up in a paroxysm of international conflict.

Later, after the Great War, and before the even worse slaughter of the Second World War, Kahn wrote of the transformation of war that had occurred in his lifetime. War had no function in the twentieth century other than "immediate, universal, reciprocal, and unlimited destruction." An idealist until the end, this horrifying prospect meant, to Kahn, that war had become an "impossibility."[28] He retained this belief even when it was apparent that war was on the way. In this respect he was a typical French intellectual, persuaded that war could not happen, and that it was just around the corner.

The use of photography in the pacifist cause helps us locate Kahn's imagination at the divide of the nineteenth and twentieth centuries. Photography had captured the attention of many intellectuals and men of affairs before 1900 but had many new uses and unlimited possibilities in the era of newsreels and moving pictures. It was the "high-tech" art of the day, filled with an unresolved mixture of the playful, the "realistic," and the dishonest.[29]

It is not at all surprising that a practical man like Kahn was drawn to photography. So was Etienne Clémentel, who, during the Great War, used to escape from boring Cabinet meetings to what is now the Musée Rodin to experiment with photographic techniques. So were many others. But what distinguishes Kahn's mind is how he decided to use photography.

Epilogue

Let us leave the Kahn of 1900 and follow his life in subsequent decades. For his mind remained resolutely that of a fin de siècle visionary until his death in 1940. In later years, Kahn's personal philanthropy took on a number of other forms. He created an international garden in his house in the suburbs of Paris, a Center of Social Documentation, a National Committee for Social and Political Studies, an Institute of Public Health in Strasbourg, alongside the Chair in human geography he endowed in the Collège de France. But at the heart of the project was the image, or rather the galaxy of images collected between 1909 and the collapse of his financial empire in 1931.[30]

The imagery of an enduring and shared humanity is what Kahn was after, but the pace of change in the period in which his emissaries operated was so great that *la longue durée* was disturbed time and again by fundamental upheavals. Not the least of these was the Great War itself. Kahn was a recorder of the timeless, but the effects of early globalization and the world war presented much else to the gaze of the traveler and the *cinéaste*. There are impressive images in the Kahn collection of Paris at war: here it is patriotism, not pacifism, which is triumphant.[31] And Kahn's patriotism was not in doubt. Germany at war represented everything he loathed; and like so many Frenchmen, he identified the cause of his nation with the cause of humanity as a whole.

In 1917, Kahn drafted a long disquisition on the rights and duties of government. This document is a plea for a Kantian world federation. "Mankind had to pass through a calamity in order to see reality," Kahn wrote. Germany had shown one path to the future: that of "the negation of morality and justice." Now it was time to forge another one, since "humanity has no rational organism to direct it, and no certain light to orient it. Security comes out of finding both." Only a league of nations, he believed, with a Federal military force to back up Federal decisions, could prevent the descent into barbarism.[32] I will discuss this vision, braided together with that of Woodrow Wilson, in chapter 2.

Kahn the banker dealt with anticipating the future of financial and other markets; that was his metier. Was it possible to anticipate the future of human societies? Within boundaries, yes, since what we could see and understand was the basis of any sound projection into the future.[33] Here his approach to knowledge dovetailed well with the work of the League of Nations, in particular its International Labour Office, headed by Albert Thomas, a member of the Société autour du monde. There are clear echoes too in the later development of movements towards intellectual cooperation, leading after 1945 to the United Nations Educational, Scientific, and Cultural Organization (UNESCO).[34]

After 1918, Kahn's overall project, so redolent of nineteenth-century positivism[35]—the search for knowledge, and out of knowledge, the search for universal laws—suffered the same fate as the League of Nations itself. It could not cope with the harsh climate of the interwar years. Kahn himself lost his fortune in the wake of the economic crisis following the stock market crash of 1929, and his projects either came to an end, as in the case of the Archives de la planète, or settled into the status of personal, and now public, archives rather than agencies of world change.[36]

In one way, his story is that of a failure. All his projects for peace came to nothing. At the end of his life, Kahn was destitute. He had three personal possessions: a bed, a table, and a chair. His house and gardens were taken over by the city of Paris, which generously allowed him to remain as a lodger in his former domain. He died in 1940, two years before the Jews of Paris were deported.

The fate of his life's work shows how much of the pre-1914 world did not survive the aftermath of the world conflict. But not all was irretrievably crushed by warfare. Elements of his beliefs survive, albeit in different forms, to this day. At their core is the belief that the world is both one and horribly divided. Gazing at the common face of humanity can help unite it. The story of Kahn's vision invites us to ponder the fate of a vision of the future, a commitment to liberal humanitarianism, born in the nineteenth century, flourishing in 1900, and forced to weather the storms of a much harsher age.

There is a theme in Kahn's project to which I shall return in this book. It is this: how is it possible to visualize, to represent in images or artifacts, a world qualitatively and palpably different from the one in which we live? This question recurred in the 1919 peace conference, in the 1937 international exhibition, and in the Universal Declaration of Human Rights, presented to the United Nations in 1948. Kahn believed in vision, in the power of sight and reflection to render a change in the way people think about themselves and others.

Here Kahn anticipated later experiments in visual pacifism. In the 1950s Edward Steichen's photographic exhibition, first shown at the Museum of Modern Art in New York, and then published as *The Family of Man,* made the same urgent appeal, deepened by the cruelties of the second world war. The subtitle of the book said it all: Here was "an exhibition of creative photography, dedicated to the dignity of man, with examples from 68 countries, conceived and executed by Edward Steichen; assisted by Wayne Miller; installation designed by Paul Rudolph; prologue by Carl Sandburg."[37] Sandburg was the American poet par excellence, Lincoln's biographer. After the Second World War, Americans claimed to be the protectors of the dignity of man, configured in these classic photographs. Forty years earlier, Kahn and his associates did the same, though perhaps with more attention to the way the world was changing at dizzying speed than is evidenced in Steichen's landmark collection.

Kahn was a mystical banker, a visionary realist. He tried to record the face of humanity as it was, and to establish a direct link between peoples through the line of sight of the camera. In this way, Kahn's work expresses both the globalizing vision of turn-of-the-century pacifism and some of its inherent contradictions. By attempting to photograph the world, Kahn faced the central question as to the character of the European gaze when European imperialism was at its apogee. Were the people whose faces he wanted us to see specimens, exotic forms of life, or were they really our brothers and sisters? And if they were kin, what did we know of their gaze, of their angle of vision about these Europeans with their cameras, their notebooks, and their grand plans? The answer is very little, or nothing at all.

Kahn the banker, Kahn the financier of South African mining ventures and Japanese munitions, was not a neutral observer, nor were his emissaries. His vision was compromised at least as much by what he did as by what he said. What his project shows us, then, are the contradictions in the outlook of a liberal visionary in 1900. His hope to banish war may have been naive; it certainly bore all the traces of an elitist view that the best and most educated members of a society could bring peace to the masses. His deployment of photography as a weapon in the pacifist armory was striking, and has lost none of its power. To see the family of man was sufficient, from his point of view, to persuade observers of the absurdity of armed conflict.

The Imperial Vision: Exposition Universelle

Albert Kahn's project of visualizing the world has a very "1900" feel about it. One reason is the affinities between his project and that of the greatest world's fair of them all, the Exposition universelle of 1900 in Paris. Following a long tradition of spectacular displays of national economic power, the organizers of this world's fair intended to project a vision of the future, one based on the nineteenth-century liberal belief that the more international commerce there was, the less international conflict there would be. Here is a liberal solution to the problem of war, one which had the virtue of marrying profit to what was termed "pacificism," or the pursuit of amity among nations.

In whose interests was the world's fair of 1900 built? Firstly, it was built in the interest of individual nations, displaying their wares, their ingenuity, their creativity, their peaceful commercial life; secondly, in the interest of multinational or national firms, able to outshine the competition; thirdly, in the interests of the 40 million people drawn to a spectacle purporting to tell them what the future would be like. All this is true, and yet incomplete. The organizers of the world's fair of 1900 had a pacifist message in mind. What they offered was a blueprint for peaceful competition, a kind of commercial Olympics, which had been revived merely four years before. The organizers of the expo decorated Paris to visualize the essential link between the expansion of capitalism and the peaceful future of the world. Their expo performed this message; they did not have to lecture, or persuade; instead they could attract, impress, and dazzle the millions who came to see it.

The impresario of this cultural and commercial extravaganza was Alfred Picard, one of the *hauts fonctionnaires* of the French Third Republic. A graduate of the Ecole polytechnique, the elite college for those destined to run the country, Picard combined a technical knowledge of construction and organization with a skillful facility to orchestrate press and parliament while using his administrator's status to shield himself and his projects from direct political criticism. His hand was evident in every part of the preparation of this massive event, and his efforts yielded an efficient blend of political propaganda, business promotion, and public edification.[38]

The imagery of the world exhibition was a veritable inventory of advertisements for a world order which was stridently commercial, Eurocentric, and unashamedly imperialist. What the designers of the exposition offered for sale was "progress," understood as the materialization and expansion of European power in a cornucopia of goods.

As we shall see, there were other ways of configuring European "progress," and some people saw imperial power in very different ways. There was an undercurrent of doubt at the great expo, for instance, in some French commentary on the German pavilion, but it remained just that—a subterranean stream of concern about relative power and an air of mutual scrutiny among the Great Powers now heavily armed with the fruits of industrialization. Still, the overall mood was ebullient. And why not? Europeans in 1900 looked on their "high tech" with the same insouciance as we do today when using electronic communication or commerce. The grand Exposition universelle in Paris, which opened 14 April 1900, was a kind of "World Wide Web" of the beginning of the twentieth century.

The organizers of the expo left enduring marks on the city. The layout of the *exposition* described a giant letter A in the heart of Paris. One leg of the letter described a line that linked two new exhibition halls, which remain landmarks in Paris today. They are the Grand Palais and the Petit Palais, and they form part of a new line of sight down the avenue Alexandre III, crossing the Seine River over a new bridge named after the czar, France's most powerful ally. Across the river the vista opened to the dome of Napoleon's Invalides, where both his bones and those of his old soldiers found a resting place.

The second leg of the giant A stressed power as well. It stretched from the large spaces adjacent to the Ecole militaire on the left bank of the Seine through the esplanade around the Eiffel Tower and then across the river to the Trocadéro. The industrial, military, and colonial exhibits were located along this line. Connecting the two legs of the A were a host of displays and exhibitions along both banks of the Seine. Further exhibitions of a more rural character were housed east of Paris in the Vincennes Park.[39]

Product obliterated process in the Parisian expo. In the Trocadéro gardens descending to the river, visitors surveyed the bounty of imperial expansion stripped of even the hint of the struggle that went on to achieve it. As the novelist Paul Morand put it: "All that survived of our many Colonial expeditions—often so disastrous—was the enchantment of mosques and minarets, the medley of all the strange races on earth, conquered and subjected to the laws of the white man."[40]

The same was true of other European exhibitions. German goods jostled with French ones, less than 30 years after the Prussian army had encircled Paris and in 1871 created, on the grounds of Versailles, the new imperial German state. Thirty years later, not a trace of these convulsions remained in central Paris, where the pavilions sprang up like mushrooms. The fantastic forms of art nouveau architecture and design formed palaces of the imagination, where war was abolished, where poverty was invisible, where strikes and social conflict never happened, and where social hierarchies, like imperial ones, were turned into God-given facts of life.

The slogan of the exhibition was retrospective: Picard and his huge staff self-consciously framed it as "Le bilan d'un siècle" (the balance sheet of a century). But the thrust of this project was clearly prospective, suggesting to its huge population of visitors what the twentieth century was likely to become. Between April and November 1900, some 50 million people attended. Half of all the displays were French. Aside from Metropolitan France and Algeria, French colonies and protectorates were represented. There were displays on the French Congo, Ivory Coast, Dahomey, Guadeloupe, French Guinea, Guyana, Indochina, Madagascar, Martinique, Mayotte and the Comoros Islands, New Caledonia, Oceania, Reunion, St. Pierre and Miquelon, Senegal, French Somalia, Sudan, and Tunisia. In every one a version of colonial life, orderly, unpolitical, deeply indebted to the noble colonizers, sanitized in every respect, was there for visitors to see.

Twenty-four European nations participated, as did four African states—Liberia, Morocco, the Republic of South Africa, and the Orange Free State. China, Korea, Japan, Persia, and Siam represented Asia. From the Americas came Ecuador, Guatemala, Mexico, Nicaragua, Peru, El Salvador, and the United States. Bolivia, Costa Rica and the Dominican Republic were invited, but were unable to mount national displays.

With the costs borne primarily by the exhibiting states, architects submitted their designs to a central French committee. Their approval was necessary before construction could begin on national pavilions. For a year, Paris was turned into a building site. Peacefully and colorfully, the East of Europe invaded the West, at least in the representation of different national cultures. The pavilion of Serbia, staffed by 408 people, was a "Serbo-Byzantine" mansion, in which visitors were invited to view exhibitions of wine, food products, and silk, including a display of silk-worm cocoons. The pavilion of Italy, serviced by over 3000 people, similarly pointed to the East. Its design was Venetian Gothic, combining details of the Doge's Palace and the Basilica of San Marco. The nine Russian pavilions, manned by over 3000, included a pavilion of Asiatic Russia in the form of a Kremlin, perhaps as a reminder of Napoleon's defeat in Russia 78 years before.

The imperial presence was everywhere. The Portuguese presented a colonial palace; three Dutch pavilions included a Buddhist cloister and two edifices representing the Dutch East Indies. The British had a colonial palace, an Indian palace, and a display of Canadian agriculture, alongside a wide array of displays of domestic industrial and commercial power. A set of colonial displays provided information on the process of colonization, on colonial materials and products.

The exotic character of the colonial project was evident throughout the *Exposition*. Here is a description of the Madagascar pavilion, a circular edifice 55 meters in diameter. Displays covered 2.6 kilometers: "On the ground floor there was a wooden island, on which in a decor of rocks and shrubs, unfolded the panorama of a forest in Madagascar, whose flora and fauna were present within the limits of the Parisian climate. Monkeys played on the rocks; ducks swam alongside different kinds of indigenous boats." Above were displays of zoological, ethnographic, and commercial interest, as well as a diorama describing the position of French troops in the act of taking Tananarive on 30 September 1895.[41] A snack bar was manned by natives from Martinique, offering to visitors to the pavilion of "anciennes colonies" a taste of local produce.[42]

Fully one quarter of the colonial exhibition was devoted to Indochina. A Cambodian temple, surmounted by a royal pagoda, rose 47 meters above the ground; it introduced visitors to the splendors of the recently discovered temple complex at Angkor. The pagoda was approached by a cascade of steps decorated by ceremonial stone dragons and Cambodian guards. To its left was a Vietnamese household and a Cambodian theater.[43] The pavilion of Sénégal and Sudan echoed to the sounds of the Senegalese Cora.

The novelist Paul Morand captured the flavor of this imperial *tour du monde*. "Paris is given over to Negroes," he remarked,

> to Breton bag-pipe players, to Yellow eaters of raw fish. The world revolves so fast that one is dizzy, passing from surprise to surprise . . . caught in a network of mythical evocations and impossible monuments, whirled in a maelstrom of progress, held in the clutches of new alliances, amidst a cacophony of weird diphthongs and incomprehensible words.
>
> I passed my days at that Arab, negro, Polynesian, town, which stretched from the Eiffel Tower to Passy, a quiet Paris hillside suddenly bearing on its back all Africa, Asia, an immense space of which I dream . . . a Tunisian bazaar where you smoke the *narghileh* and watch the dancers, the stereorama,

the Kasbah, the white minarets, surprised to find themselves reflected in the Seine, the stuffed African animals, the pavilion of Indo-China varnished with red gum, its golden dragons and its carving painted by Annamites in black robes and its golden dragons . . . The Tonkinese village nestled with its junks and its women chewing betel. [At] a Dahomey village . . . great negroes, still savages, strode barefoot with proud and rhythmic bearing, the subjects of ancient kings, old and recent enemies. . . . All this hillside exhaled perfumed incense, vanilla, and the smoke of pastilles that burned in seraglios, there you heard the scraping of Chinese violins, the click of castanets, the thin wail of Arab flutes, the mystic sadness of the Aissous.[44]

This mélange of stereotypes fits in perfectly with what we now call Orientalism, a prism of the imagination, producing distortions of a kind both denigrating to the other and flattering to the European. Contemplating the weak, the decadent, the sexually depraved "East" helped many in the "West" to glory in its strength, its progress, its civilization.[45]

And yet the gaze was not (and never is) one way. The exotic face of empire stared back at the Europeans who came to the Exposition universelle. We can only conjecture about what these Africans and Asians made of it all. The Pavilion of the French Ministry of Colonies celebrated all the key figures of French colonial expansion, including 50 busts of contemporary explorers, administrators, men of the army and navy, all displayed in the Hall of the Geographic Service of the Colonies. A sculpture of a French explorer benignly raising an African from his proximity to the beasts of the forest, and pointing to the sky, encapsulated the self-deceptions of the age.[46]

This was the common currency of colonial officials and their "auxiliaries," whose work was celebrated too in the Exposition universelle. There were many participants in *la mission civilisatrice.* "One of the most characteristic features of the progress of the colonial idea in France," the organizers proclaimed, "is the considerable and rapid development over the last ten years of private societies of propaganda, geography and scientific research which brings to French colonization a spirit of active and disinterested collaboration."[47] As in Britain, measuring the world was part and parcel of controlling and exploiting it.[48]

There were many other thematic pavilions too, in which international exchange and cooperation were the leitmotifs. Some were industrial; other pavilions were dedicated to celebrating the growth of what we now call social capital and social policy. Alongside parks presenting wonders of motorized transport, or of electricity—where the word "television" was coined—or of civil engineering, mines and metallurgy, were displays on education.[49] The Berlitz language school had a booth, as did the *Alliance française,* the Alpine club, the big Paris department stores, Bon Marché and Printemps, and the Louvre. The commercial dimension of this world's fair was hard to miss. Those with purchasing power had a cornucopia of things to buy: consumption could run riot in such an atmosphere, and that, to be sure, was precisely the point.

Power of a more martial kind was on display as well. Anyone who wanted to find out about armaments and artillery could do so; torpedoes, maps, naval instruments, and forms of military hygiene were there for the curious. The big armaments firms were in attendance: the British Vickers and Maxim; the American gun manufacturers Smith & Wesson, and the German Krupp, though its display was limited to its enlightened program of workers' welfare.[50]

The overall effect was dazzling. What could Europe not do in the future? What could Europeans not produce and sell in the future? As Rosalind Williams has argued, at the Exposition universelle, dreams and commerce became one.[51] And as in most advertising campaigns, what was left out, what was obscured about the "product" mattered at least as much as what was seen. One Catholic critic put the point succinctly. Maurice Talmeyr was struck by the array of goods and colors presented in the pavilion of British India. What visitors saw was "an India-warehouse, so magnificent and so partially true as it may be, is true only partially, so partially as to be false, and all these overflowing rooms . . . speak to me only of an incomplete and truncated India, that of the cashiers. For this land of enormous and sumptuous trade is equally that of a frightening local degeneracy, of a horrifying indigenous misery. A whole phantom-race dies there and suffers in famine. India is not only a warehouse, it is a cemetery."[52] Talmeyr put his finger on the central conjuring trick of the Exposition universelle. It was a festival of science and learning, pointing to the pure and applied arts as benefactors of humanity, but it was also a palace of fantasies, most of which were on sale. Fantasies were turned into goods; as such, their commercial appeal relied on their liberation from anything sordid or even realistic.[53] Positive advertising appeared side by side with positivist instruction.

In the Paris expo, the brutality of imperial rule inside Europe and colonial rule outside of Europe was nowhere to be seen. Stripping away these self-serving myths of beneficence was the job of novelists, not curators. One of them was an obscure Polish-born novelist, Joseph Conrad, who in 1900–1 published two novels which exposed the moral ugliness of the European reach across the world. In *Lord Jim*, the impossibility of living according to a European code of honor is the subject of an extraordinary journey across the Indian Ocean into Sumatra. In *The Heart of Darkness,* published a year later, the sheer brutality of *la mission civilisatrice* in Africa was presented as an uneasy nightmare. En route to finding Kurtz, the man in charge, the central character, Marlowe, meets one of Kurtz's subordinates, the chief accountant of the firm collecting ivory in the Belgian Congo. "The cause entrusted to us by Europe," says the accountant, "was in the hands of this great man Kurtz: 'Oho, he will go far, very far,' he began again. 'He will be a somebody in the Administration before long. They, above—the Council in Europe, you know—mean him to be.'" Marlowe's view was the same: "All Europe contributed to the making of Kurtz; and by and by I learned that, most appropriately, the International Society for the Suppression of Savage Customs had entrusted him with the making of a report, for its future guidance."[54] Kurtz would have been right at home at the Paris expo, which celebrated the world he served so brutally.

It is inappropriate to judge the Paris expo by the imperial and racial standards of the subsequent century. But those very standards were challenged within the expo itself. One such discordant note was struck in an exhibition on African-American life and culture. The American commissioners sponsored a display on Negro life in the United States. It was placed in the Palace of Social Economy, and its avowed purpose was to show that the "race problem had been solved through political compromise."[55] The vice-principal of the Tuskegee Institute, Thomas J. Calloway, was in charge and turned to the young black sociologist W. E. B. Du Bois to gather together the displays which would support this vision of racial peace.

Du Bois did nothing of the sort. He rejected what had been termed the "Atlanta compromise," the view championed by Booker T. Washington, Calloway's colleague at Tuskegee, that blacks should accept discrimination and work within segregation to achieve economic rather than political freedom. Instead, Du Bois put together an entirely different vision, one describing the world of middle-class black Americans as little different from white Americans or Europeans in their cultural and intellectual life. Black professionals were captured by a black photographer, Thomas J. Askew, in a series of arresting studies in dignity. By doing so, Askew and other black photographers, including Frances Benjamin Johnston, engaged in a powerful act of "subversive resistance" to the ideas of Calloway and Washington. As historian Shawn Smith has noted, "Contesting the colonialist and imperialist logics forwarded by living racial and ethnic displays, the American Negro exhibit disrupted the essentialized narratives that depicted people of color as the uncivilized infants of human evolution."[56]

Du Bois the sociologist deployed statistical material on black property ownership and displayed 200 of the roughly 1400 books written by black American authors. "We have thus," he wrote, "an honest, straightforward exhibit of a small nation of people, picturing their life and development without apology, or gloss, and above all made by themselves."[57] The word "nation" is the critical one; using it meant that America was not one nation under God, but two nations, a white one on top and a black one treated in ways which could not be squared with any sense of human dignity. These photographs showed the way to breaking the racial barrier; it could not be sustained on any rational grounds after gazing at the faces of the men and women displayed in Du Bois's exhibit and viewing the evidence of black achievement in Atlanta, Georgia. What would the world look like if black men and women were given the chance to break the bonds of racial prejudice? Here is the core of the book Du Bois published three years later, *The Souls of Black Folk,* in which he prophesied that "the problem of the twentieth century is the problem of the color line."[58] In 1900 Atkins's photographs and Du Bois's exhibit sketched out a vision, one in which the color line was lifted to disclose the cultural and intellectual sophistication of black Americans.

This example of the use of photography to describe a common humanity is strikingly similar to the project of Albert Kahn. As we have noted above, it informed the hugely popular *Family of Man* exhibition of the photographs of Edward Steichen.[59] But 50 years earlier, what is striking is the jarring contradiction between the Du Bois exhibit, which won a gold prize in the Paris expo, and the triumphantly imperialist vision which surrounded it. There was a Cuban exhibit in the Trocadéro palace, prepared by the American commissioners. It was covered with red, white, and blue bunting, suggesting that Cuba was halfway between a colony and an annexed part of the United States. There were displays on the civilizing mission of schools for native Americans.[60] The Paris expo offered sufficient space and opportunity for the expression of competing and entirely contradictory imaginings of race relations in the future. Whenever the nonwhite world was configured at the Paris expo, we can see the instability and contradiction of the vision the fair offered to its millions of visitors.

Not everyone found the fair to their liking. The painter Claude Monet hated it. He considered it such a "menagerie that I rushed off to see the apple orchards in blossom."[61] Henry Adams noted that, on going into the expo, he "entered a supersensual world, in which he could measure nothing except by chance collisions of movements"; it was a kind of "physics made stark mad by metaphysics."[62] The metaphysics was that of commerce and advertising, the world Walter Benjamin later described as dominated by the arts of mechanical reproduction.[63] Beneath the stated agenda of peace and progress, other, more material appeals were in evidence. Both gave to the Paris expo of 1900 its peculiar force and appeal.

Europe as a whole, Europe dominating the world, was on display, and a dazzling display it was. But it is easy to dismiss the logic of the enterprise as a simple commercial exercise. To do so is to read back into 1900 something which happened much later. Now world's fairs are advertising events, of little political consequence, and with no evident social agenda. Not so a century ago. Then the connection between commerce and peace was more evident. The claim was this: what possible use was war if the productive forces of the world's industrial powers could be harnessed to the well-being of the people of the world? War was a businessman's nightmare; in so far as it disrupted commerce, it introduced vast uncertainty, which is the enemy of finance, and tore up the fabric of international trade. While today these claims appear to be self-serving rhetoric, a century ago they made sense to a surprisingly large population. Liberal pacifism was a vision of its time, filled with contradictions, but a vision nonetheless.

Jean Jaurès and the Workers' Vision

So was socialist pacifism, drawn to the great Paris expo as was every other major social movement of the time. In this sense, Paris was indeed the capital of the nineteenth century, and of the beginning of the twentieth century, too.[64] The dreams of a peaceful and a bountiful future conjured up by a Parisian banker in Boulogne-Billancourt and by a host of architects, builders, and designers who created the pavilions of the Exposition universelle, were not the only visions of the future to emerge from the French capital. There was a third, distinctive way in which the twentieth century was imagined, far removed from the banker's world, and from that of the prefects, the industrialists, and the commercial magnates of the Exposition universelle. This vision focused on working men and women and on their grievances and their rights. This dream touched on peace and plenty, but focused as much—or even at times more—on justice and equality.

The People's Tribune

The tribune of the working people was not a Parisian, but his voice echoed throughout the city and indeed throughout the world. His name was Jean Jaurès, the leader not only of the French Socialist Party but of the social democratic movement which had spread from Europe to North and South America and beyond and which had created an international socialist organization—the Second International, founded in 1889—which was a kind of parliament of working-class organizations and a forum for the expression of working-class aspirations.

Between 1900 and 1914, Jean Jaurès did more than any other man or woman to create a third vision of the twentieth century, one based on the message of international working-class solidarity in the face of international tension and the threat of war. It is worthwhile broadening the chronological limits of this chapter to show how a third vision of 1900 developed in the years which followed.

Jaurès was a speaker without peer. His oratory embodied the moral vision behind the European socialist movement, a movement which had come into prominence by the last years of the nineteenth century.[65] Both Jaurès and the socialist project he espoused, indeed symbolized, came of age together in the 1890s. By then the French Republic had weathered its early unstable years, and the new German Empire had lifted its ban on working-class organizations. In the 1890s, a wave of labor militancy spread over Western Europe, announcing that working-class deference to their masters at work was on the wane.

This new spirit of revolt was evident in many villages and towns, including the mining town of Carmaux in southwest France. In 1892 the secretary of the miners' union, Jean-Baptiste Calvignac, was elected mayor. He asked his employers to give him two days off to fulfill his administrative obligations. They refused. To the miners, the refusal was a punitive reaction to Calvignac's socialist views; to the employers, it was because he would not do a full week's work. To defend their leader and their choice as mayor, on 16 August 1892 the 3,000 miners of Carmaux went on strike. The stalemate dragged on for two months until socialists in the Chamber of Deputies forced the mine owners to accept arbitration. Calvignac was reinstated, and the striking workers went back to work.[66]

The head of the family which owned the mines and much else besides, the Marquis de Solages, resigned from the Chamber of Deputies. In his place the people of Carmaux elected Jean Jaurès. A native of the region, born in 1859, he came from a family of professionals of some distinction. A brilliant student, he graduated from the elite liberal arts college of the Third Republic, the Ecole normale supérieure. He became a professor of philosophy and then turned to politics. He was a staunch defender of the Republic, but it was only during his period working with the miners of Carmaux that he crystallized his socialist position. He came to socialism in order to better defend the Republic.

Working people, in Carmaux as elsewhere, gave Jaurès a political education. The principles he espoused were common to many ardent Republicans who were not socialists. He believed in God as "the order and harmony of things,"[67] but favored separation of church and state. He was a patriot, devoted to national defense, but he favored a militia to defend the nation rather than a professional army dominated by a reactionary professional staff. To advance the active participation of the citizenry in the Republic, he fought to extend and develop a system of national education open to all. These were the views of the Republican center in France.[68]

What made Jaurès turn left was his contact with working men and women in southwest France in the 1880s and 1890s. Through these friendships and exchanges came a commitment to defend political freedoms by rooting them in social equality. Local politics taught him much about national and international politics. A true Republic, Jaurès held, was unreachable while social divisions along class lines were so deep. He came to see that the political framework of a Republic committed to "liberty, equality, fraternity" was bound to be subverted by those who used it to defend property and privilege. And a system of states resting on class inequalities would inevitably clash in the field of imperial and international conflict. Both domestic and international peace were impossible, he came to see, under capitalism.

The vision Jaurès created was clearly utopian. It identified what was destructive in the current order by positing an entirely different one. Here he was not alone. A multitude of men and women in Europe and beyond imagined a world in which industry was in the hands of the many rather than the few, in which the fruits of production were shared so as to eradicate urban slums and rural hovels.

How would this come about? There were those who based their notion of social transformation primarily on the gathering together in trade unions and cooperative societies of working people. These men and women contested with employers at the point of production for control over the fruits of their labor. In France such people were called "syndicalists," and they harbored a deep suspicion of anything tainted by "politics." By that they meant the struggle for control of the instruments of state power. Jaurès sympathized with their struggles, but not with their rejection of politics. He saw the political process as essential for the liberation of labor, and was prepared to work with anyone, of whatever class, in achieving real freedoms for the common people. Reforms mattered and were possible, even though they never displaced a commitment to a more radical transformation of the social order.[69]

That radical step went beyond industry and politics to a moral transformation of men and women, debased and degraded under the capitalist system. The new social order of Jaurès's utopia was imaginable only if new men and women could make it happen. This idealist vision was central to his outlook. He chose socialism because he believed that "it seeks to develop all the faculties of man, his power to think, to love, and to will."[70] These faculties were stunted under capitalism.[71] The struggle for socialism was in effect a moral education, a turning away from habits of mind based on deference, inequality, and injustice. Socialism was "a moral revolution which is expressed through a material revolution. . . . It will be . . . a great religious revolution," Jaurès continued. "I cannot conceive of society without religion, which is to say, without certain common beliefs which bind souls together and join them to the infinite, from which they have come and to which they will go."[72]

This third force in the socialist movement—more moral than industrial or political—was a powerful component of the international socialist movement, reborn after two decades of dormancy in 1889. The date of the birth of the second Socialist International is no accident. The great fair of 1889, leaving the Eiffel Tower as its permanent monument, drew to Paris those determined to celebrate the centennial of the French Revolution. Socialists like Jaurès claimed the legacy of that event, and they did so in a manner very different from that of the organizers of the world's fair. Marx himself in 1864 had helped inaugurate a first socialist international association. By 1876, that organization had collapsed. Thirteen years later, it was time to start again.

1889

The Paris conference of 1889 establishing what quickly became known as the Second International was a chaotic event. A total of 391 delegates from 20 nations or national groups attended. Poland did not yet exist, being divided among the Russian, German, and Austro-Hungarian empires, but the Polish Socialist Party was in Paris. German socialists were prominent, as were the French. Others were there to represent tendencies rather than national parties or organizations. There were Swedish, Swiss, Austrian, Belgian, British and American "delegations," though their constituencies were often unclear or virtually nonexistent. Linguistic barriers were formidable, and many people who were attached to obscure organizations or to none at all came in to intervene, heckle, or just enjoy the energy of the moment. "Crowded into a small hall," the Austrian physician and socialist leader Victor Adler observed, they managed to create "a polyglot and temporarily helpless chaos."[73]

The first order of business was to determine who had the right to attend. Which socialist organizations were legitimate delegations? Initially all delegates were allowed to vote as individuals; later congresses would face the hard question as to who actually was a socialist. At this moment, the crucial task was simply to manage a turbulent and disorganized but exuberant constituent assembly of socialist opinion, and to create a forum for the exchange of ideas, news, and information about the socialist cause wherever it arose.

Resolutions were passed about the need to achieve an eight-hour working day and for legislation to regulate conditions at work. Here was a marker for the future. These material matters pointed the new International toward reform politics. Some delegates disputed this tack, and wanted to urge total rejection of political reforms, which could delay revolutionary transformation. But initially, general statements about the rights of labor carried the day.

The second program on which all could agree was international peace. The delegates were all opposed to standing armies, frequently used by leaders to crush their own workers on strike rather than foreign enemies. The advent of socialism, they cried, would abolish war. How that would happen was left to the imagination.

The figure who both embodied this socialist vision and tried in many ways to link it to concrete proposals in both domestic and international affairs was Jaurès. His powerful rhetoric disclosed both the idealism at the heart of the socialist project and its tendency to substitute passionate oratory for effective political strategies. Jaurès was the prophet of the socialist future. He pointed the way ahead, but he did not expect to see it.

1900

In late September 1900 in Paris, while the Exposition universelle was in full swing, the Second International convened on the Avenue Wagram in the French capital. Jaurès, as chairman of the French delegation, welcomed 2000 delegates representing 16 countries. They were meeting, he insisted, at a dangerous hour, when "capitalism was trying to whip up chauvinistic bestiality and nationalistic madness." Against these artificial antagonisms, socialists opposed their sense of solidarity, their belief in the possibility of a "socialist peace."[74]

Domestic peace among French socialists was also difficult to preserve. As soon as the international delegates entered the hall, 60 or so members of dissident French groups marched in, too, singing the "Internationale." Then came a dispute over who represented French socialism. Until the question was resolved, one delegate insisted, they could not form a delegation and, as hosts, could not even open the congress. Jaurès, exasperated and furious, begged his colleagues not to "give to socialists of all countries the pathetic spectacle of their divisions."[75] Democracy was in full display, in all its chaotic glory.

An hour later, the congress opened, despite the grumbles of the minority. Clara Zetkin, a German socialist delegate, translated French into German and German into French. Someone identified only as "Citizen Smith" produced English versions of the proceedings. Everything took time. The struggle for socialism, Jaurès scoffed at the Trocadéro the next day, had nothing to do with monotony.[76]

There followed heated debates on the vexed question of the wisdom of working-class participation in middle-class governments. Co-option was always the risk of collaboration. The outcome was a compromise, accepting in exceptional circumstances the need for such arrangements, while reaffirming the ultimate aim of socialist groups—the supercession of capitalism.

To help reduce the level of friction within the international socialist movement and to create a structure which would carry on international work between congresses, held at four-year intervals, the delegates agreed to the creation of an International Socialist Bureau. This body would link groups around the world and serve as a source of information and support among widely scattered working-class organizations.

The next year the Bureau was installed in Brussels, and from 1906 its Secretary, Camille Huysmans, published reports and then a periodical bulletin to disseminate information of interest to working-class organizations and activists around the world. For instance, in the January 1910 bulletin, there is a "Circular on the events in Argentina," including documents on "the situation of our South-American comrades, whose political and syndical organizations are virtually suppressed by the government of the Argentine Republic." Mario Bravo, secretary of the Argentine Socialist Party, issued an appeal for funds to help support socialists facing martial law, imposed after the assassination of the chief of police. He also published a list of the names of exiled socialists, implicitly urging sympathizers to help with their plight.[77] Solidarity was always both moral and material.

The Road to War

While the struggle of labor for recognition and dignity went on in every country represented in the International Socialist Bureau, the movement never lost sight of its overarching commitment to work for world peace. "No peace; no justice" was the watchword of the day. In the Paris conference, the Polish-born German delegate, Rosa Luxemburg, offered the following proposals: socialists must educate youth against militarism, vote against military and naval credits and against colonial expeditions, and be prepared to coordinate international action when the risk of war becomes evident.

In 1907, at the Stuttgart congress of the Socialist International, delegates reaffirmed their commitment to take active steps in the event of international crises. But just as in the earlier dispute as to who was a delegate, there were profound ambiguities in the position they advanced. Some insisted that there be a general strike of all working people in the event of a war crisis; others argued that such a position was futile. The outcome satisfied everyone and no one. "In the case of war being imminent," the Congress declared, "the working classes and their parliamentary representatives in the countries concerned shall be bound, with the assistance of the International Socialist Bureau, to do all they can to prevent the breaking out of war, using for this purpose the means which appear to them the most efficacious, and which must naturally vary according to the struggle of classes, and to the general political conditions."[78] Would there be a general strike in a war crisis? Perhaps.

In place of precise strategies, socialists could always resort to noble words. And the noblest socialist orator of them all was Jaurès. He had what has been termed a "symphonic" approach to oratory. He could change registers with the mood of his audience, introduce cadences in his message which had both mobilizing and at times hypnotic effects. His was a rhetoric of combat.[79]

When war in the Balkans threatened to engulf Europe in 1912, the International Socialist Bureau convened "un Congrès international extraordinaire" in Basel. There, 555 delegates from all over Europe assembled on 24–25 November. A public procession accompanied the delegates to the cathedral where Jaurès spoke. It was led by the "workers" cyclists' union and drummer boys dressed up as William Tell. Following were "phalanxes of young people accompanying a chariot of peace, in which young girls in white waved palm leaves in place of olive branches." The municipal band was followed by "a veritable forest of red banners." Pacifist slogans were prominent. "It is better to shed tears than torrents of blood," read one. The procession, singing their national songs of solidarity—the "Song of Work" for the Austrians, the "Internationale" for the French—crossed the Rhine, passed the City Hall and arrived at the cathedral. Twenty-three bell-ringers set in motion the great bells of the cathedral.

Six thousand people crammed into the candlelit cathedral, and with the echoes of the "Hymn of Peace" in Beethoven's Ninth Symphony ringing in their ears, they awaited the words of Jean Jaurès. "It was a moment," the official report affirmed, "that all the comrades present will remember for the rest of their lives." The workers' chorale of Basel set the tone; but Jaurès lifted it to the firmament. He started soberly:

> It is first on the shoulders of our brothers in the Balkans that responsibility lies. Now our Austrian comrades feel the burden too. But the burden rests as much on the entire International. . . . Capitalism is reflecting on the question: is war or peace more in its interests. Governments are hesitating. The balance of destiny shifts in their trembling hands. And that is why the proletariat throws its force into the balance on the side of peace.
>
> In this struggle, I hope we will not be alone. The Christians have opened to us the gates of their Church. Our aim fits their faith and their will—to preserve the peace. May all Christians who follow seriously the words of their Master fortify this spirit. We are all opposed to those ready to deliver the multitudes to the bronze clutches of the demon of war. It is up to us, workers and socialists of every country, to make war impossible.
>
> . . . We have entered this church to the sound of bells which are a clarion call to general reconciliation. I recall the motto which Schiller inscribed as an epigram to his "Song of the Bell": *Vivos voco, mortuos plango, fulgura frango! Vicos vovo:* I call the living to resist the monster who would ravish the land. *Mortuos plango:* I weep for the countless dead, now buried in the

east, whose rotting stench fills us with remorse. *Fulgora frango:* I will harness the thunderbolts of war now breaking across the skies.

... The closer the peril comes, the more we must ask ourselves: if this monstrous thing comes about, if it becomes necessary for workers to assassinate their brothers, what can we do to prevent this horror? ... When the clouds threaten, when the waves become turbulent, the sailor cannot predict what needs to be done at every moment. But the Internationale must raise its voice for peace, and to take every legal or revolutionary step to stop war and to call the war-mongers to the bar of justice.... We must bring our message to the masses; we must confirm in all the Parliaments that we want peace.... And we shall leave this edifice swearing an oath to save peace and civilization.[80]

As it happened, a general European war did not break out at the end of 1912, though no one—including Jaurès—believed that the rhetoric of Basel had made any difference. The meeting in the cathedral mattered in another way. It crystallized the socialist vision which Jaurès made his own. It reflected his appeal to the imagination, his use of prophetic language to express his belief in reason, in persuasion, in the force of human decency, and in the necessity of justice. In these struggles, words mattered tremendously; to Jaurès, oratory had the capacity ultimately to outlaw war.[81]

Eighteen months later, war did come. A few hours before its outbreak, Jaurès was assassinated by a nationalist fanatic fearful of another address like that delivered at Basel Cathedral.[82] What Jaurès's position would have been is of course impossible to know. We can state with some clarity that Jaurès was not a pacifist, but rather a socialist patriot, steeped in the Jacobin tradition of French Republicanism.[83] A new army, of the people and serving the people, was one he championed in 1911.[84] But it was the old armies which went to war just three years later and, by doing so, destroyed much of what Jaurès had dedicated his life to achieving.

Conclusion

Paris, 1900: three very different visions of the future, each concerned in different ways with peace. Albert Kahn wanted to capture the face of humanity, and by gazing into it, to make war impossible. The entrepreneurs of the Exposition universelle of 1900 wanted to capture the muscular productivity of capitalism, and to show how a new world could be build, a world in which war was not necessary. And the Socialists of the Second International thirsted for justice, and dreamed of a world both without hunger and without the clash of arms. Each vision was utopian in that each was a way of imagining the twentieth century without the horrors of modern, industrialized warfare. And yet, these visions of a better world were unlikely to materialize, because the men and women who framed them could not evade who they were: European citizens of an imperial system controlling the globe, a system about to detonate the most devastating war in history. This was as true of workers bound to country as much as to class, as it was to bankers like Kahn or bureaucrats like Picard. In 1914, war engulfed them all.

In 1900 and in the years leading up to war, there were two competing carriers of social progress: the nation and the working class. In 1914, all combatant countries fused the two. The nation and the working class became one, united in defense against the enemy. By the end of the war, four years later, that partnership had broken down. A new working-class movement, based in Russia, confronted the victorious Allies, surveying the wreckage of Europe and a new array of nation-states, hewn out of the defeated German, Austrian, and Turkish empires.

How could a lasting peace come about? Delegates gathered once more in Paris in 1919, this time to rebuild a world order and to outlaw war. The man who seemed to hold the keys to this peaceful future was not a banker, nor a bureaucrat, nor a socialist orator. He was the American president Woodrow Wilson, and his minor utopia was couched in the language of self-determination. What this term meant and what happened to his project is the subject of the next chapter.

2 1919
Perpetual War/Perpetual Peace

The Great War of 1914–18 had torn up the map of Europe and, on account of imperial ties, the map of the world. In the first half of 1919, people from all over the world converged on Paris to join in the discussion surrounding the peace conference and to influence the outcome. Some were official delegates; others were there because during the war their people had a glimpse of freedom. After four years of carnage, this was a time of hope, some of it utopian, about the way the war had opened up the possibility of an enduring peace. Paris 1919 seemed to be a place where the people of the world, after the most destructive war in history, might indeed be offered "a second chance on earth" to avoid war. Now we know that would not be. But at the time, expectations of a transformation in the international order were high.[1]

The peace conference was a patchwork of the old and the new. The world war had been fought by states in defense of territorial boundaries. Britain went to war on the side of France and Russia when Germany violated the territorial integrity of Belgium. Those boundaries were restored. For the Allies, the critical issues were state security and the territorial boundaries of the successor states of the defeated Central Powers. These were the time-honored core of international diplomacy.

But within this history, there is another one which deserves our attention. It is the "minor utopian" vision of self-determination for all, the realization of the national aspirations of peoples to determine their political future in their own territory. Once achieved, self-determination was a form of insurance against war. Take away the imperial element in international affairs, and armed conflict would simply be unnecessary. The vision of self-determination is, therefore, a set of ideas about how to avoid war. That is how it was understood at the time, as a key element in the "new diplomacy" which would replace the failed old diplomacy discredited by the war.[2]

Nine million men lost their lives in the Great War. Three times as many men were maimed, injured in body and mind while on active service. Millions of veterans, orphans, and widows never escaped the shadow of the war. Without official prodding, a groundswell of sentiment rose in every combatant country supporting the view that the peace settlement following the war had to be of a different order from those in the past. It could not simply punish the losers and distribute the gains among the victors. It had to abolish war, or risk the total destruction of society as they knew it. What we learned through the war, said the French writer Paul Valéry, is that our civilization is mortal.[3]

"Never again" is a term we now associate with the Holocaust; but the phrase was on the lips of millions of men and women a generation earlier. The fact that "Never" lasted less than two decades should not obscure the depth of the feeling behind it. Substantial numbers of people—in and out of uniform—believed fervently that peacemaking in 1919 had to make another world war unthinkable. This chapter is about that dream of outlawing war and on the project of building the peace. On what foundations? On the platform of a League of Nations dedicated to a new world order, one based on the twin principles of the nonviolent resolution of international conflict and the slow and steady progression of subject peoples to self-determination.

"Self-determination" is the minor utopia explored in this chapter. Its prophet was the American president Woodrow Wilson. He saw in self-determination an essential key to a future without war. There were others who agreed, but who defined self-determination in ways Wilson could not or would not accept. The African-American writer W. E. B. Du Bois and the Chinese diplomat Wellington Koo were among them. Why, they asked, should self-determination be limited to the white race? Was it not a matter of universal right rather than of racial privilege?

Du Bois and Koo lost the argument. Self-determination remained a racial privilege rather than a human right. Why did this happen, and what were the consequences? This chapter explores these questions, and, in doing so, it throws light on what may be termed the dilemma of liberal imperialism. In the period leading up to the peace settlement, both before and after the Armistice, the peacemakers never made up their minds as to whether they were inaugurating a new order in international affairs or shoring up imperial power in the guise of a system of internationally sanctioned mandates. Self-determination was the order of the day, as Lloyd George and Wilson affirmed, but so were both the truncation of German power in Europe and the transfer of German colonies to Allied hands. Was the settlement a step toward self-rule or toward imperial hegemony? The answer is both. Wilson accepted this contradiction in order to secure Allied support for his central objective—creating the League of Nations. But by aiming in two contradictory directions at once, the vision of an enduring peace vanished in the process of its framing.

In Paris in 1919, the concept of "self-determination" turned out to be more a slogan than a destination. It shriveled from a "minor utopia" to a minor diplomatic adjustment of the old order. Whenever the term was used, it exposed the contradictions at the heart of liberal imperialism —a belief in democracy and in benign domination. One element in the failure of the Versailles settlement was located, therefore, in the inability of the victorious powers to realize that, after 1914, they could be democrats or imperialists, but not both at the same time. Imperialism on the Victorian model was no longer possible. The Allies could no longer afford it; the coffers of the European powers were drained by the effort to win the war and by the huge burden of debt incurred during the conflict. But trying to maintain imperial power under the guise of stewarding dependencies toward self-government could not work indefinitely. Setting in motion expectations of self-determination without intending to move in that direction was one way to ensure that conflict would recur throughout the world—in China, in Palestine, in Europe itself.

In a host of ways, an ambiguous commitment to the concept of self-determination was lethal to the settlement of 1919. The German sense of grievance about being forced to accept sole responsibility for the war, as embodied in clause 231 of the Treaty of Paris, informed a wide body of opinion on the need to revise the treaty. And one way to do so was to give those who saw themselves as German the opportunity to join together with others in the expression of their "self-determination." If ethnic Germans in the successor states of the Austro-Hungarian empire voted to join their brethren in a reconstructed Reich, then they were simply being good Wilsonians.

The peacemakers' flawed and partial commitment to "self-determination," as the term was understood at the time, undermined the effort to provide a stable peace either in Europe or in those areas around the world where Europeans and Americans ruled in formal and informal ways. The tension between liberal commitments and imperial realities—so evident in the 1900 Paris expo two decades earlier—was played out time and again in the interwar years. In this chapter I show that that outcome was imbedded in the thinking of those fashioning the peace in 1919.

"Debatable Areas and Unfortunate Peoples": The View from Above

How did the idea of "self-determination" come to dominate the Paris Peace Conference? There was little trace of it in the first years of the conflict. But after the war had been transformed in 1917 through two Russian revolutions and American entry into the war, the rights of peoples to break with the past was an issue of singular importance. The clash of empires made it inevitable that the losers would cede sovereignty and territory. Discussions of war aims now went beyond territorial and colonial questions to embrace commitments to democracy and the right to self-determination of subject peoples.

With the mobilization of an army of several million, and the promise of millions more on the way, American views on war aims took on increasing significance. American economic power gave President Wilson added leverage. In 1917 and 1918, the White House and the State Department devoted much time to these matters. The president and his advisers shared a familiar and enduring American sense of moral superiority over the combatant countries on both sides. Having tried and failed between 1914 and 1916 to act as an honest broker of a negotiated peace, and furthermore, having been provoked to go to war by the German U-boat campaign of 1917, Wilson felt entitled to develop a set of principles to govern the kind of world to come out of the war. And he expected to be listened to. In a speech to Congress on 8 January 1918, these guidelines emerged as the 14 points, including centrally the commitment of the American government to open diplomacy and to the freedom of the seas, as well as to the construction of a new international league.[4]

The central question was how to prevent Germany in future from disturbing the peace of the world; but while the war was still undecided, it was difficult to be precise about the ways to accomplish this, or about the boundary changes needed to effect an enduring transformation in European affairs.

One focus of discussion was about territorial issues. Another concerned dependent territories, and what to do with German holdings in Africa and Asia. And then there remained the still thornier issues of the transformation of imperial relationships and the construction of a League of Nations both to oversee colonial affairs and to defuse potentially explosive conflicts between its members. European boundaries had to be set, to be sure, but there were other, more structural changes in the international system mooted in the years 1917–19.

The key to these new issues was the right to self-determination. No one knew precisely what this right actually entailed. Which populations qualified for the right? Who was the "self" doing the determining? How was the "determining" to be framed and administered? And what defined a "people" whose existence by that very fact gave them this right?[5] The search for self-determination is the subject of this chapter.

The Inquiry

In the United States, President Wilson led a multitiered effort to work out both war aims and the precise meaning of the term "self-determination." He delegated much of this work to his close adviser Colonel Edward Mandell House. Neither an elected official nor an employee of the Department of State, he worked for the president alone. House's assignment was to bring together expert opinion on contested issues, the resolution of which was bound to shape the world after the war. The outcome was termed at the time "The Inquiry," a wide-ranging set of American academic explorations of the way the future could be constructed.

This investigation is revealing in many ways. Its authors came from different disciplines in the American academy and brought to the effort formidable knowledge of international affairs. But for our purposes, they show clearly how the "minor utopia" of self-determination was doomed from the start. American thinking on the subject even before the Paris peace conference fully exposed the contradictions and confusions inherent in Wilson's concept of self-determination. This episode also revealed the enduring tendency among Americans in authority to stand above and to preach to those peoples needing help to reach the promised land of liberal democracy.

To illustrate these points, we can start with a document prepared on 27 November 1917 about the activities of the Inquiry. A mere three weeks after the Bolshevik revolution, the committee set out two fields of research they intended to pursue:

> Field I. The Powers
>> The Friends—The United States, British Empire, etc.
>> The Enemies
>> The neutrals—Denmark, Holland etc.
> Field II. Debatable areas and unfortunate peoples
>> Alsace-Lorraine
>> Schleswig
>> Trentino
>> Baltic Littoral
>> Jews
>> Pacific Islands
>> Nationalities of Eastern Europe
>> China, Turkey, Middle East[6]

"Debatable areas and unfortunate peoples": what a revealing phrase to describe the assumptions of the men and women trying to imagine the contours of the international history of the rest of the twentieth century.

In the short term, these categories were set up for a specific purpose: to provide President Wilson with the best briefs possible on the shape of a world order to be fashioned at a peace conference to be convened at the end of hostilities. That was the intention. Let us consider how it was realized. At the heart of the inquiry was a group of four individuals who reported to Colonel House and who were personally approved by President Wilson. These men formed the Inquiry's executive committee. First came Sidney E. Mezes, president of the City College of New York, a philosopher of ethics and religion, and—as it happened—a brother-in-law of Colonel House.[7] The second was Isaiah Bowman, a Canadian-born president of the American Geographical Society and professor at Yale. His special interest was Latin America, where he had led the Yale expedition that reached Machu-Picchu in 1908.[8] The third was James T. Shotwell, professor of history at Columbia and a central figure in the work of the Carnegie Endowment for International Peace, itself engaged during the war in a project to write its economic and social history.[9] The fourth was the Inquiry's secretary, Walter Lippmann, a twenty-eight-year-old editor of the *New Republic* and special assistant to the Secretary of War. In May 1918 Lippmann left the Inquiry to take up a post with American Military Intelligence.[10]

Lippmann steered the committee's initial progress by setting its priorities. In December 1917, he divided the work to be done into two categories. The first was gathering information on all peace initiatives; the second was drawing up maps: "Physical, racial and economic maps for territory from the Baltic Sea to the Persian gulf. Economic and political map of Africa. Boundary maps to be superimposed indicating tentative solutions for Poland, Balkans, Asia Minor, and Africa. Economic maps of Alsace-Lorraine and occupied areas of France." There would be "social maps," too, providing data on the Baltic Provinces, Poland, Serbia, Macedonia, Palestine, and "Italia-Irredenta." From this cartography and from other information on shipping, credit, and the "immediate civil and economic needs in Europe" would flow the American position on most postwar economic issues—reparations, raw materials, boundaries.

The only specifically American objective was tacked on to the priorities as a final task, seemingly unrelated to the others. This was to work out "The relation of the Monroe Doctrine to the Settlement": in other words, how the new international system would fit in with the ironclad assumption all American presidents to date accepted as to American hegemony in its hemisphere.[11] Without an assurance that the Monroe doctrine would remain intact, untroubled by any international commitments to emerge at the peace conference, Wilson could never sell the peace treaty to the American public or to the United States Senate: America in its sphere of influence; Britain—and presumably France—in theirs. This is the limited map of world power which the Inquiry set out to draw, ensconced in their offices first in the New York Public Library on 42nd Street and then at the offices of the American Geographical Society uptown on 155th Street.

In early 1918, the work of the Inquiry was broadened to take in Austria-

Hungary, the Far East, Africa, and "South and Central America."[12] The Inquiry's initial Eurocentrism had diminished; the assignment of the Inquiry had mutated into producing a map of the world. It is this map, and this vision of the world which they offered Wilson as an archive, a repository of knowledge and argument, to be used in the Paris peace conference a year later.[13]

The Inquiry operated by delegating questions to "experts." Men and at times women would provide informed sketches of international problems and outlines of solutions. Most of these people were drawn from the professoriate at the major American research universities—Harvard, Columbia, Yale. Others joined the team because of their particular expertise or talents. Many already had or went on to have distinguished careers in the academy.

Examining the work of this intellectual and social formation can tell us much about how the vocabulary of liberal morality masked powerful and only partly hidden assumptions about imperial and racial superiority. That these commonplace early-twentieth-century notions lived in vigorous incompatibility with the Wilsonian language of high-minded commitments to democracy and self-determination is evident in these reports. After all, visionaries—like the rest of us—see the world through a social prism, a set of "unspoken assumptions" disseminated in their society.[14] By exploring their imaginings, we can understand much about their efforts to fashion the peace and the reasons why they failed. It was not the notion of self-determination which was the problem, but the historical nature of its semantics, the way contemporaries understood the term. Self-determination in 1919 was an impossible dream, dashed by the imperialist assumptions of the men who fashioned it.

The League of Nations and the "New Monroe Doctrine"
Many currents—American, British, South African—flowed into a generalized consensus on the need to construct a new international forum to secure world peace.[15] But here too we can see the contradictory character of liberal imperialism—that mix of ideas of high-mindedness and American national interest which Woodrow Wilson personally

embodied and expressed throughout the deliberations leading to the peace settlement.

One striking facet of the American approach to these questions was the way they took the principle of North American hegemony in the Western Hemisphere, enshrined in the Monroe Doctrine of 1823, and reconfigured it a century later as a foundational principle of the international order. In this context, the Inquiry's investment in research on Latin America, hardly central to the deliberations in Paris, makes sense. Here is one place where the limits to the notion of self-determination were glaringly evident. Should America's role as the "protector" of weak states in Latin America against the predatory powers of Europe be a guide, then the future of the world order could be governed—so the argument ran—by the extension of the Monroe Doctrine to the rest of the world. International "protection" on the American model thus could be offered as a means to protect small states in Europe as well as colonies and dominions elsewhere from predators and from the danger of war.

One of Woodrow Wilson's most ardent admirers, the historian W. E. Dodd of the University of Chicago, made precisely this point in his work for the Inquiry. What the Monroe Doctrine had achieved, in his view, was the enforcement of "the rule of democracy where no state encroaches on another." "The application of the Monroe Doctrine to European countries," he therefore suggested in February 1918, "may hasten to bring about a permanent peace of the world."[16]

Dodd admitted that the changed economic character of imperialism required a revision of the second facet of the Monroe Doctrine, which related to American noninterference in European affairs. Whereas the threat had come in the nineteenth century from British economic power, or from Spanish and Portuguese designs, after 1914 the situation was entirely different. Spain and Portugal were minor players in world affairs. Britain was not, but a substantial share of her economic holdings in Latin America had been liquidated to pay for the war. British bonds and equity had been sold, most going into American portfolios. Thus the Western Hemisphere was "safe" from predatory encroachments, and it was time to offer the same protective shield to small or vulnerable states in other parts of the world. Herein lay the justification for renouncing the other side of the Monroe Doctrine—the prior refusal of American presidents to accept a permanent role in European affairs.

There was a vital political point to be made through this argument. Opponents of Wilson and the peace treaty challenged him to defend the Monroe Doctrine as being beyond the reach of any League of Nations to "interfere" in American hemispheric questions. Only by squaring the League's covenant with the Monroe Doctrine could Wilson hope to defuse some of the domestic hostility to his policies. That is why he insisted on an amendment to the covenant precisely on this point. To French objections that such an amendment was unnecessary, Wilson replied testily that such wording was absolutely essential. It would reaffirm that American "policy for the past century has been devoted to principles of liberty and independence which are to be consecrated in this document as a perpetual charter for the world."[17]

Mandatory Power Within the League of Nations
The notion that the Monroe Doctrine could serve as a model for the postwar international order also attracted Jan Christiaan Smuts, the South African leader, member of the Imperial War Cabinet, delegate to the peace conference, and framer of the League of Nations. Smuts's belief in the need for such a League appealed to Wilson, who adopted the South African leader's formulations in his own drafts of the Covenant.[18] This meeting of minds extended to the framing of mandates within the League as well, though not to the subject of German reparations. Still, on the subject of the League, the two men were clearly like-minded. What Smuts envisaged was a system of benign paternalistic stewardship of former colonies and dependencies of the defeated Central Powers. What the British Dominions want, he told the Royal Geographical Society in 1918, was "a new Monroe doctrine for the South as there has been a Monroe doctrine for the West, to protect it against European imperialism. Behind the sheltering wall of such a doctrine they promise to build a great new peaceful world, not only for themselves, but for the many millions of black folk entrusted to their care."[19]

Vast territories had emerged from the breakup of the Ottoman Empire and the defeat of imperial Germany. Many of these lands lay in the Middle East and Africa. Smuts's notion was to construct a midpoint between imperial governance and self-government. That mediating role was to be played by powers given the right—the mandate—to administer these territories on behalf of the international community, configured as the League of Nations. Thus the issue of what to do with the colonial world was central to the constitution of the League.

Here is the clear link between the Monroe Doctrine and the system of mandates set up as part of the peace settlement of 1919. In both cases, the notion of an apprenticeship in independence was adopted. Its paternalistic overtones and racial undertones were plain. In the Americas, the United States purported to shield weaker states from the European predators circling around them. In Africa and Asia, the same role would be played by Allied powers, but this time, in the name not of a hemispheric order but a world order, administered by individual countries on behalf of the League of Nations as a whole. Thus France took on the mandate for Syria; Britain for Iraq and Palestine, and so on. In Africa, the role of beneficent overlordship would be played by a mix of nations: Britain for Tanganyika; Belgium for Rwanda; South Africa for South West Africa, Australia and New Zealand for parts of Oceania.

That pattern of governance was a central theme in the work of the Inquiry. The key figure in this initiative was the Columbia University historian George Louis Beer, an expert on colonial rule in Africa. His position paper on what to do with Germany's former African colonies established clear guidelines for the work of mandates. "Mandatory powers," he insisted, "must be wholly honest in this Trusteeship and forego all purely national and imperialistic ends."[20]

These two elements of thinking about the outlines of the postwar international order, evident in the work of the Inquiry and in the deliberations in Paris which followed, bear all the hallmarks of the treaty as a whole. Entirely incompatible propositions were joined together. A commitment to the nonimperialist administration of colonies en route to self-determination was accompanied by an equally clear commitment to securing their raw materials for the world's markets. These two objectives would collide, the Inquiry believed, unless both were subject to the authority of an international organization, the League of Nations.

Imagining the twentieth century in this way was a recipe for disaster, since expectations that were set in motion among subject peoples could never be fulfilled by their rulers. It is difficult to know which assumption is more extraordinary: the view that American guardianship of Latin America was neutral and not self-serving, or the view that Britain and France would administer their new holdings, under League of Nations mandate, in a way beyond any purely "national or imperial ends."

Consider the same logic in the way the Inquiry configured the League of Nations project as a whole. As a final statement of objectives, the Inquiry formulated peace terms including this proposition: "From the nations at present engaged in resistance to Germany's effort to dominate the world, there is growing a League of Nations for common protection, for the peaceful adjustment of international disputes, for the attainment of joint economic prosperity including equal opportunity upon the highways of the world and equitable access to raw materials which all nations need."[21] Note the significance given to economic freedoms, to be exercised by the developed countries of the north, in the interests of all. No one discussed ways to ensure that this outcome, however unlikely, would come about. A war of imperial powers produced a peace of imperial powers, and no flights of well-intentioned rhetoric would change that fact.

The Limits to Self-Determination

On 11 February 1918, Woodrow Wilson told Congress that following the war, "There shall be no annexations, no contributions, no punitive damages. Peoples are not to be handed about from one sovereignty to another by an international conference or an understanding between rivals and antagonists. National aspirations must be respected; peoples may not be dominated and governed only by their own consent. *'Self-*

determination' is now an imperative principle of action which statesmen will henceforth ignore at their peril" (my italics).[22] But when applied to particular cases, the contradictions in this position emerged rapidly. Self-determination was destined only for some, and not for others.

Consider the issue of Palestine. The competing claims of Arab nationalists and Zionists were scrutinized, and there is no question that the American position tilted toward Zionism. O. J. Campbell pointed to the growth in Zionism during the war, spreading support for the "inherent justice of its own aims." To Jews, Campbell argued, their collective existence in exile was configured as a state of "national incompleteness," one which the peace settlement should bring to an end.[23]

There is no reason to assume a blanket form of philo-Semitism among the Inquiry's researchers. On the contrary, a study of Austria-Hungary pointed out that "International Jewry" was interested in perpetuating the existence of the dual monarchy in order to protect its "securities and to exploit especially the Jugoslav territories." But the Roman Catholic Church and unspecified pacifists were also suspected of being participants in a plot to keep alive German powers throughout central Europe.[24] There was no trace of this brew of prejudices when the Inquiry turned its attention to the future of Palestine and other areas liberated from the Ottoman Empire.

Instead, what has been termed "Orientalism"[25]—so evident in the representations offered in the Paris expo of 1900—infused some of the Inquiry's research on Muslim and Arab populations. One noted Orientalist reported to the Inquiry that "the Turk is liable to be always inconsistent. . . . His lack of executive ability is one of his most conspicuous failings. Inconsistent reasoning is not conducive to justice or to fair and efficient administration of any kind."[26] Those Turks who were not deficient in their public duties, this expert believed, were likely to suffer from syphilis or other maladies. It would be hard to find a better summary of the twisted reasoning of "Orientalism"; whatever was supposedly wrong with the Jews was never examined through the same distorting prism of prejudice.

There was also considerable sympathy in the Inquiry with the

Christian Armenian populations, a sympathy not extended to the Muslim Kurds. To be sure, the plight of the Armenians had been well publicized in the United States, though the American administration had done little to make its displeasure felt by Turkey or her patron, Germany, while the United States was still neutral in the conflict.[27] But the ranks of those worthy of joining the community of independent states in the short term included Jews and Armenians and excluded most Africans and Asians. Throughout these investigations, it is clear that self-determination was a category reserved for those populations which shared the values and the religious tradition, broadly conceived, of the "civilized nations" or, in other words, the nations who won the war.[28]

Debatable Areas and Unfortunate Peoples: The View from Below

So far I have discussed planning for the peace conference. When it convened in January 1919, how did the contradictions inherent in the idea of self-determination unfold? To see the unstable mix of ideas that went into the negotiations, we may observe the moment not from the viewpoint of the powerful, but from the angle of vision of people who could not control their destiny but who could only await the outcome of the proceedings—those outside the circle of "civilized nations." How did they see the peace being negotiated on their behalf in Paris in 1919? We can learn much about this question by entering the precincts of the many groups who came to Paris in those first postwar months to make their voices heard.

Black Voices

Paris was a grand bazaar of ideas in 1919. Societies and organizations of many kinds emerged in the French capital to speak out, even if they were not part of the 70 delegations officially recognized as parties to the conference. Among the outsiders were black men and women who convened a Pan-African Congress in Paris. This meeting was primarily the work of the American sociologist and journalist W. E. B. Du Bois, then aged 50. He had been here before when, as a much younger man, he had framed a photographic exhibition on the American Negro in the Pavilion of Social Economy of the 1900 Paris *Exposition universelle*. Now, 19 years later, the gaze was reversed: black men and women were looking intently at the plenipotentiaries of the great powers to see how far they would go in addressing the race problem as part of their effort to offer self-determination to the subject peoples of the world.

The year 1919 paralleled 1900 in yet another way. In the earlier year, Du Bois helped convene the very first Pan-African Congress in London. At Westminster Town Hall, just across from the Houses of Parliament, 32 black men and women came together from 23 to 25 July 1900, "the first time in history," so said the chairman Bishop Alexander Walters, that blacks "had gathered together from all parts of the globe with the object of discussing and improving the condition of the black race."[29] They drew up a petition to Queen Victoria on the situation in Southern Africa, convulsed at the time by the Boer War. And they signed an appeal "To the Nations of the World," written by Du Bois, in which he affirmed that "the problem of the twentieth century is the problem of the color-line, the question as to how far differences of race—which show themselves chiefly in the color of the skin and the texture of the hair—will hereafter be made the basis of denying to over half the world the right of sharing to their utmost ability the opportunities and privileges of modern civilization."[30]

In Paris in 1919, Du Bois posed the same question, this time in the context of the refashioning of the international order. There was a sense of hope, even of euphoria, in his anticipation of the deliberations of 1919. This mood rested on the assumption that the military participation of black Americans after 1917 had given them an unanswerable argument against white supremacy. No one knew what black men trained in combat would do when they returned to a country which had mobilized them to defend it. Would they put up with humiliation and subjugation? The same question was posed in other countries and other contexts about working-class men who had fought and who returned to poverty and severely constricted lives.

No wonder many men with a romantic temperament would leap to their feet at the possibilities that appeared to beckon in 1919. The field of action in which both struggles were set had been broadened radically by American participation in the war. Black soldiers—American and African—had fought and died in a just cause; their example, their sacrifices, could not, would not, be ignored.

In 1915 Du Bois made his views clear on what he termed the African origins of the war. Since the path to war began in Africa, so, he argued, did the pathway to peace after 1918.[31] Du Bois tried to get official approval for his plans to speak for the black man in Paris. He wrote to Wilson hoping to be appointed an official American delegate; Wilson never replied. Du Bois was not deterred; he would find another way. "It seems to me," he wrote to Newton Baker, Secretary of War, "it would be a calamity for the two hundred million of black people to be absolutely without voice or representation at this great transformation of the world."[32]

Unsanctioned by his government, Du Bois convinced the National Association for the Advancement of Colored People (NAACP) to send him to France both to look into reports of the mistreatment of black American troops and to speak for black interests at the peace conference.[33] He sailed on board the *Orizaba* on 1 December 1918 in a large group of journalists en route to Paris.

Once there, he joined a Senegalese deputy, Blaise Diagne, who had helped recruit *la force noire,* black troops for the French army, and who organized a second Pan-African Congress, this time to be held in Paris in 1919.[34] The intention was to bring together delegates from the United States and the West Indies, from African colonies and dependencies, as well as from Abyssinia, Liberia, and Haiti. Invitations would be extended also to India, China, and Japan, but the primary focus of the meeting was Africa and Africans.

The official American delegation to the peace conference had no interest in being tested on the race question; Wilson, ever a Virginian, never lost sight of the racial limits to self-determination. It was—at least for the foreseeable future—the white man's business. To avoid embarrassment to the president, passports were denied both in the United States and in Britain to prospective delegates to the Pan-African Congress. The American expert on African questions, George Louis Beer, was totally unsympathetic to the cause of African self-determination.[35] Du Bois and Diagne persevered, and rallied some well-placed support. Walter Lippmann offered to help. A progressive Frenchwoman, Madame Calmann-Lévy, offered Du Bois her salon.[36] And more importantly, the organizers received a tepid but valuable endorsement from Clemenceau for their meeting. "Don't advertise it," he is said to have remarked, "but go ahead."[37]

And go ahead they did, in the Grand Hotel on the boulevard des Capucines on 19 February 1919. Opening the Congress with a paean of praise for French colonial practices, Diagne set the positive tone for the proceedings.[38] Delegates decried discrimination, but with an eye toward the inevitable police report on the meeting they voted for a resolution urging League of Nations supervision of Africans and people of African descent, during the period of apprenticeship when Africans would learn to govern themselves. Moderation was the order of the day.

At this stage Du Bois shared *la mission civilisatrice* assumptions behind the politics of self-determination. "The principle," he affirmed, "could not be applied to uncivilized people."[39] Instead, a trajectory of gradual self-government would emerge under League of Nations supervision and would be driven by increased educational provision for Africans.[40] Here his ideas merged with French notions of the role of intellectuals, teachers, and administrators in bringing the fruits of European culture to those in the process of forming a "self," as Europe understood the term. Intellectuals like Du Bois were the vanguard of "Pan-Africanism"; they saw the future, and could help those with lesser education and lesser vision to realize it. It is intriguing to see in Paris the bifurcation in the black voice—between the educated Negro, African-American like Du Bois or African like Diagne, and the uneducated subjects for whom they spoke. Elite guidance of the masses was their watchword; what Du Bois and Diagne among others wanted was to ensure that among those elites, black men like themselves would be prominent.

"We caught the ear of the civilized world," Du Bois proclaimed in May 1919.[41] But in the evolution of the peace conference itself, little came of the Pan-African meeting. The plenipotentiaries carried on deciding the fate of black Africa and Africans as if they were insensate and illiterate, and essentially ignored those in Paris who claimed to speak for them. The delegates at the Pan-African Congress of 1919 took the limited step of creating a permanent committee, with Diagne as president and Du Bois as secretary. The major achievement of this group of men and women was simply to be there. Paris was where the future was being set, and that was where the voices of black people had to be heard. However faint the echoes, these voices established the claim that blacks had a right to join in the deliberations on the fate of Africa.

Asian Voices

Chinese delegates in Paris in 1919 also claimed that they had a right to a voice in their own future. Their position was different from that of Africans, in that China was an ally and an official participant in the peace conference. Her position, though, was in no sense that of a sovereign state among other sovereign states. This anomalous state of affairs was recognized by the Inquiry, which categorized China as sovereign without the rights of a sovereign power.[42] Partly this was the result of the predatory nature of Western powers, which had treated China as a series of fiefdoms, but partly her fragility was a function of the ongoing civil war between northern and southern political and military factions. A truce had been declared in 1918, and negotiations between the parties went on while the peace conference in Paris was in session.[43]

The weakness of a fractured state coincided with the wish on the part of the Allied powers and the United States to offer something substantial to the Japanese, one of the Big Five powers at the conference, whose naval contribution to the Allied cause had been substantial. And that meant concessions in China, in particular over the former German holdings in Shantung, already promised to Japan in treaties signed by

Chinese representatives in 1915. The question remained, would these treaties be honored in the new environment of peace-making?

For many Chinese, the peace negotiations in Paris were first of all a test case as to the meaning of self-determination. Was Wilson to be held to his word, to his commitment to set aside secret treaties and imperialist bargains? Or was he to be exposed as a hypocrite, rendering China subordinate to Japan?

The men who asked this question in Paris were two American-educated diplomats. V. K. Wellington Koo was a 32-year-old diplomat, with three degrees from Columbia University. At the time of the Paris peace conference, he was serving as Chinese ambassador to the United States. C. T. Wang, three years older than Koo, received his undergraduate education at Yale. He had been a minister in the first Republican cabinet in 1912.

Both men used their American training and contacts to advance the position of independent China. In particular they cultivated an understanding with David Hunter Miller, a member of the Inquiry and close adviser to President Wilson on the issue of the League. The Chinese objective was clear: to transfer to China as a sovereign right all concessions and agreements made before 1919 with Germany and Austria-Hungary, and in particular the railway concession in Shantung province.

The problem was that Japan insisted on the transfer of former German concessions not to China but to her. This was the dilemma both the Allies and the Americans faced in Paris. How to square the claims of the two Allies? Koo and Wang framed the Chinese case in terms of Wilson's 14 points; if ever there was a chance to take the measure of the man and his ideas, here it was. "China is now at the parting of the ways," Koo wrote in his memorandum to Wilson on 23 April 1919. "She has come to the West for justice. If she should fail to get it, the people would perhaps attribute its failure not so much to Japan's insistence on her own claims as to the attitude of the West which declined to lend a helping hand to China merely because some of its leading Powers had privately pledged to support Japan."[44]

Wilson's answer was clear: Japan's claims and demands took precedence. In a series of meetings with Wilson and his aides, Koo tried to make the point that a Japanese presence in Shantung would give her effective military control over the northern railways of China, and thereby dominate Peking itself. Feeling in China about this outcome of the peace conference was running high. But none of these arguments persuaded Wilson to change his mind. Thus evaporated the Chinese hope that a new order would emerge in Paris, based on the Wilsonian notions of open diplomacy and self-determination and support for the rights of weak states. Koo and the other Chinese delegates refused to sign the peace treaty under these humiliating circumstances.[45]

Many compromises emerged in Paris, but the denial of the Chinese claims was one of the most striking and most severe, and not only from the Chinese perspective. To be sure it was difficult for Wilson to defy Japan, and see her walk out of the conference, as she threatened to do, shortly after President Orlando of Italy had left the deliberations in high dudgeon over the failure of his claim to Fiume. One walkout was enough. But it was also important to note the Americans' ongoing anxiety about Japan's territorial ambitions. It would be better, they thought, to accept Japanese expansion to the west, in China, than to confront Japanese moves to the east, where a collision with the United States might loom.

Finally, there is the president's own order of priorities. He placed more weight in the architecture of the peace than in its individual elements. Getting the League of Nations approved was his sine qua non, and all other issues came second. Wilson knew that he would be accused of violating his own principles, and the accusation is valid.[46] He did compromise his previous stand on self-determination in the belief that securing the League was paramount.

The Chinese were well aware of this fact, and addressed it in their protest over Wilson's decision to support Japan on the Shantung question.

> If the Council has granted the claims of Japan in full for the purpose of saving the League of Nations, as has been intimated to be the case, China of course would have less to complain of, believing as she does that it is a

duty to make sacrifices for such a noble cause. . . . The Chinese delegation cannot, however, refrain from wishing that the Council had seen fit, as it would be far more consonant with the spirit of the League now on the eve of formation, to call upon strong Japan to forego her claims animated only by a desire for aggrandizement, instead of upon weak China to surrender what was hers by right.[47]

The Chinese delegation was right; there was little reason to back off from concluding that they had been betrayed. They had high hopes that the Paris peace conference would be a new departure in diplomacy. The principle of self-determination, if it meant anything at all, had to preclude imperial horse-trading of the traditional kind. They were mistaken.

Horse-trading was inevitable in getting imperial powers to accept the very existence of the League. Wilson's reasoning was transparent: once a structure for the defusing of explosive international conflicts had been built, then and only then would many issues be resolved according to principles that could not be applied in 1919. Japanese claims in China were one such issue.

A structuralist approach to both domestic and to international affairs, so central to the Wilsonian vision, helps us to see why his choice of Japanese over Chinese interests in the disposition of Shantung reflects less hypocrisy than a set of calculations surrounding his priorities in Paris. Individual claims mattered less than the institutional transformation of the international order. Self-determination would come later, in the long run.

The Chinese differed. In the long run, as Keynes put it, we are all dead. Their position arose from a belief, shared by millions of people in many different countries, that 1919 was a unique moment, a time to move away from conventional practices and secret diplomacy, into a new democratic age, one in which all nations had the inalienable right to self-determination. This was the hope Wilson initially represented, and the hope he failed to realize. In surveying the negotiations in the spring of 1919 in Paris it is difficult to avoid the conclusion that very rapidly "self-determination" became a pious phrase, whose content varied according to the race, power, and location of the people espousing it.

One issue binding together the views of Japanese and Chinese delegates, among others, was racial equality. On 13 February 1919, Baron
Makino, one of the leading Japanese delegates to the peace conference,
read the following amendment to delegates considering the Covenant
of the League of Nations: "The equality of nations being a basic principle of the League of Nations, the High Contracting Parties agree
to accord, as soon as possible, to all alien nationals of States members of the League equal and just treatment in every respect, making
no distinction, either in law or in fact, on account of their race or
nationality."[48]

Wilson's attitude to this matter when it was first raised is unknown.
He had the advantage of leaving the conference just at this point to
return to the United States; he therefore could duck the issue, which
was bound to be divisive at home. In addition, Wilson's own views on
the matter were what might be expected from a civilized Southerner.
In 1914 he had virtually thrown out of the White House Wilfred Trot-
ter, an angry black man determined to tell him a thing or two about
racial discrimination. But the American president was much more
open-minded than members of the British and Dominions delegations.
Lord Robert Cecil opposed the amendment. "White Australia" was not
negotiable, prime minister Billy Hughes insisted with his usual lack of
subtlety. "Sooner than agree" to the amendment, Hughes said, "I would
walk into the Seine—or the Folies Bergères—with my clothes off."[49]

When the issue was brought forward again by the Japanese on 11
April, Wilson was back and had to engage with it. Colonel House passed
him a note urging a negative vote. Should the amendment go through,
"it would surely raise the race issue throughout the world." Wilson
urged the Japanese to withdraw the motion, since everyone knew the
League of Nations was based on equality. They refused, and on a vote,
a majority supported the amendment. Wilson as chair pointed to the
strong opposition which still existed, and ruled that the resolution
was not carried. Consensus came before democracy, and with an eye
toward other issues the Japanese let the matter drop.[50]

They had effectively used the resolution as a bargaining counter. As we have seen, satisfying the Japanese demands for Shantung became a way of avoiding a Japanese-sponsored resolution which would have exposed the racial limitations to the principle of self-determination for all. Britain, no less than the United States, wanted no part in a resolution affirming the principle of racial equality. Japan was well aware of this fact and used the "race card" to secure its own imperial position. Yet another nail in the coffin of self-determination was hammered into place by the Japanese, who realized that imperialism had emerged alive and well from what has been termed the "Wilsonian moment."[51]

Conclusion

By 28 June 1919, the hopes of a new world order, which had greeted President Wilson on his arrival in Europe six months earlier, were gone. Peacemaking in Paris in 1919 was a renewal of the old order, with some new rhetoric to accompany it. No one could miss the echoes of the past—the ending of one war in the very site of the ending of its sequel. The Hall of Mirrors in Versailles was where the German Empire was born in 1871 and where its demise was certified 48 years later. Alsace and Lorraine became part of Germany in the first peace treaty and reverted to France in the second. France was forced to pay in short order five billion francs in war indemnities in 1871, and it returned the compliment with interest, German interest, in 1918.

The reversal of the humiliation of 1871 required a similar staging of the humiliation of the defeated power in 1919. Newsreels captured the German delegation, vilified and cowed, filing into the Hall of Mirrors, suddenly grown silent and under protest, signing the document that was supposed to establish peace.

The terms of the treaty were emphatic. The German army and navy were severely truncated; parts of Prussia were ceded to the new Polish state; the new states of central and southern Europe replaced the old Austro-Hungarian empire, and a system of League of Nations mandates supervised the transfer of German colonies and Ottoman provinces to effective control by the Allied powers, Britain, France, Australia, Japan, and Belgium.

The creation of the League of Nations announced something new, something unprecedented in international history. It was not an attempt to create a world state, or a federation of republics of the kind Immanuel Kant had posited in his 1795 essay on "Perpetual Peace."[52] Instead, it was a start, a point of departure in the collective resolution of international conflicts between sovereign states and between what we now term the developed and the developing world. The system of mandates set up in the Wilsonian mold was a new idea in the management of dependencies, resting on the concept of the self-determination of peoples, their right to determine their own futures when deemed able to do so. But when would that be, and who would make the decision that the "self" was ready to "determine" its own destiny?[53] These questions were not answered and could not have been answered even if the United States Senate had ratified Wilson's treaty. The contradiction between democratic impulse and imperial aspirations was not resolved in 1919; it remained unresolved throughout the twentieth century and beyond.

The peace settlement unraveled rapidly. First, if security was the goal, then the failure to address the problem of Russia other than by military intervention of a halfhearted sort ensured that insecurity in the east of Europe would be endemic. If the economic and political shackling of Germany was the destination, then the effort failed, by ignoring the integral nature of German economic activity for European recovery, and by creating in Germany a wide consensus that the Treaty of Versailles was unjust. If the aim was the slow and steady passage to independence of colonies and dependencies, whose development was to be fostered by disinterested administrators holding in trust the human and material capital of subject peoples, then the effort was a failure even before the treaty was signed.

The Indian holy city of Amritsar was the site of a massacre on 13 April 1919. Fifty riflemen under the command of the British general Sir William Dyer shot into a crowd of civilians in the square of Jillianwalabagh, wounding 1,500 and killing 379. A few weeks later, on 4 May 1919, approximately 5,000 students protested in Beijing against the proposed Versailles settlement. Anti-Japanese demonstrations and strikes spread in China, preparing the ground for the emergence of new nationalist and social movements, including the Chinese Communist Party. In early 1919, the first Palestinian national congress convened in Jerusalem to affirm its opposition to the plan to create a Jewish homeland in Palestine. A visiting American fact-finding commission, appointed by President Wilson, visited Palestine in the summer of 1919; its report, emphasizing the incompatibility of Zionist plans and Arab rights, was ignored by the British mandatory powers, to whom authority was ceded a year later. Other instances could be cited. The prospect of a peaceful path to the self-determination of subject peoples, central to the Wilsonian vision, was an illusion.

No one can place the blame on one man's shoulders for the failure of the Versailles settlement. And yet at the heart of the disorder of the international system created in 1919 was a contradiction which President Wilson embodied and which was never resolved. The liberal commitment to self-determination of peoples, one he repeated time and again, stood in rock-solid opposition to the imperial vision of benign European and American stewardship of the rest of the world in its slow and steady apprenticeship in democracy and good government. Wilson was no admirer of imperialism red in tooth and claw, but the new order which he helped to inaugurate further imbedded Great Power control—be it British, French, Japanese, or American—over less-developed and less-powerful dependencies. "The old hag of colonization," Salvador de Madariaga baldly observed, "puts on a fig leaf and calls itself mandate."[54] The irony was that while informal or mandatory empire was the outcome of Versailles, the European countries which benefited from it were so weakened by the 1914–18 war that they could no longer pay for their imperial privileges.

The focus of this brief survey of visions of peace in 1919 is not on the diplomacy of the interwar years, but on the moment of hope which preceded it. There were many other groups whose vision of outlawing war emerged at this time, and who failed to realize their aspirations. Veterans' organizations affirmed the moral authority of those who could condemn war by virtue of their own participation in it.[55] Women's organizations continued to agitate for peace, as did trade unions and socialist parties.

All these people shared the view that a convulsion on the scale of 1914–18 was so terrifyingly cruel and destructive that no one in his or her right mind could countenance its recurrence. Wilson spoke for a wide body of opinion in 1919. He believed that he owed it to the American soldiers who had died and to their bereaved families to make war unthinkable. Millions of people looked to him to bring about a new order; in that hope they were profoundly disappointed. The failure of his policies is well known, and as I have argued, some of its roots lay in the contradictions of his own vision and that of his liberal supporters. But that failure did not destroy the dream of proscribing war. That vision returned time and again in Europe and beyond.

Was the effort to construct a peace based on self-determination a "minor utopia" in the sense I have used in this book? I believe it was. Compared with the convulsions following the birth of the new Soviet regime, the notion of self-determination appears limited in scope and in scale. The transformation of colonized and dependent peoples into self-governing populations was intrinsically valuable, but it was not, and was never intended to be, a recipe for the elimination of all conflicts or for the transformation of the social order. Instead, the vision conveyed by men like W. E. B. Du Bois and Wellington Koo was the hope that an imperial war of unprecedented destructive power would be the occasion for the construction of a postimperial peace. They were wrong, not because the idea of self-determination was impossible, but because the men who wielded power—including Wilson—prevented its realization. The failure of that project should not blind us to the utopian hopes it triggered, hopes of a better future for the subject peoples of the earth.

3 1937
Illuminations

The world's fair of 1900 was an exuberant celebration of the muscular dynamism of imperialism and capitalism. But in fourteen years, these nations' creative force on display turned bellicose and produced the worst bloodbath in history. The peace of Paris was framed to avoid a recurrence of industrialized violence, but by the 1930s it was obvious that the hopes of a new world order, more stable than the pre-1914 balance of power, were misplaced. In chapter 2, we explored some of the inner contradictions within the thinking behind the peace treaty which ensured this somber outcome. But the shadow of war refused to go away. The Kellogg-Briand Pact of 1928 had spoken of the renunciation of war as an instrument of national policy. Nine years later, to many, war was both unthinkable and just around the corner.

It was in this paradoxical setting that another great fair was organized in Paris in 1937. This fair presented a map of the world, as it was and as it might be. The organizers of the expo provided a cartography wrapped in moral values. Their world's fair told a story filled with paradoxes. Ostensibly the expo expressed in space a set of social relations and practices out of which a bountiful future and peaceful future could emerge. Enlightenment, science, peace: these were the watchwords of the fair. But there were other stories unfolding in the midst of the expo which exposed the frailty of the enterprise and its glaring inconsistencies. The Paris fair of 1937 provided less a description or a destination than a critical point at which the contradictions of the time were exposed. The "minor utopia" of 1937 was peace based on the exuberance of science and technology, literally illuminating the world.

What a spectacle of enlightenment. The 1937 expo was a grand parade, a worthy successor to its predecessors. But if we look more closely at it, the fair still projected the future from a particular past, a particular point of view, that of the major European and imperial powers. Other nations were there, to be sure, but very much in a subordinate capacity. The expo was a *fête,* a European carnival, held precisely at the site of earlier grand exhibitions. The organizers of the world's fair of 1937 tried to re-inscribe earlier itineraries, to reaffirm earlier values, and thereby to legitimate them.[1] But they failed. It was simply too late. Too many contradictions had to be faced. Enlightenment for whom? And under whose national or imperial gaze? Science for what? And under whose control? And as for peace: war was not a distant threat, but a reality, built into the exhibition itself.

The organizers of the world's fair of 1937 knew that a world war was close, that the precipice was there. Many nevertheless clung to the belief that the disaster could be averted, and that "minor utopias" could still be dreamed and, from time to time, actually built. But when war came, a war of unprecedented ferocity and destructiveness, the premises on which such fairs as the 1937 expo rested were blown away forever. World's fairs were held thereafter. There was one in New York in 1939 and in Brussels in 1958, for example, but their political and social agendas were entirely different. The grand fair of 1937 was the end of an era.

The 1937 expo opened on 17 May and closed on 25 November. It had been unable to reach the record 40 million visitors recorded by the 1900 expo, but the total of 32 million visitors was impressive enough. The books of the organizers were balanced, and Paris was now graced by a number of permanent buildings constructed for the fair. The Palais de Chaillot, opposite the Eiffel Tower, and the new museum of modern art of the city of Paris were there. So was the Palace of Discovery, turned into an enduring museum of science.

Within 20 months of the fair's closing, war broke out. In 1940 the Nazis conquered Paris. Where the expo's Tower of Peace had stood, Hitler now surveyed his dominions. The world's fair had vanished, and in its place an infinitely harsher reality unfolded.

During and after the Second World War, utopian hopes of various kinds germinated. And after 1945, they emerged, as utopian visions do, at precisely the point of their previous failures. On 9 December 1948, on the steps of the Palais de Chaillot, and only a few kilometers away from the Hall of Mirrors in Versailles where the doomed Treaty of Peace of 1919 was signed, the disabled French veteran of the Great War and hero of the French Resistance, René Cassin, unveiled to the United Nations assembled in Paris a Universal Declaration of Human Rights. He had been here before, as one of the leaders of the pacifist movement dedicating the Tower of Peace which stood over the 1937 world's fair. A decade later, he returned. That story, full of utopian echoes and promise, is the subject of the next chapter of this book.

Illuminations

Between May and November 1937, Paris, the city of light, became the city of illuminations. The international exhibition of the arts and techniques of modern life literally lit up the capital.[2] Submerged barges enabled the mundane business traffic on the river Seine to proceed unhindered during the day, but every night at 10 p.m. they rose to the surface and on them a panoply of searchlights brought the riverside of the Seine into sharp relief. And on both banks of the river was a dazzling array of illuminated pavilions.[3] The verticality of some of the more grandiose designs added to the sense of spatial radiance. Facing each other, the pavilions of the Soviet Union and of Nazi Germany, appropriately massive in daylight, became beacons when night fell. They pointed to the sky, and to the diverse futures they both foretold and claimed as their own. So did 40 other national pavilions. Similarly bathed in white light were the thematic pavilions arrayed in front of the Eiffel Tower, which itself was illuminated. The pavilions of radio, the cinema, and the press brought a horizontal glow to the center of the world's fair.[4]

All this nocturnal radiance was essential to the message of the exhibition. Here was the Enlightenment of the eighteenth century visualized, materialized, festively celebrated through the central dynamic element of the twentieth century—electrical power and artificial illumination. Visitors were brought to the various gates of the expo on the Metro, powered by electricity. They enjoyed the exhibits by day and could move between them by electric train. And at night, along with fireworks, the visionary world of the nineteenth-century world's fair took on a new and luminous character. Here were science and light and beauty and gaiety merged in a moment of celebration of practical reason transformed into an urban landscape which itself was a work of art.

Why 1937? Because a century before, the first train had traveled between Paris and Saint-Germain. And in 1637, Descartes had published his "Discours sur la méthode"; the exhibition would therefore mark important anniversaries in French scientific history, configured as "the triumph of scientific method over prejudice." The last public event in the life of the exhibition was the transfer of the ashes of Descartes himself to the Pantheon in the Latin Quarter near the Sorbonne.[5]

The central theme of the expo—the symbiosis of art and technology—was manifest during the day, but even more spectacularly at night. The Palace of Discovery, a lasting legacy of the 1937 expo, presented "a living exhibition where the fundamental discoveries which have widened the field of our intelligence, ensured our mastery over matter or increased our physiological security" were on display.[6] There white-coated scientists presented the great experiments and discoveries of science through film, exhibits, and practical demonstrations. This was the plan of Jean Perrin, Nobel laureate, president of the French Academy of Sciences, undersecretary of state for science, and a communist, who wanted to highlight the significance of French contributions to science, as well as to reinforce further investment in applied and pure research.

In this domain, the expo left two legacies. First, the Palace of Discovery itself, occupying one wing of the Grand Palais, became a permanent museum of science, a "Louvre of the sciences."[7] Secondly, Perrin mobilized popular and political support in the Popular Front to continue and deepen the French role in scientific work. This led directly to the founding after the Second World War of the CNRS, a vast institute of French scientific research, constituting a university without students.[8]

The compatibility, the essential partnership of art and technology, were visible in other parts of the expo. There was a Palace of Aeronautics, entirely transparent, the interior of which was decorated by the artists of the "Art and Light" collective, including Robert and Sonia Delaunay. The same group decorated the railway pavilion.[9] Perhaps the most striking marriage of art and technology was to be found in the Pavilion of Electricity and Light. Here the French artist Raoul Dufy decorated the walls of this pavilion with a mural of positively Pharaonic dimensions.

This work of art may be the largest painting in history, measuring in total over 200 feet long and 32 feet high. It was commissioned by the Paris Electricity Company in 1936 on this grand scale, and Dufy accepted the challenge of producing it within a year. And this is precisely what he did, with the assistance of his brother Jean Dufy and André Robert. Dufy listened to scientists; visited workshops, generators, and factories; and then proceeded to paint 250 panels on the subject of electricity.[10] These panels were assembled in a hangar in the Paris suburb of Saint Ouen and were produced with such efficiency that—unlike many other elements of the world's fair—the ensemble actually was ready for the opening of the exhibition.

The pavilion was placed in the Champ de Mars adjacent to the Eiffel Tower. The pavilion was dominated by a tower bearing the beacon of the Breton lighthouse of Ouessant, the most powerful searchlight in the world, with a range of 80 kilometers. Entering the pavilion, visitors came upon a 20-foot-long electrical sparking current, joining two copper spirals; here was the longest continuous electrical current of its kind in the world.[11] This gigantic display was only a prelude to what visitors saw at the heart of the building. Entering a huge hall painted black, they confronted Dufy's mural on the "spirit of electricity," a spectacularly colorful and illuminated mural. The majesty of science was there in all its splendor.[12]

Here was a heroic narrative set in space and time. The story reached from the Greeks to the present, and was embodied throughout the expo. As the poet Pierre Camo put it, the ensemble was "a vast and magnificent garden of forms and colors in which, as in a world of make-believe, the gods and goddesses, the sun and moon, the stars and comets, the thunder and the rainbow, preside over a varied picture of the attributes of nature and the inventions of the human mind."[13] Below this Olympian world, fittingly graced by the Greek gods themselves, paraded 109 men and one woman of science (Marie Curie), all inviting us to marvel at the ingenuity of these benefactors of humanity. It was as if Dufy had taken a medieval representation of the elect going to heaven and secularized it. The gods of science stood before us, and their good works floated in space above their heads.

There could be no better embodiment of the Enlightenment tenor of the great world exhibitions than this grandiose painting. It was a catalogue of progress, fit for Diderot's *Encyclopédie,* tracing the stages of man's conquest of the elemental power of electricity. It constructed a time horizon from great achievements in the past to a future of limitless mastery of the environment, and it obliterated any sense of a divide between the applied sciences and the arts.

The echoes of this paean to electricity were worldwide. The Soviet drive to industrialization had a slogan in the form of an equation: communism equals electrification plus Soviets. In the United States, the construction of great dams and the electrification projects of the New Deal were symbols of how the state could overcome the Depression through vast investments in electric power. The spread of radio and cinema highlighted the significance of electricity. The pavilions of the Press, and of Cinema, Photography, and the Phonograph, placed under the arches of the Eiffel Tower, all testified to the reliance of information flow on electricity. Power stations, not great industrial machines, were the centerpieces of this exhibition.[14]

Dufy's "Spirit of electricity" captured much of the forward-looking spirit the organizers of the expo wanted to cultivate. But the fate of the mural suggests another story entirely. Disassembled after the expo of 1937 was closed, the mural passed into the hands of the nationalized French electricity industry after the Second World War. The mural was then donated to the Museum of Modern Art of the City of Paris and displayed from 1961 in a building which itself was constructed for the 1937 exposition. There it remained until 2001, when curators discovered that every one of the 250 wood panels that made up the work was covered in asbestos. Whether Dufy used this substance or it was added later as a fire retardant is not clear. But the dangerous effects of asbestos made the painting a health hazard, and required its removal from public display for extensive restoration.[15] Ironically, this encomium to science has produced its mirror opposite: here was a carcinogenic vision. Utopia has turned into dystopia.

The notion that science was not easily controlled, that it was a golem, a monster created by man but ultimately outside the command of human agency, was a theme with many contemporary echoes. It is there in the dark novel of utopia gone wrong, *Brave New World,* published in 1932 by the British novelist Aldous Huxley, grandson of one of the pillars of the Darwinian revolution. It is vividly present in Abel Gance's film *J'Accuse,* released in 1938, telling the story of a war veteran turned scientist who discovers the ultimate weapon so terrible that it would make war impossible. But the weapon is stolen by evil men intent on adding it to their nation's arsenal, and to prevent catastrophe the hero calls the dead of the Great War to rise from their graves and confront the living with the horror of war. Anti-technological rhetoric was common in America as well.[16] The 1937 Paris world's fair, like the 1939 New York fair after it, stood against such naysayers, but the essential role science played in re-armament and in preparations for war as a whole was so evident that doubts were bound to remain as to what the long-term legacy of applied science would be. Now, if you will, please fast-forward to 2001, when the painting was quarantined. If a great painting about the wonders of science could transmit cancer-causing asbestos to those who came to admire it, then anything is possible.

Of course this particular problem emerged long after the end of the 1937 expo, but it was foreshadowed by other elements in the world's fair which enable us to see how fragile was the visionary impulse in the later 1930s. Consider the imagery of the electric light, so central to the ambiance and the message of the 1937 expo. That image, that symbol was at the center of a second major work of art which was created for the 1937 Paris exposition, the *Guernica* of Picasso.

Visions of Violence

This mural is the most lasting legacy of the 1937 international exhibition. The story of its creation has been told often, and entire libraries are devoted to unraveling its symbolic universe. I want to draw attention to a few features of this project and, by locating them within the exhibition and within the political context of 1937, throw some light, as it were, on its power and its contemporary resonance.

Picasso was invited to produce a mural for the Spanish pavilion in January 1937. He chose the site for the mural and its dimensions while the architects worked on the final design of the building.[17] The subject matter emerged only later in the spring. This is how Picasso himself described the evolution of his thinking on this project: "The Spanish struggle is the fight of reaction against the people, against freedom.

My whole life as an artist has been nothing more than a continuous struggle against reaction and the death of art. . . . When the rebellion began, the legally elected and democratic republican government of Spain appointed me director of the Prado Museum, a post which I immediately accepted. In the panel on which I am working which I shall call *Guernica,* and in all my recent works of art, I clearly express my abhorrence of the military caste which has sunk Spain into an ocean of pain and death."[18]

Picasso's *cri de coeur* followed the destruction of the Basque market town of Guernica on Monday, 26 April 1937. On that morning, the city center was destroyed by aerial bombardment. One hundred thousand pounds of explosives were dropped on the town by bombers of the German Condor Legion. Approximately 1,600 people, or one-third of the population of Guernica, were killed. A small arms factory and the town's railroad station were not hit; the target was civilian life itself.

On 30 April, three days after the attack, the story appeared in the Parisian newspaper *Ce soir,* along with black and white photographs. The next day, Picasso began drawings for his mural. Within a few days he was transferring them on a white canvas, measuring 3.5 by 7.5 meters. This surface divided in half his atelier at 7 rue des Grands-Augustins, a few meters from the Seine. In early June 1937, only four weeks after it had been begun, the painting was transported to the Spanish pavilion of the expo. Picasso himself offered his drawings and sketches for sale in the pavilion; postcards of the work were also available.

The mural remained there until the end of the expo, which coincided with the last days of the Spanish Republic. The painting went on tour to raise money for the victims of the war; then it migrated to the United States, where it was displayed at the Museum of Modern Art in New York. It rests now behind bullet-proof glass in a hospital transformed into a major modern art museum, the Reina Sofia in Madrid.

Picasso rarely produced statements with direct or overt political content. *Guernica* is therefore an exception.[19] But then, the Spanish Civil War, going badly for the Republican side, was exceptional enough. At the time he produced *Guernica,* Picasso had begun to write plays and had developed his interest in poster art and ambulatory theatrical productions; both played an important role in Spanish Republican and French artistic experimentation. In January 1937 he wrote a pamphlet entitled "Dreams and Lies of Franco," and illustrated it with 14 watercolors showing the Caudillo as absurd or terrible. These images had some of the features of a comic strip, yet again prefiguring elements absorbed into the *Guernica* painting. Here is a sample of Picasso's verse in "Dreams and Lies of Franco": "cries of children cries of women cries of birds cries of flowers cries of buildings and stones cries of bricks cries of beds and chairs and curtains and casseroles and cats and papers cries of smells that scratch cries of smoke."

Guernica is an extension of these ideas; the poster, the newsreel, the satiric simplification of form are all there. But the painting is more complex than that. His distinctive figuration paralleled and reproduced the dismemberment of the human body in war, just as Picasso's poem in "Dreams and lies of Franco" dismembered sentences into fragmentary cries.

Picasso is mixing elements of immediacy—the dashes on the horse, for instance, suggesting newsprint or the newsreel—and of eternity. The mythic and Christian references are visible, though problematic. On the left side of the painting is a Pietà; the mother grieving over the child is palpable. Below this ensemble and to the right is the cruciform figure of the dead male figure, with a broken sword and severed arm on one side, an outstretched hand on the other. Where hope may lie is uncertain: perhaps in a flower, perhaps nowhere.

All these elements of the painting are well known. But what about the electric bulb or eye at the center of the painting? Might it not be possible to read this part of the painting in a straightforward way, in the context of illumination and the world's fair of 1937? To be sure, there are many other readings of this puzzling image. It may be seen as a divine eye, a Mithraic eye. Or it may be an interrogation. Perhaps Picasso was forcing us to ask the question how to look, where to look, at disaster: from a balcony, from afar? The eye of Picasso's painting may describe the predicament of seeing the horror of war.

These references and readings are persuasive, but they may miss something more immediate, more obvious. If the eye is god-like, then it is striking that Picasso constructs this facet of divinity in the form of a lightbulb. As we have seen, the god of electricity is all over Dufy's mural, painted at precisely the same time. These two artists knew each other, and Dufy's construction of his immense paean to electricity was widely publicized. Similarly, the overarching theme of light and of enlightenment was ubiquitous in the preparation of the world's fair. Enlightenment was one of the most powerful themes of the Popular Front government elected in 1936 and which used the expo to broadcast its ideas about equality and the democratic character of the cultural *patrimoine* of France. Picasso and everyone else in Paris were well aware of the massive illuminations being constructed along the river and in the adjacent neighborhoods. The visionary, hopeful, progressive character of this demonstration of the mastery of nature was built into the fabric of this expo, as it had been in the grand exhibition of 1900, which Picasso had seen as a young man.

In 1937, with the murder of innocent civilians clearly in mind, and with the perpetrators of this crime, there in Paris, proudly bathing the German and Italian pavilions in the light of progress, Picasso seems to have turned the issue of illumination inward. It casts its light not on progress but on war and innocent suffering. Guernica was destroyed by planes dropping bombs—planes which could not fly without electricity, and bombs constructed through the scientific genius of chemists and engineers whose skills were harnessed to kill rather than to heal or warm or enlighten. It is tempting, therefore, to locate Picasso's placement of an eye at the center of his *Guernica* in the context of an exhibition elevating, celebrating, praising the applied sciences of vision and light. The lightbulb at the heart of *Guernica* illuminates horror. It is a dark sun.

Dufy's mural retained some of the utopian charge and the naive faith of the previous century. Picasso's use of the lightbulb, and the absence of a sky from which death had descended, inverts the optimism of Dufy and many other artists whose work appears in this world's fair. In the mural of Picasso, hope turns dark, and enlightenment fuels murderous barbarism. There are many narratives in this astonishing work of art, and all I claim is to suggest one text that may be imbedded in it. What a way of exposing the contradictions within and the frailty of the hopefulness of the 1937 expo, and of peeling away its glittering exterior to reveal another face of the contemporary world, an uglier face, one capable of crimes almost beyond description.

The Pacifist Challenge

The two murals—exercises in public art—encapsulated the collision between hope and despair which created massive fissures in the 1937 expo itself. In other ways, we can see how, under the pressure of contemporary events, the dream of a peaceful future began to dissolve.

The principal entrance to the expo was on top of the hill of Trocadero, facing the Eiffel Tower on the other side of the river. There, at the pinnacle of the entire fair, surveying the entire panoply of pavilions, was a Tower of Peace, erected by the international veterans movement. This tower was 164 feet high and had a diameter of 17 feet. It was covered in bronze and decorated in a spiral motif of olive leaves interspersed with words of peace in six languages. This columbarium, an echo of Trajan's column, showing not the spoils of war, but the glories of peace, stood in front of a semicircular building, the Peace Pavilion. In it were illustrations of the horrors of war, and of the efforts of the League of Nations to outlaw it. This was the only multinational pavilion, reflecting efforts to supersede national conflicts leading to war. It was a pavilion broadcasting the message of the League of Nations, already paralyzed by its inability to stop warfare from disfiguring Ethiopia, Spain, and China.[20]

What is most striking about this part of the expo is its direct confrontation of the logic of national self-representation and assertion unfolding in the national pavilions below. Here international politics entered the expo in a way not visible in previous fairs. The choice was there, in front of the visitors: national differences could be asserted to the point that they led to war, or they could be contained, superseded as it were by a higher cause, an assembly of nations dedicated to peace.

Although the outcome of this choice soon became evident, in the mid-1930s the hope that disaster could be averted was still strong. In May 1935, during the final preparations for the exhibition, the newspaper *Le Matin* told its readers

> The 1937 exhibition will be the triumph of Paris, of peace and of international solidarity. Since the last exhibition in Paris, the world has completely changed and every day this change accelerates. We are marching forwards (with a stunning rapidity) towards a new world, one we can hardly imagine. It is good to call a halt in the midst of this vertiginous course and to seek out not only where we are heading (which is impossible) but also where we are today. . . . Men, all blind, remain separated by their absurd national prejudices. That is why it is important that through the marvels of this exhibition, we have a magnificent opportunity to make everyone see that among men, whether they like it or not, whether they know it or not, there remains a profound solidarity.[21]

Initially, the fair as a whole was supposed to demonstrate this point. No overt pacifist statement or pavilion was planned for the exhibition. But the outbreak of the Spanish Civil War in 1936 and the victory of the Popular Front in the elections of the same year changed the political climate. The organizers of the expo had made no provision for a Pavilion of Peace, and when the Popular Front government envisaged that it favored the construction of such an international pavilion, the commissioners agreed to provide only one-third of the funds needed to build it.[22] Outside money was raised to pay for the design, construction, and decoration of the column and the Pavilion of Peace. The group which raised the cash was the *Rassemblement Universel pour le Paix* (RUP), the Universal Alliance for Peace, a French-dominated organization of veterans of the Great War, intent on using the expo to pass on the pacifist torch to the young generation.[23] Among its prominent members were many veterans of the peace movement, including the French jurist René Cassin, about whom we shall hear more in the next chapter.[24]

The international veterans movement was an anomaly. It turned military service into a commitment to international peace, and therefore moved in exactly the opposite direction from that of veterans' movements in Germany and Italy. The membership of pacifist organizations among ex-soldiers numbered in the millions. Here was a vast population who spoke with the moral authority that only soldiers had, and who saw themselves as men reprieved from a death sentence carried out on nine million of their brothers. Many of the bureaucrats who ran the expo were among these survivors. So were countless visitors. Yes, Hitler and Mussolini were war veterans, though Mussolini invented much of his "heroic" military record. But there was another outcome of war service, a pacifist outcome, and the centerpiece of the 1937 expo was one of its last expressions.[25]

Ironically, labor troubles delayed the completion of many buildings designed for the 1937 expo, including the Pavilion of Peace. When the fair opened in May, the city was a veritable construction site. By the time the Pavilion of Peace was completed, the Popular Front had fallen. The former prime minister, Léon Blum, inaugurated the Pavilion of Peace on 8 July 1937. There, at the entrance to the fair, the attack on Guernica was condemned as an abomination, the antithesis of everything for which the 1937 expo stood.

Oddly, and perhaps as a sign of the times and of the deeply fractured character of French politics as a whole, on the very eve of its inauguration, the pavilion was damaged by a fire. Since the entire expo was still under construction, it is possible that this fire was an accident. More likely it was an act of arson which expressed in criminal form some of the deep hatred of the Popular Front, and everything it stood for, shared by many on the right of French politics.[26]

All the guests of state who entered the expo passed the Peace Tower and Pavilion, including the Italian and German ministers, whose forces were fighting alongside the Nationalist rebels to overthrow the Spanish Republic. The Japanese delegation passed the Tower of Peace while its armies were engaging in atrocities in Nanking and elsewhere in China, which made Guernica appear comparatively minor. And yet, we cannot simply dismiss the pacifist message of the 1937 expo as simple lip service. In Paris, many people stood out against another war as both unthinkable, and alarmingly just around the corner, and used the platform of the 1937 world's fair to say so.

On 10 September 1937, an eternal flame was deposited at the Tower of Peace by veterans of the Great War who had transported it from Fort Douaumont at Verdun, the scene of the longest and one of the bloodiest victories of the Great War, then to the tomb of the unknown soldier under the Arc de Triomphe.[27] On Armistice Day 1937, the RUP led a procession to the Tower of Peace. There the vice-president of the organization told the crowds that "peace is in the hands of every one of us."[28]

Here was the challenge to the 32 million visitors to the 1937 expo. They were presented with evidence of ingenuity and cultural brilliance on every side. Art and technology promised a future of unlimited bounty, but none of it would be possible if another world war were to break out.

Collisions

One large difference between the Paris expo of 1900 and that of 1937 is that the later fair confronted head on the ideological and political conflicts of the contemporary world. No less could be expected from a celebration orchestrated by a French government of the left, besieged as it was on all sides. The world's fair of 1937 brought together in a literal sense antagonisms and fault lines in international affairs, with the implicit aim of demonstrating that reason and harmony could contain such conflicts. The Tower of Peace rose above all the national pavilions. It stood as a last, desperate sentinel, a reminder that all the ingenuity and beauty displayed below would be swept away in the event of war. The fair was a Popular Front against war.

Yet, the organizers and designers of individual pavilions had other things to say on the subject. Their buildings were symbolic statements of national achievements, explicitly excluding even the slightest reference to the violence either on or just under the surface of daily life.

What is intriguing in the work of cultural representation here is what they excluded. The silences of the world's fair of 1937 pointed to the powerful tensions which would tear the world apart.

Palestine

In 1931 there had been a massive colonial exhibition on the outskirts of Paris. Among those pavilions was one celebrating the progress of the Jewish settlement of Palestine.[29] Now, six years later, a Pavilion of the Land of Israel stood among the nations. The international pavilions were divided into two groups which rose from the Seine to the Palais de Chaillot above them.[30] The Pavilion of Palestine was placed behind the pavilions of Japan, Romania, and the Soviet Union in the southern cluster; facing them were the pavilions of Spain, the Pontifical States, and Germany, among others.

The proximity of a Zionist and a Nazi pavilion was no more incongruous than the proximity of a pavilion celebrating the Spanish Republic and one dedicated to the Pontifical States, in which hung a mural by the Catholic painter José María Sert to the Catholic martyrs of the Spanish Civil War.[31] And, as we have seen, Picasso's *Guernica* was placed a few yards from the Nazi pavilion, the proud statement of a regime directly responsible for the war crimes depicted there.

The Zionist pavilion was constructed to refute every calumny the Nazis and their fellow travelers had leveled against Jews. The four sections of this two-story building were dedicated to showing the strength of Jewish settlement in Palestine in agriculture and industry as much as in intellectual life and technological research.[32] As one French Jewish observer put it: "Everyone talks about the struggle against anti-Semitism through positive propaganda. It is essential to show to world opinion that Judaism is capable of creating useful and original works in all the domains of human culture. The 1937 exhibition in Paris gives us the possibility of doing just that: the creation of a Pavilion of Judaism, through which we can have artistic, literary and theatrical productions which will highlight the genius of Israel in modern civilization."[33] And that is precisely what they did. A series of musical evenings and theatrical events brought to Paris elements of the new state in the making in Palestine.

This pavilion was an act of defiance at a time when anti-Semitism was ominously on the rise. The French prime minister Léon Blum was the target of a tide of anti-Semitic abuse, and no one coming to the expo could have been unaware of the racial ideology of Nazi Germany. The Pavilion of the Land of Israel was anti-Nazi propaganda, and like all the other pavilions, what it represented was highly selective. No mention was made of the convulsions occurring in Palestine at the time, following an Arab revolt over increasing Jewish immigration, which itself was precipitated in large part by Nazi persecution.

Nazi Germany

All the pavilions in the world's fair were conjuring tricks. They presented their national narratives in censored and highly selective form. The exhibition organized to represent the new Germany at the 1937 expo was expressly framed to exclude any direct or explicit reference to the racial character of the regime or to its character as a police state. The swastika was present, but only as an internal decorative motif. Nevertheless, the pavilion's architecture conveyed Nazi messages of a powerful, though unstated, kind.

The pavilion, designed by Albert Speer, was called the "Deutsches Haus," more a pantheon of the German spirit than a simple pavilion of Germany.[34] By 1937 the Nazi regime had consolidated its hold on power. It had successfully defied the French and the League of Nations and proceeded to rearm and to reoccupy the Rhineland, an act specifically forbidden under the peace treaty of 1919. Germany had escaped the bonds placed on its power after the Great War and was once more the dominant military force on the European continent. This is what the building meant.

Nothing could have been further removed from the Tower of Peace and the pavilion dedicated to the work of the League of Nations, which Germany was then in the process of demolishing. The German pavilion was five times more expensive than any other national pavilion. It presented a three-columned massive face to the world, a tower of Germanic myth and national self-assertion atop which perched a very unpacific eagle. The pavilion's design drew upon many different traditions.

The classical reference of the facade gave way to a secularized cathedral within, replete with stained glass windows and a nave in which visitors could inhale the spirit of German culture.

There were echoes too of funerary architecture. The German pavilion had elements of the Temple of Honor built in Munich to house the graves of Nazis killed in the abortive coup d'état of 1923. This reference to the Nazi cult of death and sacrifice inverted yet further the message of the Tower of Peace above it. This pavilion was "a quasi-religious monument, sombre and imperial."[35]

Here was a defiant statement of the "national spirit" which had brought the Nazis to power and had transformed international politics. In September 1937, the Berlin Philharmonic Orchestra under Wilhelm Furchtwängler performed in the pavilion Beethoven's Ninth Symphony and Wagner's Tristan and Isolde.[36] It was this Germany, the nation of myth and vision, which was celebrated.

This message had power and appeal. The illuminations of Nazi ceremonial choreography may be seen as precedents for some of the events of the 1937 expo itself. The torchlight parade of 14 July along the Champs Elysées, illuminated at night, recalled the extraordinary power of the film *The Triumph of the Will,* made by Leni Riefenstahl the year before. Here was a form of Nazi aesthetic which was imitated by the French organizers of the expo.[37] Karen Fiss suggests that the Popular Front, haunted by the fractured character of French political opinion, found much in the German self-representation to admire and to imitate. The Nazis were the masters of spectacle, and in the framework of the 1937 expo, the Popular Front could show that the drama of movement and mass action was not restricted to right-wing political movements.[38]

The French organizers of the fair went out of their way to accommodate German demands. A planned display of German culture interpreted by exiles and enemies of the Nazi regime was scotched, while the organizers gave their blessing to a separate floating pavilion of the city of Cologne.[39] *Commissaire général* Labbé affirmed that these displays were the foundation of "a solid bridge of peace." As a gesture of solidarity, Hjalmar Schacht, Hitler's Minister of Economic Affairs, ordered the *Tricolore* flown next to the German flag in front of the pavilion.[40]

The designers of the interior adopted a style which Jeffrey Herf has termed "reactionary modernism."[41] Though many of the objects were strikingly modern, their presentation and setting were classical and conservative, like many of the other buildings constructed for the expo including the Palais de Chaillot itself. Advanced technology was "spiritualized" by its location within a national project of reconstruction and renewal.[42] Two huge mosaics on "Work" and "Strength Through Joy" projected an entirely idealized image of a unified nation, one in which the labor movement had been completely destroyed.[43]

Bear in mind that over 1.5 million French soldiers had died 20 years earlier in the defense of their country against German invasion. Paris itself had been shelled. What had come of the sacrifice and the victory the blood of so many Frenchmen had purchased? Here too the 1937 expo was eloquent in its silences. The German pavilion was powerful, ominous. It represented a cultural arsenal, a place of preparation for war and domination.

The Popular Front government took a calculated risk. They took the decision of the Germans to spend massively on this display as evidence that they were minded to limit their expenditure on armaments. Trade as a barrier to war was another slogan of the French organizers of the expo; the more commerce flourished, the less risk there was, so they reasoned, of international conflict turning into war. These were vain hopes, based not on a clear analysis of Nazi plans, but on a deep sense of the reluctance of the French population as a whole to go to war again.

Soviet Union

Powerful and ominous were words that suited the Soviet Pavilion, facing Speer's edifice at the heart of the expo. The Soviet Pavilion was designed by Boris Iofan, a Ukrainian architect. He created a series of ascending galleries 450 feet long, and the building had an impressive sweep of an ascending curve. The walls were lined with Samarkand marble, and the entire edifice was capped by a 79-foot-high sculpture by Vera Mukhina. This statue portrayed a male industrial worker and a young woman collective farm worker. It was cast in 65 laminated stainless steel sections and weighed 75 tons.

This ensemble was just slightly lower than the German pavilion. This was the result of a bit of minor espionage by Albert Speer. When he came to Paris to research the site of the German pavilion, he "found" a copy of the Soviet plans. He was able to locate the German eagle at an angle and an elevation which made it appear ready to withstand whatever challenge the Communist pair offered to Germany. Indeed the three vertical columns of stone were ideal representations of a Teutonic wall, holding back the Slavic tide rising just across the Chaillot gardens at the fair.[44]

The mirror imaging of the two great totalitarian states at the heart of the 1937 expo was a calculated gamble on the part of the organizers of the fair. The pairing of the two adversaries was made more emphatic by the construction of an underpass at the point where the two pavilions intersected with the Pont d'Iéna, thus highlighting their spatial equivalence, above the flow of visitors along the Seine. That the Soviet Union and Nazi Germany were enemies was no secret. What possible linkage could there be between these pavilions and the Tower of Peace at the top of the hill, completing the spatial core of the entire international ensemble? Was there a message in this triangulation of Germany, Russia, and peace, suggesting that peace superseded nation? Perhaps, but another way to interpret this pattern is to suggest that, whatever the intention of the organizers, the 1937 expo represented the fragmentation of the European and international order so well that it undermined the pacific message it was at pains to deliver. The organization of space, highlighting antagonism, was at least as emphatic as the rhetoric of peaceful coexistence.

Colonies

Spatial decisions tell us much about the final set of contradictions at the heart of the world's fair of 1937. These surround the issue of colonialism. The presence in the expo of what the French euphemistically call "La France d'outre-mer," overseas France, was concentrated on an island in the Seine, the Ile des Cygnes. There 16 pavilions were crowded into a relatively small space. It was evident at this expo that, compared with the 1900 world's fair and the 1931 colonial exhibition, held on the outskirts of Paris, both the space of representation of empire, and the empires themselves, had shrunken considerably.

Unlike previous world's fairs, this exhibition presented displays on French territories only—British, Dutch, and Belgian imperial possessions had vanished from the show—and so the space accorded to imperial populations, their cultures and their products, was limited. There was no trace either of newer colonial powers like Italy. One reason for this narrowing of the imperial field of representation was political. The contradictions between universalism and colonialism in French Republican thought and policy were accepted wholeheartedly by the organizers of the conference. Here was *la mission civilisatrice* in all its supposed glory. According to this view, other imperial powers were exploitative; the French were engaged in Enlightenment. The fact that a Socialist government was in power in the months leading up to the opening of the expo made no difference at all.

In the very layout of the Paris expo of 1937, the dilemma of the Enlightenment posture with respect to subject peoples was exposed, not for the last time.[45] The colonies were dwindling, but they were still there. They were slightly off-center, slightly liminal, just to the south of the main axis of the expo linking the Eiffel Tower and the Tower of Peace. And to the French organizers of the exhibition, the presence of these pavilions attested to the benevolent nature of French colonial rule.

In the British case, this conjuring trick was not so simple to perform in 1937. France's colonial travails were still to come, but by the late 1930s, Britain faced insoluble problems in several of the territories under its control. Palestine was torn by bitter fighting between Arabs and Jews, with the British mandatory power in the middle. How fortunate for Britain that the issue of Palestine was presented in a national, rather than a colonial, context in this exhibition. India was much more problematic, since it was not a mandate but an imperial possession. But the Indian National Congress solved the problem for the organizers of the expo by refusing to come unless granted national status. Ceylon declined the invitation for the same reason.[46]

Ethiopia refused to come to Paris "due to the present circumstances," meaning Italy's colonial conquest of it. Italy invaded Ethiopia in 1935 and annexed it on 9 May 1936. The impotence of the League of Nations to stem this aggression, and the atrocities to which it led, was the beginning of its final demise. To salute Italian colonialism was simply unthinkable.[47]

In 1937, after the world's fair had opened, Mussolini plundered the Axum obelisk from Ethiopia and had it delivered to Rome, where it has stood to this day, despite repeated promises of its return.[48] But what was the difference between Mussolini's display of the fruits of colonialism in Ethiopia and the French display on the Ile des Cygnes (or the Elgin marbles in the British Museum for that matter)? The only differences were in the Republican framework of colonialism in the French case and in the temporary nature of the display in Paris.

The line of reasoning was familiar. Since the eighteenth century, a long line of "cosmopolitan" Republicans have constructed their mission in the world as bringing the fruits of their system of government and administration to non-Europeans. The 1937 expo was squarely in this tradition. France overseas was Republicanism transplanted and supposedly flourishing in the Levant, the Maghreb, in Africa and in Indochina.[49] And in return for the "gifts" of good governance and lessons in citizenship, the colonies offered France her art, her culture, and her indigenous handicrafts.[50] The exotic aromas and colors of Moroccan cuisine or textiles were both attractive to visitors and of interest to French merchants. Here the commercial side of imperialism was legitimated for yet another reason: its potential to help the French economy emerge from the shocks of the world economic crisis, felt in France later than in other countries.[51]

Now we tend to see this kind of exchange as simple exploitation, as in many respects it was. But in the 1930s many Europeans could believe that their dominion was benign. The subject peoples who came to

Paris in 1937 to demonstrate native handicrafts were just as exotic and colorful as their predecessors had been 37 years before. The world was still organized around a core, and it still had a far-flung periphery. At the 1937 world's fair, this remote world was drawn into the "metropole." There national, ideological, geopolitical, and commercial interests came together at a moment just before another world war swept it all away.

Conclusions

After the Second World War, decolonization accelerated to the point that no celebration of enlightened imperialism could be configured in the same way as in the 1937 expo. Similarly, the cult of science of the liberator was compromised by the uneasy response of many scientists themselves to the emergence of atomic energy and the atomic bomb. Two of the core beliefs of the 1937 expo—the dedication to the European *mission civilisatrice* and to expanding the benevolent power of science—were shaken or transformed by the events of the subsequent decade.

So was the commitment to pacifism, which also helped determine the geometry of the 1937 world's fair. The replacement of the League of Nations by the United Nations announced the beginning of the American half-century, that time when, after the earthquake of the Second World War, the balance of power shifted across the Atlantic. International exhibitions could not even hint at the kind of pacifism present in the 1937 expo. The Brussels world's fair of 1958 highlighted the power of atomic energy, which America dominated, and which peace activists feared like the plague.

Paris 1937 was therefore the last stand of a much older tradition of thought and action, one deeply parochial in its geography of the world and in its implicit sense of racial and cultural superiority. The spatial organization of the world's fair exposed the contradictions in this way of looking at the world. A pacifist tower cast its thin shadow on two totalitarian pavilions below it, the Soviet and the German. Both presented a profile to the world which offered not a hint of the murderousness of either regime. Around the corner, as it were, from the German pavilion, stood the Spanish Republican pavilion and the *Guernica* of Picasso, an enduring indictment of the lies these pavilions told. By the time the Spanish pavilion had been dismantled, the Spanish Republic had been destroyed. In fact, when the organizers of the expo tried to recover the costs of taking down the Spanish pavilion, they were politely informed that the committee responsible for the display no longer existed, nor did the government which had appointed it.[52]

Science was visible everywhere—in the new Palace of Discovery, in a host of pavilions, and in the illuminations which turned this parade of culture and products into a carnival. But the limits of Enlightenment could not have been more obvious. During the 1937 expo, in an obscure corner of the French *Bibliothèque Nationale,* the philosopher and German refugee Walter Benjamin, a student of spectacle, exhibitions, and utopias,[53] reflected on these themes, and three years later, in 1940, he produced a powerful judgment on the cast of mind reflected in the world's fair. "There is no document of civilization," Benjamin wrote, "which is not at the same time a document of barbarism."[54] Just a few months after Benjamin wrote this sentence, barbarism had indeed conquered Europe. Benjamin was dead, a suicide on the Franco-Spanish border, but his statement, which has been published as part of his seventh thesis on the philosophy of history, endures.[55] It is inscribed on a memorial tombstone to Benjamin and others in the cemetery in Port Bou where—so it is said—his remains had rested at one time. It could serve as a fitting epitaph to the Paris exhibition of 1937.

4 1948
Human Rights

Many people have described the Universal Declaration of Human Rights as a utopia, understood as a pipe dream, a fool's vision. In this book, I have tried to reclaim the term "utopia" and to define it in a limited and positive way as a mode of describing where we are by describing where we have not yet reached. The term "minor utopia" is more restrictive still in locating the boundaries of these visions, their tendency to rethink not all of the world, but parts of it which can be transformed.

One minor utopian in the sense I am using the term was René Cassin. I will interpret his work on the Universal Declaration of Human Rights here as a dark utopia, one located very specifically in the history of the Second World War. Placing this document in this particular historical perspective has advantages other than the purely biographical.

It enables us to identify some of the darker shades of meaning inherent in the document, and the paradoxical context in which that meaning emerged. Why paradoxical? Because it discloses the tendency of many figures, great and small, to dream dreams, to erect new edifices, to imagine futures at precisely the moment when those dreams, structures, and futures were least likely to be realized. The Universal Declaration of Human Rights is one such dream, born out of catastrophe, and yet strong enough to transcend it.

I want to insist upon the multiplicity of such visions, on the temperamental affinity of many people who decided not to make a linear extrapolation of the current balance of power, but to leap over it at difficult times. This is the environment in which the Beveridge Report of 1942 was born, released, and disseminated when the Nazis were approaching Alexandria and Stalingrad, and when only a clairvoyant could have predicted an Allied victory in the Second World War. This is the field in which Jean Monnet imagined a European community, with the border between France and Germany as porous as that between Connecticut and Massachusetts. This is the terrain in which the French resistance dreamed of social justice and Dietrich Bonhoeffer celebrated the possibilities of doctrineless Christianity, and where an imprisoned Antonio Gramsci wrote that the more constrained his circumstances, the wider his field of vision. In this context, imagining a different world is an act of defiance, a rejection of the likely in the search for the necessary.

My first argument is that the Universal Declaration of Human Rights is one such vision, with a particularly European origin. Accepting this framework offers us a distinctive reading of the document and its political and cultural meaning at the time of its creation. It is a dark utopia, one with tragedy and failure written all over it.

That tragedy had a particular meaning to one of its chief draftsmen. René Cassin lost much of his family in the Holocaust, but he also witnessed the wholesale dismantling and humiliation of the French Republican tradition. My second line of argument is that the particular form of utopia he designed is intrinsically French. It was aimed to resurrect French political culture by turning back to the Universal Declarations of 1789 and 1793, and thereby to revive the duality of French Republican thought, which was (and remains) both deeply patriotic and aggressively universal.

It is hard from this distance to realize how shattered the French Republican project in the Second World War was. No other occupied country collaborated in the same way—directly, legitimate government to legitimate government—with the Nazis; no other occupied country enacted Nazi policies on deportation and forced labor, for example, within the parameters of the old civil service. Thus one of the chief administrators of the prefecture of the Gironde, Maurice Papon, initialed receipts for taxi fares paid by the parents of Jewish children, brought from outlying villages to Bordeaux for deportation and death. He did this (and many other things) as an agent of the French state.

How to confront this calamity was an issue of both domestic and international importance. I want to set the Universal Declaration in this specifically French context. To do so requires attention to the life's work of René Cassin. In 1948 he stood at the podium at the Palais de Chaillot in Paris, in a building designed to mark the 1937 international exhibition of arts of modern life. It was at this expo, as we have seen, that Picasso's *Guernica* was displayed for the first time. A decade later in the same public space, Cassin came to offer another cri de coeur against war and the indignities that produced and accompanied it.

To tell the story of how he got there we must return to an earlier calamity, the outbreak of war in 1914. Thirty four years separate that date from the signing of the Universal Declaration of Human Rights in 1948. But the pathway leading from the trenches of the First World War to the Palais de Chaillot is worth noticing, for it frames an interpretation of the work of one of the central figures who drafted the document.

Attending to this narrative also enables us to explore more fully aspects of what I would like to call the utopian temperament. The kind of person I have in mind is one with an initial ideal, a commitment to a mission. That calling is a given, but so is its partial or complete frustration. Utopians are those who commit, and then hit a brick wall.

What distinguishes them from others is that they then get up and (perhaps against reason or logic) do not turn cynical or passive, but manage to take a leap in the dark, and despite all, they dream dreams which reconfigure their initial commitment in new and imaginative forms.

In this book, I have examined the ideas not of all utopians, but of particular people in search of "minor utopias." René Cassin was one of them. He was a "minor utopian." Why the adjective *minor*? The reason to avoid accepting the term *utopian* without qualification is its contamination through association with the great murderers of the twentieth century. Hitler and Stalin wanted to transform the world and murdered millions in the effort. Instead I adopt a more circumspect view and consider those with a vision, though not a vision of transforming the whole world, or of weeding out the "base elements" supposedly standing in the way of a glorious future. Instead I want to recover the visions of those who sketched out what García Márquez termed "utopias for life," utopias "wherein no one can decide for others how they are to die," and "where the lineal generations of 100 years of solitude will have at last and forever a second chance on earth."[1]

The minor utopia of the Universal Declaration of Human Rights is one such vision. It was the product of the work of many men and women, but one individual in particular must be credited for its form and much of its substance. This person is not Eleanor Roosevelt, whose name is indelibly associated with the project, but rather the French jurist René Cassin. To understand the document, we must understand his life and its trajectory. First I will go back to his military service in the Great War. Then I will explore his role in the international veterans' movement and the League of Nations. Thirdly, I will follow him in his escape to London from France after the debacle of 1940 to work with de Gaulle and the Free French movement. Fourthly I will sketch out some of his work to recast the French Republic as part of his contribution to the drafting of the Universal Declaration of Human Rights.

La Boucherie

In August 1914 René Cassin was a 26-year-old lawyer, born in Bayonne
to a prominent Jewish family living in the southwest part of the country.
The outbreak of war found him in Paris, from which he immediately
journeyed south to join the 311th Infantry Regiment in Aix.[2] In September he was promoted to the rank of corporal and served near Saint
Mihiel in northeast France. He remained in this sector, where on 12
October he was ordered to take a squad of 16 men and advance toward
a German strong point near Chauvencourt on the outskirts of Saint
Mihiel. German emplacements made such a probe suicidal. All 16 of
his men were hit by flanking fire from well-entrenched machine guns
and artillery. He himself was hit in his side, abdomen, and left arm. He
knew that a stomach wound was almost always fatal. Cassin refused
evacuation, but told a passing soldier to inform their commander of the
strength of the German positions in his sector. In addition he begged
this man, Sergeant-Quartermaster Canestrier, to write to Cassin's father
that he had died painlessly (which was a lie) and to send to his family
a leather cigarette case, two gold pieces of 100 francs, and some small
bills that he handed over to Canestrier. Canestrier vanished, and so
did Cassin's valuables.

Clearly Cassin thought he would never survive. He asked a priest if
someone could say Hebrew prayers with him. The priest replied that his
prayers were for everyone, and gave him the benefit of his company.[3]
He survived the night and was then handed over to the French army
medical services.

The way these units were organized in the early days of the war almost killed him. The rule was that on mobilization you reported to your
regiment in the region where you were assigned. After battle, you returned to *that* site, either intact, wounded, or in a coffin. Consequently,
Cassin would not be treated in northeast France but in Provence, 600
kilometers away. He was sent south, first by wagon and then by train,
and after a 10-day journey he arrived in the regiment's hospital in
Antibes on the Mediterranean. The surgeons there were astonished to
see that he was still alive, despite the wound to his abdomen, which

had been torn to shreds (Cassin wisely drank virtually nothing on the trip, knowing that to do otherwise likely would have been fatal). Still, they told him that he might not survive more than a few hours and that they needed to operate immediately—there was no time to anesthetize him beforehand. This Cassin accepted, and he somehow endured an hour under the surgeon's knife. He later said he was fortunate that the operation was on a less than sensitive part of his anatomy.

While in convalescence, he wrote the story of his service and framed it in terms of a conventional French patriot and a Jew. One of the Jewish men with whom he served had told him that a Jew had to be more courageous than non-Jews in order to evade accusations of cowardice. This bravery was Cassin's trademark. But for our purposes what is intriguing in his own narrative is how laconic it is. Nowhere does he dwell on the hideousness of being wounded, of the incompetence of his own medical service, of the appalling cruelty inflicted on him by it. His journey alone, during which he had to physically hold his intestines in his stomach, is a middle passage which might have broken many other men. He saw and felt what battle was and yet managed to frame his part in it without feeling that it had undermined his own identity.

The courage of his war service was palpable, but so was the miserable treatment he received. This was hardly exceptional among the wounded or among those disabled and discharged. Here is an early instance of Cassin's capacity to work through a traumatic event, to retain elements of his idealism despite institutional obstacles, and to recast his commitment in new and broader terms.

What followed his convalescence was a fight not against the enemies of the French state, but against the callous, inhuman bureaucracy of the French state itself. He was a founder of the French veterans movement and worked tirelessly to ensure that men who had been wounded in the service of their country would have a decent pension, or that the orphans of the men who did not return would be given a start in their lives.[4] This work brought him up against recalcitrant and indifferent authorities. These rights were earned, not only by military service and the shedding of blood, but thereafter by harsh political struggle. French veterans, like others in Europe, were given their pensions grudgingly, not as a right but as a privilege, wrested from the hands of unfeeling administrators and the physicians who served them.

This struggle for natural justice for the lame and the blind, for men who had answered their countries' call but then found that few nations were prepared to heed the voices of the wounded, created something new in European affairs—a pacifist veterans' movement. The notion of soldier pacifists may seem like a contradiction in terms, but in inter-war France it was not at all oxymoronic. French Republicans like Cassin saw it as their life's work to ensure that their sons would not have to enter *la boucherie*—the slaughterhouse—of modern warfare. They knew what it had been like and were determined that the young would be spared the fate they had suffered. In striking contrast to the myth of the war experience and lies about the nobility of armed conflict conjured up by the Nazis—veterans too—the French *ancien combattant* movement made war on war. On 11 November they marched to the war memorials in every tiny village; they did so in civilian dress and deliberately out of step. They had been civilians in uniform, and they bore a message from their comrades who had died to the young: war must never return.[5]

The League

This political program was crippled from the start. The focus of the veterans' movement in France was justice for their brethren, and for the widows and orphans they had left behind. But their mission extended into the field of international relations as well, and that meant struggling with and through the League of Nations.

As a leader of the French veterans' movement, Cassin had much to do with International Labor Organization (ILO), headed by Albert Thomas, the successor to Jean Jaurès, assassinated leader of the French Socialist party. This association, building on welfare work in munitions factories in wartime, was committed to ensuring the right to work of all those disabled in the war. On 2 September 1921, Cassin was present at an international veterans' discussion of work for war invalids. The meeting was sponsored by the ILO in Geneva. Cassin represented the largest French veterans movement, L'Union Fédérale, with two million members, and it was at this venue that he and his colleagues met for the first time (without a gun) with enemy veterans from the defeated Central Powers. Such contacts convinced Cassin that veterans had to work within the League of Nations if their voice was to be heard in international affairs.

Here is Cassin's point of entry into politics of a very peculiar kind. It was a kind of nonpolitical politics, filled with contradictions that ultimately destroyed it. Cassin was among a host of French veterans who felt that their vision was *above* politics. These were angry men, men who had formed what they termed the generation of fire and who were not prepared simply to let the old merry-go-round of politics go on its way. Politics was a word they used as an insult, and they played with it and mutated it into a host of venomous rhetorical forms, all filled with vitriol—*politicaille, politicailler, politicaillerie, politicaillon*—and roughly translated as political scum, criminal rabble, wily, shady, scandal-ridden little piggies at the trough, vulgar, partisan, blood-sucking shits. The vulgarity of this language is not to be missed: we are dealing with ex-soldiers, and however high-minded their motives, their anger descended to the gutter, where they believed their opponents, the politicians, were to be found.[6]

How to get around them without joining in their miserable game was an open question. Cassin refused the offer of a post in the cabinet of Herriot, who came to power as head of a left-center coalition in 1924. Instead, Cassin was glad to join the French delegation to the League of Nations as the representative of the veterans movement, as if that institution were free of all the faults of politics at home. At the same time, he took the initiative in establishing an international veterans organization, CIAMAC, which met for the first time in Geneva in September 1926.[7]

Cassin's first speech was on international intellectual cooperation, and, wearing his hat as a professor of civil law in Lille (and from 1928 in Paris), he worked to transform the League of Nations from a forum for world peace into a juridical assembly.[8] The starting point was the construction of a center for international intellectual cooperation, an idea sponsored by Henri Bergson and the ancestor of the United Nations Educational, Scientific, and Cultural Organization (UNESCO). The midpoint was the construction of a protocol for the peaceful resolution of international disputes. Once this was drafted and approved, the League would reach the end point, as a kind of forum of international justice, a tribunal, whose moral authority would rest in large part on the support of tens of millions of veterans, who knew a thing or two about war. "A world marked by the blood we shed would do well to accept the imprint of our ideas," he noted.[9]

Disarmament was one of them. Cassin served on the French delegation to the League of Nations for 14 years, from 1924 to 1938, and much of his work in this body concerned arbitration and disarmament. "It isn't enough," he wrote in 1929, that veterans are represented at the League. What mattered more is that "in each nation burned by the war, organizations develop public opinion and that of youth to struggle against the mundane and the murderous language" of armaments and national defense. Only then can they "stand for the principles of Geneva: the defence of peace and security."[10]

The Assault on Sovereignty

It was during his service at Geneva that Cassin began to formulate notions which ultimately bore fruit in the Universal Declaration of Human Rights. In Geneva Cassin had a front-row view of the fragility of an institution which challenged the supremacy of state sovereignty as a principle of international political order. He saw how entrenched were conventional approaches to unbridled state power as the ultima ratio of international affairs. No one could question his patriotism, but he had no time for what he termed "the ordinary obstinacy of old ideas which, in the name of the absolute sovereignty of states flow directly into the construction of armaments, to the politics of prestige, and then to war."[11]

Cassin discerned that there was an immense gap between the thought of conventional nationalists like Clemenceau or Henry Cabot Lodge and the notions of those like Briand or Wilson, who were prepared to sacrifice some elements of state sovereignty to the League of Nations, if that were the necessary price to erase war from the international political agenda. In the first round, Lodge won the argument, and older notions of state sovereignty prevailed. If a more robust League of Nations or any similar venture would ever succeed, it would do so only after a sea change had occurred in both academic and popular notions of the indivisible sovereignty of the state, and of the power of the duly elected statesman, acting like a "châtelain dans son château" (lord of the manor in his castle).

Two major events led to the undermining or refashioning of this older definition of sovereignty. The first was the Nazi constitutional and lawful seizure of power in 1933; the second was the legal transformation of the French state in 1940 under Philippe Pétain and Pierre Laval. These episodes would open the door to a new kind of thinking on state sovereignty, and these developments are discussed below. But first it is important to note that Cassin—among others—was active long before these two political earthquakes in the effort to provide an alternative view of state sovereignty. And that view ultimately bore fruit in the 1948 Universal Declaration of Human Rights.

Cassin made the argument explicit in the course of a series of lectures he gave in 1930 at the Academy of International Law at the Hague.[12] He titled his series "The New conception of Domicile in the Resolution of Conflicts of Law," which aimed to "desacralize" claims of state sovereignty. Only then, he believed, was it possible to create an environment in which the all-powerful state cannot by its own fiat and with impunity trample on the rights of the individual.

Before turning to the structure of the argument, it is useful to note the echoes of Cassin's earlier battles. He joined up in defense of a state whose meanness to the disabled men it had sent out to fight had to be resisted through a vigorous campaign originating in civil society. That struggle first for and then against the state is a stance to which

Cassin returned throughout his life. It ensured that he would resist conventional views of political authority and state sovereignty and look to revising them in order to establish a just order.

In the Hague he sketched out how such a new system might operate. To this end he juxtaposed the law of domicile to the law of citizenship and argued that each has merit as a basis of political rights: "The tie of nationality is not a primary or a unique bond among the members of a nation: there are other more elementary ones . . . the home, the town, the city. It is precisely because the right of domicile rests on a universal and permanent fact, the concreteness of a place where one lives, a place were families reside, that it has been taken into consideration everywhere to determine the point of juridical attachment of persons and to order more or less completely the status of the individual."

Regimes change, but (with luck) domiciles remain. People remain attached to their homes whatever happens at the political level. This has always been the case among minorities and refugees, as long as they respect the laws of the land. The right of alien residence (while obeying the laws of a land) in a host nation is therefore based on the prior and superior force of domicile over nationality. One reflection of this principle, Cassin argued, is that married women in France could have more than one nationality; in deciding which applies, her domicile could be the point of reference. Cassin here cites explicitly the plight of over one million Russian and Armenian refugees whose personal status was thrown into doubt by war and revolution. Their standing, he insists, must be based on a right of domicile independent of nationality.

To Cassin, the choice between nationality or domicile had evolved over time. Throughout the latter part of the nineteenth century, in an era of state-building, those standing on claims of nationality grew in number. By the third decade of the twentieth century, most European states took this approach; in contrast about the same number of people lived in a state where domicile trumped nationality. These were the Anglo-Saxon countries and Latin American states, in which immigration played a powerful role. Cassin's point is that it was time for the pendulum to move back toward the claims of domicile over nationality in a continent riven by powerful political and ideological quarrels exposed during the Great War. Jurisprudence had to follow events, in order not to be overwhelmed by them.

The implications of the argument are far-reaching. A commitment to internationalism describes the bonds of the veterans of different countries who came together to work with Cassin in his international veterans' organization. The same commitment is the principal defense of vulnerable minorities stalked by powerful nationalist movements in states worried about their ethnic composition. Domicile over nationality helps correct the imbalance in then current international law "which confers to the sovereign nation a competence which is too exclusive, simplistic, and ill adapted to satisfy the complex needs of international life."[13] What is worse, despite having done its job well in the period of state formation, "the principle of nationality has exhausted its beneficial effects and has become a germ of doctrines destructive to the international community and oppressive to the individual." And finally, by privileging the concept of domicile over nationality, Cassin points the way to establishing the standing of the individual within international law itself. This same line of argument was adopted by the Institute of International Law in New York in October 1929, when it drafted a "Declaration of the international rights of man."[14] It was not Cassin's view that nationality had vanished as a principle of law, but that in some cases domicile should prevail.

Note the date of Cassin's disquisition. Three years before the Nazis came to power and used sovereign law to destroy every single trace of natural justice, Cassin constructed a powerful argument against the extremes of state sovereignty then still unrealized. How much more powerful then, his argument against the all-powerful state once that state under Hitler had made war first on millions of his own citizens, and then on the rest of Europe.

Free France

Political thought rarely follows straight lines. Before returning to his mission to reinterpret and reduce the pretensions of state sovereignty, Cassin turned to its defense. He also abandoned the bankrupt anti-political politics of the veterans' movement and moved into the center of political life as he would not have done in the interwar years.

The circumstances in which he had to act were unusual. In May 1940 he was the legal advisor to the Ministry of Information of the besieged French government under Reynaud. When, after the military collapse of May 1940, Raynaud asked the 84-year-old Marshal Pétain to take over the government, Cassin went back to his family in Bordeaux, and after Pétain had sued for peace, he fled the country with his wife.

This turn of events was a catastrophe on every level. Cassin was among the many French Jews who had no idea that their Jewishness compromised their Frenchness. After May 1940, they had to rethink both. Cassin did not hear the famous broadcast wherein Charles de Gaulle, then a minor figure who had been undersecretary of defense and who had a certain reputation as a controversial author on strategic and military policy, announced that France had lost a battle but not the war, and invited all patriots to join him in a Free French movement in London. Cassin learned of the appeal the next day and decided to respond. This decision was not easy for a man with little or no English. But after paying his taxes, finishing the composition of a lecture on civil law, and saying farewell to family members, he left France on board an Australian troop transport and landed in Britain on 28 June. The next day he met de Gaulle in a small office in South Kensington. Cassin recalled the exchange vividly: "General, I have come directly from Bordeaux in response to your appeal of 18 June which I know only by hearsay. I had decided definitively not to accept defeat which signifies the ruin of liberty in the world as a whole. . . . I believe that France needs all its sons and I consider it my duty to join you immediately. I am a jurist, a professor of law, I am also an invalid having served in the infantry in the war of 1914–18. Finally, I presided over one million disabled ex-servicemen in the Union Fédérale. Do you think my support will be of use to you? 'You have come just in the nick of time,' de Gaulle said. These were his first words." Then he added: "If Hitler could hear this, he would say, 'these two are completely mad.'" And perhaps they were.

What Cassin offered de Gaulle was priceless. At this dark stage of the war, de Gaulle's office was virtually penniless and entirely dependent upon the British government. His role was not at all fixed, but the British were prepared to support a lawful, fully functioning alternative to those who had just made peace with the Nazis in France. Cassin's training as a professor of law and his standing in the veterans' movement were precisely what de Gaulle needed. Cassin first drew up an indictment of the new Vichy regime as illegitimate, a rogue state whose writ was legally null and void. Pétain's government was *de facto*, not *de jure;* therefore, the Republic had not died; it had been usurped by the traitors who had signed the Armistice with the Nazis. This document de Gaulle presented to Churchill 48 hours after his first meeting with his new jurist colleague. Then de Gaulle asked Cassin to sketch out the structure of a shadow Republic, an administration in exile. This body claimed the legitimate authority to speak for France and to continue the traditions of the French Revolution and the Republic betrayed by the collaborators of Vichy. This political coalition the British were prepared to fund, and to promote as part of the alliance against Hitler. And so Free France came into being.

In this organization, Cassin was everywhere, and his role was dignified further by the decision of a Vichy court to convict him of treason and sentence him (and de Gaulle and all other Free French leaders) to death in absentia. According to Jean Lacouture, it was Cassin who won de Gaulle over to Republicanism, and damped down the embers of his earlier Bonapartist tendencies.[15] On 29 July 1940, Cassin started broadcasting for the BBC. He was responsible for the publication of the *Journal Officiel de la France Libre,* the Congressional Record of the government in exile. He opened an Office of French Nationality in London, where, in the tiny corner of France which was his office, domicile and nationality were reconciled. Being in London was itself a certificate of freedom. Then in November 1940 he was named permanent secretary of the new French Council of Defense, and in that capacity joined many meetings on the future shape and reconstruction of Europe. He was the architect of the Administrative Conference of Free France, the group planning for the return of the "true" Republic to the Continent. He was responsible for maintaining ties with France overseas, her colonies and dominions. In 1944, he held three portfolios in the new French national committee, Justice, Law, and Public Instruction, all essential agents for the restoration of French political culture after the nightmare of defeat, occupation, and collaboration.

Through these posts he joined Allied discussions on war crimes trials and on the shape of the postwar world. For the purposes of this book, the most important were the two St. James conferences of 1941. The first, held in June and July 1941, was a gathering of Britain's occupied Allies in exile—Poland, Yugoslavia, Greece, Czechoslovakia, the Netherlands, Norway, and Luxemburg. Cassin wrote the following declaration, adopted by the conference: "The sole solid base of a durable peace will be the spontaneous collaboration of the free peoples of the world who, once the menace of aggression is eliminated, will be assured of their social and economic security."[16] This statement is significant in two respects. First, it was made by a Frenchman, representing Free France on equal terms with all the other allies. Secondly, it anticipated by just a few weeks the broad terms of the Atlantic Charter, which on 14 August committed Britain and the United States to work for "the final destruction of the Nazi tyranny" and for the establishment of a peace "which will afford that all men in all lands may live out their lives in freedom from fear and want." No one (including Hitler) missed the force of this declaration, coming four months before Pearl Harbor. The Grand Alliance was about to be born, and Cassin was there at the birth.

The second St. James conference, held in September 1941, enabled Cassin to put human rights on the agenda of the future world order. This was not without its difficulties, in that other members of the French delegation, in Cassin's opinion, were not at all happy that a Jew was speaking for France.[17] All the anti-Semites were by no means on the other side of the English Channel. Still, Cassin managed to retain his position and offer this summary of the French position: "The French consider of equal importance in the establishment of a real peace, the consecration of essential human freedoms and the concerted use of technical progress for the social and economic security of all peoples."[18]

Note the melange of peace, human rights, and social security: the general outlines of the postwar mission of the embryonic United Nations are evident here. Note too the date: this statement was made at a time when the Soviet Army had suffered a catastrophic set of defeats, when the German army effectively controlled the entire European continent, and when the German air force was still making life dangerous and miserable for Londoners and others. The Blitz of 1940 was over, but no one could have predicted that the Allies would win the war. Much of the discussion at the St. James conference of September 1941 concerned the provisioning of civilians once the Allies reclaimed the Continent. Yet less material issues were there, too. It was precisely when victory was so remote that visions of a different future began to emerge. René Cassin was one of the visionaries, who based the path from waging war to creating the United Nations on securing a linkage between human rights and world peace.

After the liberation of France in 1944, Cassin returned home. He found that 27 members of his family had died during the occupation, either of natural causes or as deportees. This was not an exceptional number among French Jewish families. What was particularly difficult to take was that their deportation was administered by French bureaucrats serving the French state. How could French political life be revived? One task, entrusted to Cassin by de Gaulle, was to give the Conseil d'Etat a new role, that of defender of the individual against the depredations of the state. As president of this important institution, as ombudsman of the French bureaucracy, Cassin worked to systematically dismantle the administrative latticework of collaboration.[19]

But the task Cassin set himself was wider still. The only way to restore French political culture, he believed, was to restore its international standing as the carrier of the central messages of the French

Revolution. And at the core of those ideas, at their very heart, was the concept of human rights.

There is a Jewish dimension to this story, though it was not always central to Cassin's outlook. Jewish emancipation was a by-product of the French Revolution. By returning to the sources of that event, and reaffirming the values which lay in the documents and institutions it created, Cassin and others helped reconstruct French Jewry as a constituent part of the French nation after the worst calamity in its modern history.

Human Rights

This return to origins is where Cassin's human rights project must be set. Once again a paradox: it is precisely at the moment of the most spectacular failure of the French Republican tradition that Cassin set himself the task of universalizing one of its central messages.

Cassin's participation as French delegate to various inter-Allied commissions brought him into contact with the general ferment of ideas surrounding the shape of the European world after the defeat of the Nazis. What he manifested in these deliberations was what I have termed the utopian temperament: the capacity to take the measure of extreme conditions by leaping over them. Thus in 1940–43, when the war was not going at all well, the welfare state of the Allies arose out of the domestic needs of the warfare state. Rations were limited but aspirations were not.

In London in September 1941 Cassin made the point that a future peace could be secure only if it were based on a set of international commitments on human rights. His central proposition is that the domestic behavior of regimes like the Nazis'—what he termed, in a reference to Hobbes, "Leviathan-states"[20]—was a threat to world peace. Here Cassin's critique of the notion of state sovereignty found practical expression. There were two overlapping lines of argument he developed during the war. First, a war which was being fought to restore territoriality, to liberate nation-states from occupation, had to fashion a peace which went beyond territoriality. The fatal flaws of the League of Nations could not be replicated. Secondly, nations could no longer be the sole arbiters of the rights their own citizens enjoyed, since those rights were the property of humanity as a whole. Fashioning a new international order required the recognition that older notions of sovereignty had to be revised in those areas where domestic injustice and international order overlapped. Chief among them was the domain of human rights.[21]

This is the position Cassin developed during the Second World War and in its immediate aftermath. His work in preparing the Nuremberg Tribunal further deepened his commitment to the principle of transnational jurisdiction in cases of gross violations of human rights. Human rights were clearly on the agenda when the United Nations assembled in San Francisco in June 1945. The third provision of its charter stated that it aimed "to achieve international co-operation in solving international problems of an economic, social, cultural, or humanitarian character, and in promoting and encouraging respect for human rights and for fundamental freedoms for all without distinction as to race, sex, language, or religion." Shades of the St. James's conference of 1941, indeed. But what instruments would be fashioned to realize this objective?

Three years later, at the Palais de Chaillot in Paris, Cassin provided the answer. How he got there, in collaboration with Eleanor Roosevelt and others, is a story already told authoritatively by Mary Ann Glendon.[22] Cassin left his own account of these deliberations in a set of lectures he delivered at the Academy of International Law at the Hague in 1950.[23] I will have a word to say in a moment about the symbiotic relationship he developed with Eleanor Roosevelt, but first I want to examine the precise language Cassin used in his formal presentation in Paris. "I have the honor" he began, "to report the firm adhesion of France" to the Declaration,

> an act which, 100 years after the revolution of 1848 and the abolition of slavery on all French territory, constitutes a step on the global level in the long battle for the rights of man.
>
> Our declaration is the most vigorous, the most essential of protests of

humanity against the atrocities and oppression which millions of human beings suffered throughout the centuries and more particularly during and between the two last world wars.

In the midst of this torment, heads of state, Pres. Roosevelt, Pres. Benes, both no longer with us, proclaimed the meaning of this crusade, and in the name of France, then imprisoned and gagged, I had the honor at the international conference held at St James Park on 24 Sept 1941, to join my voice to theirs, in order to proclaim that the practical consecration of the essential liberties of all men is indispensable to the establishment of a real international peace.[24]

Once again, the Frenchness of the occasion is unmistakable. Humiliated, compromised, eroded in a myriad of ways by the German occupation and collaboration, French political culture here rose out of the ashes. In the presence of the assembled United Nations, Cassin introduced not a Bill of Rights, not a Formal Commitment or Protocol, but rather a Universal Declaration of Human Rights. Here, in the shadow of the Eiffel Tower, within sight of the Place de la Concorde, the French Republican tradition was renewed.

At this moment, in that place, a particular political tradition, injured but intact, was performed. The content of the two documents mattered less than their family resemblance. The 1789 document affirms in article 1 that "Men are born and remain free and equal in rights"; the 1948 document states that "All human beings are born free and equal in dignity and rights. They are endowed with reason and conscience and should act towards one another in a spirit of brotherhood." Equality in dignity *and* rights opened the door to social and economic perspectives on the question of what was needed for liberty to be realized. Thus the twentieth century went beyond the eighteenth. Such reformulations were important, but they hardly obscured the reaffirmation of the integrity, the wholeness of the French revolutionary tradition and its legacy to the world. By standing up and telling the world in French that the Nazis had failed to destroy this legacy, Cassin was helping to heal the wounds (some self-inflicted) his nation had suffered during the war as well as pointing the way toward a new set of principles in international affairs.

This emphasis on the French, domestic setting of the creation of the Universal Declaration of Human Rights helps us to account for other features of the document. The fact that it was not initially a convention becomes clearer in this light. It took 20 years for France herself to ratify the European convention on human rights. There were too many colonial skeletons in the French closet, as well as a vicious guerilla war in Algeria, not a colony but an integral part of metropolitan France, to enable French leaders until the 1970s to sign on.

But Cassin's position on this point arose from other considerations. He had seen the collapse of Wilson's initiative in 1919. Together with Eleanor Roosevelt, he worked to form a commitment which could bypass the dangerous corridors of the United States Senate. A nonbinding declaration was unlikely to draw American isolationists into a life or death struggle; that could come later, but by then, Cassin hoped, other pressures would turn human rights into practical politics. Secondly, the cautious tactic of aiming at a declaration rather than a convention enabled Roosevelt, Cassin, Charles Malik, and others to absorb and blunt Soviet bloc criticism of the Declaration as suffering from all the faults of liberal individualism and "democratic formalism." There was some force in this charge. Cassin was interested in asserting the rights of the individual as against the state, and Soviet delegates could not possibly go along with that. The Soviet Union had lost 20 million men and women in defense of their territory, and they were reluctant to engage in intellectual arguments about flaws in the theory of state sovereignty. Other delegates, moreover, had little sympathy for the content or character of the Declaration, but, to protect their claim for American aid after 1948, they were prepared to hold their peace. Delegates from Islamic countries may have gone along for this reason.[25] But for whatever reasons, the Universal Declaration of Human Rights was adopted by the United Nations, and it remains one of its foundational texts.

Conclusion

The Greek poet Kafavy liked to say that the best way to approach a problem is at a tangent. This point has some bearing on the question of the origins and meaning of the Universal Declaration of Human Rights of 1948. From an American perspective, it appears to carry on the work of FDR, whose mantle his widow bore with dignity. But from a European perspective, there were other shadings, other colorations, to the framing of the document. Many people constructed it; the Canadian lawyer John Humphries was one; the Lebanese diplomat and scholar Charles Malik was another. There are draft documents of the Declaration in Cassin's own hands in his personal papers in the Archives Nationales in Paris.[26] It would be wrong, though, to say that he was the author of the document. He created one of its personae, that which arose from the French Republican tradition.

That tradition was in fragments in the years between 1941 and 1948, when the preparatory steps were taken before the Declaration was formally drafted. During the Second World War, the legally constituted French state collaborated with the Nazis at every level and committed staggering crimes as part of that collaboration. After the Liberation, the execution through rough justice of 15,000 French collaborators settled some scores, but it hardly effaced this disaster. Instead, during the war itself, another kind of resuscitation began, which created a vision of human rights as one of the pillars of international peace. That imaginative leap moved in a manner which defied realism; how could one speak of human rights when the ovens of Auschwitz were working to full capacity? And yet that is precisely what Cassin did. He managed to absorb the shock of a massive failure of the French Republican tradition, and then to leap over that failure to reaffirm the values of Republican France and to extend them to the rest of the victorious alliance.

There are other dimensions of this story which take us beyond France and beyond 1948. Cassin's critique of sovereignty and his work for disarmament moved forward earlier developments in international law, that "Gentle Civilizer of Nations," as Martti Koskenniemi has termed it.[27] Cassin's vision overlapped as well with that of Jean Monnet and others in the construction of the European community. Cassin also played an important part in the elaboration of the European human rights convention. From 1965 to 1968 he presided over the European Court of Human Rights. At the end of his term, he was awarded the Nobel Peace Prize.

How far he had come from his time in London during the war, when he was a refugee and fugitive with a price on his head. Utopian energies have unforeseeable outcomes that are hard to predict. Located in the context of the two world wars, Cassin's was indeed a dark utopia, a minor utopia, one born out of humiliation, to be sure, but from that inauspicious beginning came an initiative which over time took on a life of its own.

5 1968
Liberation

The one decade in the twentieth century marked most strikingly by utopian initiatives was the 1960s. Some entailed individual freedom, defined in terms of individual dress, comportment, music, drugs, sexuality. Others took the form of collective experiments, more focused on communal ways of living than on changing the social order as a whole. But there were broader visions, too. Many groups of people organized and attacked enduring patterns of prejudice and discrimination in Soweto, Birmingham, Londonderry. Warfare—in Algeria, in Vietnam, in the Middle East—brought out mass movements of protest against French or American or Israeli imperialism. But by the 1960s the energies of minor utopians had shifted away from the pursuit of peace and toward the pursuit of different kinds of freedom. In this chapter I focus on a number of instances in which moral thinking and liberation were braided together. To me this is the essence of a transnational, transcontinental phenomenon we now know under the label of "1968."

The Moral Road to Redemption: Liberation Theology in the 1960s

Many of these utopian visions were religious in character. Some originated in Latin America, although the vectors of global culture and education linked such developments in Colombia, Nicaragua, and Peru to parallel developments in European centers of thought. A global dialogue emerged in these years, therefore, which promised to transform the face of theology and to reconfigure Christian thought on social problems. No account of "minor utopias" in the twentieth century can avoid this strand of thought and action, commonly termed "liberation theology."

The trajectory of this innovative movement was complex. In the 1950s in Latin America and in a number of European universities, committed Catholic students began to formulate a set of propositions aimed at resituating Catholicism in the harsh material conditions of their home countries. The key issue for these people was to place the reality of poverty at the heart of Christian teaching. Making the Church not only for the poor, but of the poor, had radical political implications, not lost on those in authority, both secular and ecclesiastical.

What came to be called liberation theology is the collective product of this generation of Christian activists. Their beliefs cost the lives of a number of those who joined the movement. Still more were imprisoned, exiled, or silenced in other ways. But such persecution did not stop the spread of the message that liberation of the body and the spirit was a matter for this world, and that such liberation was an urgent necessity for millions of poor people, for whom "development" meant a drastic worsening of their lot in life.

A refashioning of the Christian message in the 1960s thus accompanied the convulsions of economic development in general. But more particularly, this intellectual and social ferment arose out of the political and social upheaval of the 1950s and 1960s. The Cuban revolution of 1959 formed the backdrop for many of the debates surveyed below. But there was another, more directly material, source of these reflections on what it meant to be a Christian in the 1960s. Anyone with eyes to see confronted a crisis of subsistence in the major urban centers of Latin America. In Lima, Bogota, Mexico City, Buenos Aires, and elsewhere a population explosion followed the decline in mortality brought about by the control or elimination of a number of major infectious diseases. This gain in life expectancy produced a "bulge" generation, born on the land but able to find work and subsistence only in the cities. Their arrival exacerbated chronic problems of overcrowding, illiteracy, and the exploitation of unskilled labor. The entire logic of "development" was to move such people away from the land toward areas of industrial growth, but once they got there, millions found themselves in even worse conditions than those dominant in the countryside.

Against the background of chronic rural poverty and an apparently unstoppable urban catastrophe, a number of Catholic thinkers in Latin America began to pose a set of questions about the place of poverty in their religious thought, and about the place of the Roman Catholic Church in this world of dramatically increasing misery visible alongside dramatically increasing wealth. The original and subversive answers they offered to these questions opened up the project which came to be termed "liberation theology."

This movement of ideas was not the product of one man or a few individuals. It grew out of the experience of many devout Catholics within the Church itself.[1] The role of men in Catholic orders was significant in crystallizing this movement. These people lived their lives relatively independent of the hierarchy of the Church, and in their orders they constituted a kind of utopian community apart from the world. In the 1960s men in these religious orders—Dominicans, Franciscans, Jesuits, Trappists—fashioned many of the pillars of liberation theology.[2]

These people formed a cohort of Latin American Catholics who came of age immediately after the Second World War. Their intellectual formation was both domestic and international, originating in Peruvian, Colombian, or Argentine traditions as well as in facets of European thought—philosophy, psychoanalysis, literary theory, as well as theology—which were also brought to bear on their pastoral work and on their broader activities as public intellectuals.[3]

Gustavo Gutierrez came from a poor parish in Lima, Peru, to Louvain and then to Lyon; Juan Luis Segundo, a Jesuit who had studied philosophy in Buenos Aires, traveled to Louvain and Paris, where he wrote his *thèse d'état* on the "religious communism" of the Russian emigré philosopher Nicholas Berdaeff.[4] Ernesto Cardenal was born in Nicaragua. He studied in New York and in 1956 became a novice at Gethsemeni, a Trappist monastery in Kentucky, where the mystic and poet Thomas Merton resided. Cardenal, a poet himself, was ordained as a priest in 1965.[5]

This ferment was not restricted to Catholics. The Argentine theologian José Miguez Bonino, a Methodist minister, moved from Buenos Aires to Emory University and then to Union Theological Seminary in 1958. He too was touched by the wind of change in theology, returning to Argentina, where he published "A Protestant Interpretation of Vatican II" in 1967.[6] Clearly, "north" and "south" were not segregated in the ongoing dialogue among religious men and women in these years.

The intermingling of different currents of Christian thought in different parts of the world was evident. It was not exposure to European or North American ideas which was decisive, but the use of these ideas by Latin Americans to better equip them for understanding the tasks they faced, given the reality of poverty and inequality in Latin America. What was most significant was their commitment to renew the Church by listening to the voices of their parishioners, the voices of the poor.[7]

The key that opened the door to this movement was provided by Pope John XXIII and the Second Vatican Council. Convened in 1962, this *Aggiornamento,* or gathering for the purpose of the "modernization" of the Roman Catholic Church, stimulated much reflection by priests on the need to uncover how to express their faith in a manner their parishioners could understand and accept.[8]

This meant considering the point of view and predicament of the vast majority of Latin Americans. To be sure, Latin America was only one such place for reflection on what Catholicism meant to the poor, but it was there that many of the first tentative steps toward what came to be termed "liberation theology" were taken.

The braiding of different religious traditions and strands of thought is evident in the history of liberation theology. The spirit of openness in religious thinking inaugurated by Pope John XXIII was of fundamental importance. So too was the sense that the Church was there for the poor as well as for the rich, for unskilled workers as much as for the well-to-do. Such convictions were central to other initiatives within the Catholic world. Among them were the Catholic youth movements in Belgium and France, in particular the JOC (*Jeunesse ouvrière chrétienne*), founded in 1925 by the Belgian priest Joseph Cardijn.[9] Latin American students who came to Europe in the 1950s and 1960s were confronted by many different forms of Catholic social action.

After their years in Europe and America, these Latin American Roman Catholics returned home with a deepened sense of their mission and, in light of the misery around them, of the urgency of the task that awaited them. To bring the Gospels to the impoverished city dwellers of Lima, Gutierrez, along with other Catholics in other cities, began to reinterpret them.

This is how Gutierrez did so in the 1960s.[10] The sources and rhythms of his thinking are Latin American in general and Peruvian in particular, though with many echoes of European traditions.[11] One of the most important influences on his ideas is the work of the Peruvian Marxist José Carlos Mariátegui, who wrote of the "organic intelligence of ordinary people" and their essential role in the future life of the country. Mariátegui was a Catholic who believed that the church had betrayed the people by its alliance with the ruling elites. Of equal importance was the friendship Gutierrez developed with the Peruvian novelist José Mariá Argueda, who similarly indicted the Catholic Church for abandoning the poor. His work gave voice to the Quechua peasants and their search for the solace of God. Although a freethinker, Argueda shared much with Gutierrez and his mission to reach out to the Peruvian poor.[12]

In 1964 Gutierrez attended a meeting in Petropolis, Brazil, on the future of theology in Latin America. Here he raised the difficult issues of the Church's attitude to violence and revolutionary struggles.[13] Then in Chimote, Peru, in July 1968, and the following year in Cantigny, Switzerland, Gutierrez formulated some of the ideas he contributed to what became known as liberation theology. He insisted that Latin America was in the throes of a whirlwind called "development," which he understood as potentially opening up the liberation of man from poverty.[14] Living in the world of development, experiencing its convulsions, meant "that we cannot separate our discourse about God from the historical process of liberation."[15]

A closer look at his emerging outlook discloses the analytical power as well as the expressive appeal of his writing. A radical rethinking of what is meant by the term "development" is at the core of Gutierrez's message in his address to the National Office for Social Research in Chimbote.[16] Here he suggested that the term took on new significance when it moved from the realm of economic modernization to theological regeneration. He told this group of priests and laymen that "it is not possible to live in today's world without a commitment to the process of liberation." Their dialogue with God, their theology as Christians, rested on their faith in Christ. Indeed, "to have faith in Christ," Gutierrez affirmed, "is to see the history in which we are living as the progressive revelation of the human face of God." Here is "a sign of the times," "which calls Christians to action."[17]

Refusing to choose between a theocentric and an anthropocentric point of view, Gutierrez held that "it is much more exact to say that we are passing from a theology that concentrated excessively on a God located outside this world to a theology of a God who is present in this world." Here Gutierrez found support both in the writings of Karl Barth and in the words of Pope Paul VI about the presence of God in history and "in the midst of human beings." What these texts proposed was a theology exploring the links between "human emancipation—in the social, political, and economic orders—and the kingdom of God."[18]

Gutierrez drew out of Paul VI's encyclical *Populorum progressio* the notion that development is the passage from "less human conditions to more human conditions." Among these "less human conditions" are "the lack of material necessities for those who are without the minimum essential for life." "Less human" also means "oppressive social structures, whether due to the abuses of ownership or to the abuses of power, to the exploitation of workers or to unjust transactions." Thus "less human" are oppressive structures, something Christians are generally unaware of. Here Gutierrez adopts a dialectical approach. Yes, structures must change, but so must human beings. It is futile to argue as a priest that "we can only change the structures by changing human beings. . . . After Marx, it is no longer possible to say first change the human beings and then the structures." They must change together or they will not change at all.[19]

This idea is a critical one, pointing to a fundamental difference between the human rights utopia surveyed in the last chapter, and the utopias of the 1960s, which focused less on the individual than on the collective—the church, the party, the trade union, the "movement."

This unusual movement was religious and ecclesiastical, coming from within the Roman Catholic Church itself. What could be more orthodox, argued Gutierrez, what could be more consistent with the Messianic promise of the Church of Christ, and of the Old Testament prophets who pointed the way to Christ, than the theology of liberation? "The prophets announce a kingdom of peace. But peace supposes the establishment of justice, the defence of the rights of the poor, the punishment of oppressors, a life without the fear of being enslaved by others. . . . The elimination of misery and exploitation is a sign of the coming of the messiah."[20]

The European texture of Gutierrez's position is evident in the way his oration in Chimbote drew on Descartes and Hegel, as well as on twentieth-century Catholics: "To use an image of Teilhard de Chardin, God is not at our back, pushing us along on our journey. God is before us, revealed in the thousands of faces of human beings in the different circumstances of life. As Péguy says, 'The faith that I love is hope,' the hope of encountering God in my encounter with human beings." That encounter for Gutierrez is with his neighbors who suffer injustice and poverty; that encounter is at the core of his belief that "one cannot be a Christian in these times without a commitment to liberation."[21]

And without a commitment to the poor. This is a central message of the Medellín conference of 26 August–6 September 1968 in Colombia. It is a message which Gutierrez anticipated by a few months, and which found validation in this General Conference of Latin American bishops, opened by Pope Paul VI himself. This was the first time a pope had set foot in Latin America.

The social outlook of the Medellín conference had many sources. Its brief was to examine "The Church in the Present-Day Transformation of Latin America in the Light of the Council." Brazilian bishops, like Helder Camara, then locked in a bitter struggle with their military dictatorship, and Brazilian priests, such as Camara's adviser Joseph Comblin, a Belgian-born professor in the Theological Institute of Recife, provided many of the preliminary studies out of which the conference documents emerged.[22] Gutierrez was there, too, and found in Medellín a wide body of opinion in sympathy with his views.[23]

Gutierrez himself was a principal author of the Medellín document on peace.[24] Bishop Camara was also on the committee that drafted this document. It affirmed that "Latin America finds itself faced with a situation of injustice that can be called institutionalized violence," depriving millions of their fundamental human rights. Those in power who insist on "jealously retaining their privileges . . . are responsible to history for provoking 'explosive revolutions of despair.'" Gutierrez spoke for a Church committed to social change, even open to the possibility that "revolutionary insurrection can be legitimate in the case of evident and prolonged 'tyranny that seriously works against fundamental human rights, and which damages the common good of the country,' whether it proceeds from one person or from clearly unjust structures." To be sure, Gutierrez added to the Medellín document on peace the statement that "armed revolution" generally "generates new injustices," but even to countenance arguments for revolution was a breathtaking shift in the public position of the Church in Latin America.[25]

For Gutierrez, the Medellín meeting was most significant as a powerful endorsement of the preference for the poor, the notion at the heart of his theology.[26] In 1967 he had taught a course at the University of Montreal on "The Church and Poverty" and developed some ideas that can be traced directly to the language used by the assembled bishops and clergy at Medellín.[27] The document on poverty, adopted on 6 September 1968, indicted the "inhuman wretchedness" of millions, and called for a commitment to stand alongside the wretched by affirming "poverty as a commitment, through which one assumes voluntarily and lovingly the conditions of the needy of this world in order to bear witness to the evil which it represents and to spiritual liberty in the face of material goods." "Solidarity with those who suffer," a time-honored Christian mission, is here focused on the misery evident throughout Latin America. And in particular those, like Gutierrez, in religious orders "ought to witness to the poverty of Christ" and to encourage the formation "from among their members small communities, truly incarnated in the poor environment."[28]

Gutierrez lectured in Switzerland the following year to a combined Protestant and Catholic audience of theologians dedicated to the study of problems of society, development, and peace. The group was known by its acronym SODEPAX. His theme was theology and liberation. The struggle for liberation was not a matter of choice; it was under way. The churches had to do nothing less than recover their "prophetic role." They must point out not only what liberation meant but also how divided the Christian churches were over the causes of and remedies for suffering in Latin America. Pious words about brotherhood fall on ears deafened by the sound of the victims of oppressive regimes. The Church is split; and "the hardening of the situation [has] put some Christians among the oppressed and others among the persecutors, some among the tortured and others among those who torture." The denunciation of injustice is a prerequisite of liberation, but this is only one step among many. Unavoidably, the liberation of Latin America "will have to pass, sooner or later," Gutierrez wrote, "through paths of violence. Indeed, we recognize that the armed struggle began some years ago."[29] How it would end, no one could say, but Christians who tried to separate their faith from their understanding of the upheavals through which their society was passing were living in a fool's paradise. Here again Gutierrez insisted that the root causes of violence were structural, not political, and that the existence of mass poverty was built into the way wealth was distributed. "Latin America," he concluded, "cannot develop within the capitalist system." Liberation inevitably entailed a collision between Latin Americans and the capitalist countries which dominated them, as well as "with their natural allies: our national oligarchies."[30]

Gutierrez brought together many of these ideas in a book he published first in Peru in 1971, entitled *A Theory of Liberation: Perspectives*. It is dedicated to his friend the Peruvian novelist Arguedas. In the preface to the original edition he called the book "a theological reflection born of the experience of shared efforts to abolish the current unjust situation [in Latin America] and to build a different society, freer and more human." The book was the product of his effort to "think through" his faith within a Christian "commitment that seeks to become more radical, total, and efficacious."

How did he do so? The central element, foreshadowed in his Cantigny lecture of 1969, was to shift the discussion of the Latin American predicament from the misleading concept of development and to fashion in its place a multifaceted concept of liberation. The effort to undermine a positivist view of development, located solely or primarily in rates of growth of manufacture or gross domestic product, was not original. Many economists had faulted tendentious stage models of "the breakthrough to self-sustained rates of economic growth," which were both simplistic travesties of history and paeans of praise to the American/Western superiority in wealth and power. What Gutierrez offered was a reorientation of the entire notion of development by linking it to a multifaceted notion of human agency.

Development happens to people collectively, not just to economic institutions, sectors, or entire economies as if they were inanimate objects, reified and separate from the people who inhabit them. Underdevelopment is also a collective experience, with crushing burdens unequally distributed as between north and south, between different nations, and between different social groups within nations. These inequalities are politically structured and enforced by armed forces, law courts, and political authorities at every level of society. Thus while "development" is a word that masks the unavoidably painful and strife-riven nature of economic change, liberation confronts that "tragic and conflictual reality" head on.[31]

The first dimension of what Gutierrez meant by the term "liberation" is imbedded in the social and political conflicts subjugated people face within their own boundaries in the course of development. This was a conventional position in the late 1960s, and covered a multitude of choices from peaceful protest to the path of the guerrilla chosen by Gutierrez's friend from Louvain, Camilo Torres, who left the priesthood to join the armed struggle and who was killed in an ambush in Colombia in 1966.[32]

More originally, what Gutierrez offered was an understanding of both the sociological and theological dimensions of the notion of liberation. By doing so, he moved the concept away from the struggle of armed groups or political parties to a more philosophical and psychological domain. This philosophical move was not the only way he defined liberation. He also defined it in terms of the ways people can progressively take on conscious responsibility for their own destiny. To give people a sense that they have a history, that they can make a different history, is to dignify them as free men and women. Thus a program of action aiming at liberation had to be informed by a theory of history, a set of ideas about the unfolding of human potential over time. This unfolding was a product of human agency, of the ways people "make themselves throughout their life and their history." The new men and women who would emerge from this process of liberation, aware of their own autonomy and its limitations, were both the architects and beneficiaries of "a qualitatively different society."

The dialectical relationship between the first, intellectual, level of liberation and this more concrete one is apparent. What he understood as praxis was the never-ending dialogue between daily, mundane political and social activity and more abstract, theoretical issues about the way individuals and collectives could create their own free lives. He thereby avoided the dilemma of having to choose between making better people one at a time and changing social structures. Isolating either of these two options destroys the possibility of realizing both of them.

To braid together a theory of social action with a theory of secular history was of great importance, but left there it was not enough. What was needed, Gutierrez affirmed, was an additional dimension of the notion of liberation, in terms of that unfolding of a communion with God understood as a communion with other human beings. His argument was the same as that of the German theologian Dietrich Bonhoeffer, who died at the end of the Second World War, and to whose ideas I shall return below. As Bonhoeffer put it, "Freedom is not something man has for himself but something he has for others. . . . It is not a possession, a presence, an object, but a relationship and nothing else. . . . Only in relationship with the other am I free."[33]

If Gutierrez's position can be reduced to one guiding assumption, it is that such a relationship must be forged between those who call themselves Christians and the masses of Latin America. This kind of theology reverberated throughout the world; for Gutierrez's voice was one among many which reached European, North American, African, and Asian Christians, intent on framing their own versions of liberation theology in the 1960s.

This utopian moment was by no means restricted to the writing of conference documents or learned texts on theology. Gutierrez was the first to affirm the significance of the lived experience of Catholics in the emergence of liberation theology. That the priests who framed liberation theology learned their Christianity from their parishioners was perhaps best illustrated in Nicaragua. There the poet and priest Ernesto Cardenal established a utopian community, or lay monastery, Our Lady of Solentiname, on one of the islands of the Solentiname archipelago on Lake Nicaragua. This became Cardenal's home shortly after his ordination in 1965.

In Solentiname, every Sunday, Cardenal dispensed with a sermon and instead engaged in a weekly dialogue with the people of his community on whatever biblical passage they had heard read aloud. Most were locals; others came from afar, such as the Colombian poet William Agudelo. The people of this community, many illiterate, brought their own sense of religious experience and their own vernacular language to express it. Cardenal recorded some of these exchanges from memory; others were lost—"carried off by the wind of the lake"—still others tape-recorded. These fragments of the religious life of the community were published by Cardenal as *The Gospel in Solentiname*.[34]

Several of these conversations convey the sense of a shared religious vision within this community. In response to a reading of Luke 9:28–36, on the Transfiguration of Christ, Olivia said this:

> As I see it, the resurrection is something you can already begin to have in this life. Christ was still made of mortal flesh, and they already see him with that brightness, that light so beautiful, the way he'd be after his death, resurrected. The others hadn't seen this, only these disciples had this vision. They've seen Jesus this way, already transfigured in life because of the death he was going to have. And what they saw there you can apply to the people, the people still suffering. They're transfigured like Christ even though we can't see it, because the people are Christ himself.[35]

Oscar responded in this way to John 4:1–42, on Jesus's drinking from the well in Samaria:

> I believe the rest that God took after the creation, you know what it is? It's humankind. And the rest is the same, it's getting together. Like we are today, which is a day of rest, but it's so that we can all get together, so we can feel happy. But the body always works, right? Rest is being happy; it's looking at each other's faces and greeting each other and if possible, well, having a drink. Well, that's a rest for me, I don't know about you. Look, when I go to have a drink with another guy I feel happy. When I'm working I'm talking, but I'm working; and it's different to be at rest for an hour, and to see their faces, and to be talking, like we are now. We spend six long days of the week all split up, not seeing our friends; here we're seeing each other and greeting

each other: how you doing? This is a rest that God created, to be together here. But God isn't resting, he's always giving us his spirit, pouring it out so there'll be this love among us.[36]

And Alejandro took this angle in response to a reading of Luke 14:7–14 on a wedding party:

A party . . . isn't just giving food, like we were saying. It's also something spiritual. There are elegant people and rich people that you can't get together with at a party because they don't have anything intelligent to say to you. I'd rather be in the midst of thinking, poor people, people like here—right?— than in the middle of elegant people, mental cripples, with shitty ideas, as we say, because you can't understand them.[37]

This exchange among three peasants can serve to summarize the character of this utopian experiment in Christian life:

OSCAR: We must admit, Ernesto, that Jesus Christ has done this: I was a man that maybe had something important to say, and I didn't say it out of fear. But it seems that Jesus Christ performed this miracle and without realizing it he even spat on my tongue so that I could talk without any hesitation and hear what they were saying to me. If I understand and if I talk it seems to me it's because he spat on my tongue and I didn't even realize it. He performed the miracle.
PANCHO: But it doesn't mean we all should be talking like parrots in a mango tree.
FELIPE: Friend Pancho, don't you think that if we all talked, even though it was only one little word, this meeting would seem livelier?
PANCHO: Lively, sure, but we'd be here until six in the afternoon.[38]

Or, indeed, much longer than that. The utopian moment is one in which the silent learn they have the right to speak, to dream of resurrection, to value the "thinking, poor people" of the world, and to share their love of Christ and of each other.

In Brazil, other liberation theologians worked to construct similar communities. These were not isolated in villages but were located in the midst of the urban sprawl of Brazilian cities. These groups were known as base ecclesial communities (BECs).[39] Initially they arose out of a shortage of priests. To keep the communicants within the church, and out of the hands of the Protestants and the Marxists, lay catechists were trained to hold meetings in specially constructed huts, where the faithful would meet two or three times a week. The experiment was a success. Dom Agnelo Rossi sponsored the creation of over 400 such small centers of Catholic life in the city of Barra do Piraí alone.[40]

This stopgap measure, fostered by the Church, suddenly took on added significance when, at the Medellín conference of 1968, the bishops applauded these groups and encouraged their development as the kind of face-to-face community needed to reinvigorate Catholicism. Decentralization of the Church as an emergency measure now became a policy for the church as a whole, and base communities were targeted as "the most important source of human advancement and development."

After the Medellín meeting of August 1968, the crackdown of the Brazilian military dictatorship on dissent was in full force. Under extremely harsh repression, those priests and laymen in the Catholic Church who opposed the brutalities of the authorities had no choice but to work at the local level. There clergy trained local people as "animators," and through the Catholic University Youth and the Base Education movements, they helped inculcate a view of Catholicism very close to that advanced by Gutierrez and other liberation theologians. When material grievances were placed on the agenda of every base community, it was possible for Catholics to join in movements at the local level to try to relieve the plight of the poor.

Many of these groups resembled the community at Solentiname, but with a difference. Through a pastoral approach labeled "See-Judge-Act," these groups would meet during the week and hear of the pressing problems of the neighborhood. Then Scripture would be read, and, as in Nicaragua, ordinary Catholics would offer their thoughts about the light shed by the Scripture on their day-to-day difficulties. The third stage was action, outside the base ecclesial community, a theme not touched upon in *The Gospel in Solentiname*. Here the members of the Brazilian base communities cast off the yoke of passivity and entered the wider world of local politics, which—given the dictatorship—were the only politics tolerated by the regime. By 1974, there were over 40,000 BECs in 40 diocese in Brazil, and the number grew rapidly thereafter.[41]

What happened to this movement in later years is beyond the limits of the present discussion.[42] But what is significant is the way in which liberation theology informed a movement dedicated to the refashioning of the Roman Catholic Church. Individual base communities had none of the idyllic breezes or poetry of Solentiname, but they did offer something equally powerful—a vision of liberation through community. After all, it was only by joining together that the children of Israel escaped from Egypt. Liberation is collective or it is an illusion. Here is the key message of the theology of liberation, developed in the 1960s as a striking and powerful vision of what the future might be.

Betrayal and Transcendence: The Road to 1968

There was another way in which the theology of liberation helped constitute utopian visions in the same period. In this context the name of Bonhoeffer is essential.[43] Dietrich Bonhoeffer's words brought to Europe a different kind of liberation theology, but one with equally powerful political and social ramifications. "We have learned," Bonhoeffer wrote, "to see the great events of the history of the world from beneath—from the viewpoint of the useless, the suspect, the abused, the powerless, the oppressed, the despised. In a word, from the viewpoint of the suffering."[44]

And from the viewpoint of the Jews of Europe. The words of Bonhoeffer helped ignite a disturbing debate in Germany and elsewhere in Europe not about development or European achievements, but about European barbarism, and about the supine response of many Christians and their churches to the Nazi tyranny and to the extermination of the Jews. In the 1960s this debate produced accusations that crossed generational lines and provided much of the moral ammunition of the student revolt of 1968.

The influence of the work of Dietrich Bonhoeffer in liberation theologians both in Latin America and Europe raises an issue of central

importance in our understanding of the upheavals of the 1960s.[45] Bonhoeffer symbolized a radical critique of existing moralities, in particular
those based on religious conservatism and nationalist beliefs. His life,
and the echoes of his writing in the 1960s, help us to understand much
about 1968 as a moral indictment of the generation of men and women
in power in the post-1945 decades. From this angle 1968 appears as
a moment when many people, especially young people, expressed a
widespread sense of the betrayal of moral principles by ruling groups
with a shady past to hide. But some of them went further and saw
in protest or painting or play writing or in living experimentally the
means of transcending these failures. This powerful mixture of anger
and imagination is what is usually termed the spirit of '68. The remain-
der of this chapter will examine this moment in terms of the student
revolt of 1968 and the Prague spring of the same year.

Let us pause for a moment to reconsider the meaning of the term
utopia in light of these movements. In this context, a utopian vision
arises out of a moral indictment of a set of institutions or beliefs which
have been corrupted. But instead of leading to quietism or despair
or nihilism, such a cri de coeur becomes utopian when it informs a
vision of a different world, one with a moral order remote from that
evident in the debased present. Thus 1960s utopians of different kinds
and in different places found organized Christianity wanting, or state
socialism a hollow shell, or liberal institutions a sham. What made
them visionaries was the strength of their convictions that these ways
of living could be reconstructed in authentic and radical ways.

We have had a brief look at liberation theology in Latin America
in this context. In Europe similar currents of thought can be seen,
currents which link the activism of the 1960s with the crimes of the
1930s and 1940s. Here is a generational link of central importance to
an understanding of 1968.

The Pastor

If anyone symbolized the struggle against the moral bankruptcy of
the German people under the Nazis, it was Dietrich Bonhoeffer. As a
Lutheran clergyman, he represented a theological tradition steeped in

a culture of respect for secular authorities. As a member of a prominent family with aristocratic ties, he was hardly an obvious recruit to
revolutionary causes. And as a pacifist, he ruled himself out of direct
action in political life. And yet, he managed to break all these conventions and join a conspiracy to assassinate Adolf Hitler in July 1944. The
failure of that plot led to his arrest and execution a few days before the
end of the war.

Bonhoeffer was the most unlikely revolutionary conspirator, a fact
which made him a particularly compelling inspiration for those who
grew up after the Second World War and who confronted their parents
with questions about their own complicity in the crimes of the Nazi
era.

Bonhoeffer's decision to risk his life and ultimately lose it in the
struggle against the Nazis is one reason why his name was honored
in postwar Europe and beyond. But his presence in the cultural life
of the generation of the 1960s had two other sources. The first was
his philo-Semitism. The second was his radical critique of Protestant
theology, a critique all the more remarkable in that he fashioned it in
the shadow of the gallows.

Bonhoeffer made conservatives uneasy for a host of reasons. First
and foremost was that he was a traitor to his country. This was no
easy matter for those still clinging to the belief that most of those who
died in the Second World War in German forces were honorable men,
unsullied by contact with Nazi crimes. Secondly, he was a theologian,
a man of the cloth and the university, who left his cloister to join in a
conspiracy to overthrow the regime. As a model for German youth,
Bonhoeffer was a controversial figure. And that is another reason why
his stance and his writings had such appeal in the 1960s and beyond.

Bonhoeffer's life and death forced people to confront the Nazi past
in difficult and disturbing ways. He did so by turning again and again
to the Jewish question. This was not his choice. In the 1930s he was a
young pastor in a Berlin parish, with a lively academic interest in theology, in particular that associated with Karl Barth. The Jewish problem
was simply not a significant matter for him and his family until the

Nazis made it so. Their ties with liberal, assimilated Jews were numerous and deep. Among his dearest friends was Franz Hildebrand, a Lutheran pastor whose mother was a Jew. The vulgarity of the Nazi movement was simply from another world, one which brought out the aristocratic disdain of many who came to take a stand against the new regime. When Hitler came to power in 1933, these nascent dissidents were all forced to think about the Jews again.[46]

In 1933, as the machinery of anti-Semitic persecution was being assembled by the new regime, Bonhoeffer wrote about "The Church and the Jewish Question." At issue were the "Aryan clauses" barring from the Lutheran Ministry in Prussia anyone who had been born a Jew and later converted to Christianity. This Bonhoeffer could not accept. He traversed some familiar terrain in the Lutheran tradition as to the limits the Church accepts in its critique of the laws of the state, and then threw down the gauntlet. The Church has three roles to play at such times. First, it "can ask the state whether its actions are legitimate" in promoting law and order rather than lawlessness. Secondly, "it can aid the victims of state action." Thirdly, it may be moved "not just to bandage the victims under the wheel, but to put a spoke in the wheel itself."

The context here is the question of the relevance of race to faith, and for this reason, Bonhoeffer returned to the writings of Luther to show the absurdity of a Lutheran Church banning converted Jews from acts of Christian worship. In his *Table Talk*, Luther had written that the Jews "nailed the Redeemer of the world to the cross" and therefore bore "a curse for its action through a long history of suffering. But the history of the suffering of this people, loved and punished by God, stands under the sign of the final homecoming of the people of Israel to its God. And this homecoming happens in the conversion of Israel to Christ."[47]

Here Bonhoeffer is on conventional grounds as a Lutheran. He is still focusing on converted Jews, rather than on Jews as fellow human beings. That shift happened soon enough. The seeds of this ecumenical position were there in 1933 when, in rejecting the Aryan clauses, Bonhoeffer wrote, "The people of Israel will remain the people of God, in eternity, the only people who will not perish."

From 1933 on, Bonhoeffer more and more placed the Jewish question at the forefront of his anti-regime activities and his Christian teachings. And as time went on, it became apparent that, for a Christian, the mission to the Jews was no longer to try to convert them but to share the misery of their predicament. In 1935 the Nazis promulgated the Nuremberg laws, statutes of racial difference. Stupefied that the German churches offered no protest over this set of measures, Bonhoeffer penned this challenge: "Only he who cries out for the Jews may sing Gregorian chants."[48]

The attempt by the Nazis to create a "German Church," racially pure and politically reliable, pushed Bonhoeffer and others into forming an alternative Christian position, expressed through what they called the *Bekennende Kirche,* the confessional church. Among its prominent spokesmen was Martin Niemöller, former U-boat commander and Nazi supporter, whose stubborn refusal to accept the Nazification of the Lutheran Church enraged Hitler. "When blood, race, nationality and honor are regarded as eternal values," Niemöller and his colleagues affirmed, "the First Commandment obliges the Christian to reject this evaluation."[49] The Church belonged to God, Niemöller said, and not to the regime. He became Hitler's "personal prisoner" for the next eight years, and managed to survive the war.

By the time of Niemöller's arrest, Bonhoeffer had gone to London to work as a Lutheran minister and to gather support among British clergymen for the struggle against the Nazis. Bonhoeffer spent time, too, in New York, at Union Theological Seminary, and could have remained there if he had chosen to do so. But how could he live in New York when so many of his family and friends were in danger at home? On 20 June 1939 he wrote to Reinhold Niebuhr that he had to return to Germany: "Christians in Germany will face the terrible alternative of either willing the defeat of their nation in order that Christian civilization may survive, or willing the victory of their nation and thereby destroying our civilization. I know which of these alternatives I must choose; but I cannot make that choice in security."[50] He returned to Germany, though retaining his international contacts, who became of great use to him as he became more and more involved in "putting a spoke" in the wheel of the Nazi machine.

The majority of German churchmen took a different line, and Bonhoeffer had no illusions as to the isolated position he occupied. Most churchmen either supported the Nazis or tacitly bowed to their will and their racial policies. His denunciation took the form of a confession written in 1940 as to the Church's complicity in the persecution of the Jews of Germany. Since the Church "has not raised her voice on behalf of the victims and has not found ways to hasten to their aid . . . she is guilty of the deaths of the weakest and most defenceless brothers of Jesus Christ." Even allowing for some circumlocution in a theological text sure to be scrutinized by the authorities, it is still astonishing to see a Lutheran pastor standing with the reviled victims of the regime in 1940 and crying out that "an expulsion of Jews from the West must necessarily bring with it the expulsion of Christ; for Christ was a Jew."[51]

Between 1940 and 1943 Bonhoeffer joined a group around Admiral Wilhelm Canaris of prominent and well-placed men who used their cover as intelligence agents to construct the conspiracy to kill Hitler. Bonhoeffer traveled abroad as a double agent to find out what the Allies might do in the event of Hitler's death. On 20 July 1944 their attempt failed, but Bonhoeffer had been arrested much earlier, in part over suspicions—valid ones—that he had used his position in German intelligence to smuggle Jews out of the country and make other contacts with foreign nationals while abroad, ostensibly on business for German intelligence. Bonhoeffer's arrest was part of an elaborate power struggle within the German intelligence, army, and police hierarchy and did not initially indicate that the authorities had any clear idea as to what Bonhoeffer and his colleagues were up to. But there was the matter of smuggling Jews to Switzerland as well as the money used for this kind of activity—unusual, to say the least, in the work of a German intelligence agent.

When the July plot unfolded, and the plotters were arrested, the full extent of Bonhoeffer's anti-Nazi activities ultimately emerged. His execution was inevitable and duly took place on 9 April 1945. For our purposes, what is most striking about Bonhoeffer's part in the conspiracy against Hitler is its theological meaning. His ethics of responsibility required action, even violent action, to make it possible for him or anyone else to be free and a Christian again. And that meant leaping across the denominational divide and standing alongside the Jews, the most despised, the most wretched victims of the regime. "I pray for the defeat of my country," Bonhoeffer wrote in 1944. "Only in defeat can we atone for the terrible crimes we have committed."[52] He did not live to see this moment, but alongside his brother and two brothers-in-law executed with him, he offered up his life willingly in the hope that, sharing the fate of the Jews, he could affirm and renew his faith as a Christian. As Bonhoeffer's student and biographer Eberhard Bethge put it, by the time Bonhoeffer died, "the 'Jewish question' had become, entirely and unavoidably, the 'Christian question.'"[53]

Coming to Terms with the Past
Bonhoeffer the German Christian stood with the Jews and died with them. This is precisely what made Bonhoeffer's work significant to a generation of young Germans and other Europeans in the 1960s troubled by the Holocaust and the shadow it cast on their parents' generation. In the early part of the decade, the subject of the Nazi extermination of the Jews was beginning to escape from the veil which had obscured it over the previous decade. This was now a subject of direct moral and political relevance, and contributed much to the background of the 1968 revolt. This was so despite being complicated by the 1967 war, which initially caused images of Jewish extermination to resurface, but which in the end placed Jewish soldiers in command of a defeated and devastated Arab population. Prior to June 1967, the subject of the Jews in Europe meant the Holocaust and its consequences.

And in this context, Bonhoeffer was the exception—the exception that vividly sketched out the majority rule of indifference, collusion, or active participation of millions of German men and women with the Nazi regime and its anti-Semitic program. It mattered little that most of the people associated with radical movements in the 1960s were secular. Moral thinking had ceased long before to be the sole property of religious belief.

In this respect, one way of understanding the upheavals of the 1960s is to see them as generational in form and moral in character. Such indictments were framed by those born after the war, who took a long look at their parents' generation and were appalled at how much had been buried, how little had been faced. To be sure, silence about the recent past had its geopolitical logic. In the interests of fighting the Cold War, the few score prominent war criminals convicted after the war were released from prison, and the tens of thousands who were guilty of similar crimes faded away quietly.

By the 1960s, with the German economic miracle well under way, who wanted to reopen the ugly history of the war? A new generation did, and when they did so, they began to ask questions that few wanted to answer. Sometimes the targets of this kind of retrospective scrutiny or indictment were very prominent; Pope Pius XII is one such person whose wartime record was raked over the coals in the 1960s. Most of the time, suspicion fell on lesser folk, "ordinary men" who had done or seen or looked away from terrible things. Their betrayal of law, religious beliefs, social solidarity, or just common decency was the great secret of the postwar decades. It was a secret exposed once the veil covering it was ripped away in the 1960s.

In the 1960s in Germany there were many voices that cried out for a reckoning, for an accounting of the moral and political corruption that made the Holocaust possible. Many German students who came of age in the 1960s looked back on their parents' lives and wondered, not only about the war years but also about the post-1945 period when they themselves grew up.[54] Dagmar Herzog and Robert Moeller have shown how young people reacted against the conservative project of German reconstruction under Konrad Adenauer, when Christian and family values appeared to blot out the stain of the Nazi period.[55]

These young people followed the paths of those who resisted fascism into areas remote from the outlook of men like Bonhoeffer. The resistance, after all, was a mixed group, composed (in the poem of

Paul Eluard) of "celui qui croyait au ciel et celui qui n'y croyait pas" (those who believed in heaven and those who didn't).[56] By the 1960s, the courage and radical rejection of authority such men and women manifested two decades earlier offered models to the revolutionaries of a very different age.

The delay in confronting the Nazi past was not specifically German in character. The need for healing myths locating collaboration in a tiny minority of misguided men and women or fanatics was evident throughout Europe. The passing of this myth is one of the features of the French student revolt of 1968, to which I shall turn in a moment. But first I will touch on facets of the German road to 1968, which led through Auschwitz.

There was a series of events in the early 1960s which forced German public opinion to reopen the question of complicity and culpability. The first was the trial of Adolf Eichmann in Jerusalem, the first such trial which shifted attention from the perpetrators to the victims. Time and again individuals testified to their personal experience in the concentration camps and in the death camps, opening up a sphere of cruelty that seemed, in the words of one survivor, Ka'Tzetnik, to come from another planet.

Eichmann's war record was not in dispute; what was more troubling was his defense that he was just carrying out orders. He was the loyal German if there ever was one. Furthermore, he had lived in Germany for five years after the war, before escaping to Argentina. There Israeli agents kidnapped him and brought him to Israel for trial. He was convicted and executed in May 1962. The whole incident rekindled a sense of shame among young Germans not just that such monstrous crimes had occurred, but that so many criminals had evaded judgment. How many were still on the streets of German cities, in the boardrooms of companies, prominent among the increasingly prosperous population of the new Federal Republic, or within their own families?

By the mid-1960s, the subject of Nazi war crimes was a matter of public debate. In 1963, two photographic exhibitions were displayed in the Frankfurt Paulskirche. The first was on the Warsaw Ghetto uprising. Between 23 November 1963 and January 1964, 61,000 people saw the visual record of extermination. The second exhibition was entitled "Auschwitz—Photos and Documents." It opened on 18 November 1964 and drew about the same number of visitors before closing at the end of the year.[57]

The exhibition included photographs of a number of men who were on trial in Frankfurt at the time. They had been guards at Auschwitz, and the organizers included in the exhibition photographs of these men entering the court house and elements of the prosecution's indictment against them. The prosecutor, Fritz Bauer, believed that such images helped persuade Germans of the guilt of the accused. Of the 20 people on trial, 17 were convicted and jailed for their crimes. At this trial, one German student later recalled, "a whole generation stood accused."[58]

The Auschwitz trial was by no means the only public display of the men and women who had served in the Nazi "univers concentrationnaire," or, roughly translated, "Kingdom of Death Camps." On 8 August 1963, eight men who had served in Belzec went on trial in Munich. Seven were acquitted for lack of evidence; only one surviving witness could be found to testify against these men. In Düsseldorf on 12 October 1964, ten members of the personnel running the extermination camp at Treblinka went on trial. Nine of the ten were convicted. In Hagen, on 6 September 1965, 12 men who had served in Sobibor went on trial. Six were convicted, five were acquitted, and one committed suicide before the conclusion of the proceedings.

The ominous feature of these trials was less the detailed description of the crimes these people committed than the nagging doubt as to how many others had blood on their hands and had never been (and would never be) brought to justice. Here the propaganda machine of East Germany helped fuel accusations that West Germany was run by men and women whose crimes had been covered up. In 1957, the East German government produced a film on the life of one such man, Heinz Reinefarth. He was an SS general in charge of the suppression of the Polish Home Army uprising in Warsaw in August 1944. After the war he became mayor of the North Sea resort town of Westerland.

In 1958 he entered the Schleswig-Holstein parliament as a member of a right-wing party. Local prosecutors opened a file on him but never brought him to trial.[59]

Other incidents raised doubts about other institutions. Students at Göttingen University protested the appointment of a former Nazi as education minister in Niedersachsen in 1955. The police chief of Rheinland-Pfalz, Georg Heuser, resigned abruptly when it emerged that he had commanded a death squad in Belarus. Theodor Oberländer was a prominent Nazi who was active on the Eastern front in 1941, but this record did not preclude his serving as Minister for Deportees under Chancellor Adenauer.

For our purposes, these cases are important not only intrinsically but as part of a broader context within which student radicals questioned the legitimacy of the state and the moral order of German society after 1945.[60] The radicals of 1968 grew up in these uneasy years, and time and again hurled at their elders accusations that their conventional moralities were rotten to the core.[61] Rolf Hochhuth's play *The Representative,* produced in 1963, offered a controversial portrait of Pius XII washing his hands of the blood of the Jews of Rome, deported from that city under his very eyes. In 1968 the poet and survivor Paul Celan visited the retired philosopher Martin Heidegger in his rural cottage outside Freiberg. No one knows precisely what they said to each other. But the poem Celan later produced, "Todnauberg," suggested that Celan's "hope, today, for a thinker's word to come in the heart" was dashed during this visit; Heidegger remained silent. This incident coincided with other developments in 1968, though the controversy surrounding it blew up only later.

By the later 1960s a generation of young Germans had grown up in this atmosphere of half-truths and partial silences about the past. If Heidegger, the great philosopher could have been so debased as to oversee the expulsion of his own teacher, Edmund Husserl (who was a Jew), from a university where, he, Heidegger, served as rector under the Nazis, and if Heidegger continued to remain silent about this in the 1960s, then the rot was everywhere.

It should be apparent why the term "alienation"—so central to the generation of 1968—has a specifically generational meaning. The gap between the young and their elders was one that spanned the divide between Nazism and liberalism. Did the latter really extirpate the former, or was Nazism a virus, dormant perhaps, but one which could return? Studies of the "authoritarian personality" by Theodor Adorno and others provided the young with a checklist of rigidities their parents may very well have embodied. The fact that German parents had no monopoly on the authoritarian style was neither here nor there; the recent past gave young Germans reason to fear the particular form authoritarian politics might take again in their own time and in their own country.[62]

Radicalism meant a complete break with this authoritarian past, a tearing out of corruption root and branch, and, to do so, student groups looked to past examples of defiance of the legal order—the defiance Bonhoeffer personally embodied—while by and large ignoring his Christian beliefs. The East German state was little better, despite its protestations. Both East and West were corrupt. The first reeked of Stalin's gulag; the second was infested with ex-Nazis.

Berlin 1968

No one can fully comprehend the student revolt of 1967–68 in Germany without setting it in the context of its attempt to come to terms with the Nazi past.[63] There were other sources of revolt, to be sure, related to the vast expansion of university education in the 1960s and the anonymous, deeply hierarchical system that students knew and deplored. But it would be a mistake to locate student attitudes exclusively within the milieu of university life. Young people born between 1938 and 1948, who entered university in the 1960s, shared many early experiences in common. The hardships of the immediate postwar years, the broken families, the physical upheavals associated with forced migration and the recasting of domestic life, all marked their outlook. But instead of turning toward a life of materialistic rewards, some stopped short and questioned the moral character of the world they had inherited.

By the mid-1960s the older party of protest, the Social Democratic

Party, had become so imbricated in the parliamentary system that it could not represent the search for alternatives these young people undertook. Instead, they formed an extra-parliamentary opposition, best understood as a negative alliance of alienated groups rejecting most of the mainstream political ideas, East or West, of their day.[64]

This current of opinion drew on the anti-nuclear movement, whose Christian character was evident in the silent, four-day Easter march it organized. By the 1960s, this movement merged with more radical elements of the SDS, or the former youth wing of the parent Social Democratic Party, which had expelled it in 1959. These dissidents moved away from older socialist thinking on the role of the working class in the transformation of society. Students and other marginal groups were not yet "commodified" or corrupted by the material goals of capitalism. They could challenge authority in the institutions where they worked, namely the universities.

Here there were specifically German features of higher education which accounted for the force and persistence of these protests.[65] The hierarchical and politicized nature of teachers in higher education in Germany was particularly striking. There are similarities to the French system, but the vertical structure of power within German universities was both visible and vulnerable. Student radicals in Berlin took over the student council of the Free University of Berlin in 1965; similar groups soon followed in other cities.

The appearance of these groups precisely at the time of the Auschwitz trial and after the emergence of the National Democratic Party on the right-wing fringe of German politics meant that the SDS could claim that it was carrying on the anti-fascist struggle. The only way to do so was to engage in a collective coming to terms with the past, a *Vergangenheitsbewältigung*. No more comfort from anti-communist slogans, no more evasion of the past in school textbooks and curricula. The sins of the parents had to be faced.

What triggered radical protest in Berlin as elsewhere in the university world was the escalation of the American war effort in Vietnam. And as elsewhere, pacifist objections to war were mixed. Some stood against war per se, others identified with the Vietcong. But in Germany a second issue galvanized student opinion: the so-called Emergency Laws, passed in the spring of 1968 by the "grand coalition" of socialists and conservatives in power. This measure convinced many young activists that the old SPD, the party of Marx, the party smashed by the Nazis, was a hopeless, inert institution.[66]

These two overriding issues—war and repression—dominated the emergence of the student revolt in the late 1960s. Repression in Berlin took on a particular meaning in Berlin, when on 2 June 1967, a student, Benno Ohnesorg, was shot by an undercover policeman during a protest over the visit of the Shah of Iran to Germany. "Political murder" cried the students, inevitably bringing up memories of the way the police had operated under the Nazis. Discussions went on and on about the legitimacy of violent opposition to the state.

Then another violent incident increased the tension in student circles. The SDS leader Rudi Dutschke was shot three times by a right-wing fanatic on the main shopping street of West Berlin, the Kurfurstendamm. In response mass demonstrations turned the annual Easter march into a bloody confrontation between police and demonstrators. Once again, the nightmares of the Nazi past returned with a vengeance.

Although few people knew it at the time, this was the apogee of student unrest in Berlin. As we have noted, time and again utopias emerged in two stages. First, there is the rejection of an older, bankrupt moral code. This is evident in 1968. Second is the transcendence of the older order by a vision of liberation. The student radicals of 1968 were too anti-authoritarian to work out such a vision, though there are elements of one in the writings of Herbert Marcuse, among others. They were not guerrillas in the rice paddies of Vietnam or fellaheen in Algeria or persecuted priests in Brazil or Nicaragua. They faced a grayer, colder enemy, and they came up with little in the way of an alternative social order to offer in its place. Freeing the university from some of the feudal hierarchies was no mean objective, though here too the progress made through protest was painfully meager. Like most utopian outbursts, the real significance of these events was to keep alive the possibility that there could be an alternative reality. What had been performed was a simple assertion: what is, is not what ought to be.[67]

May '68 in Paris

The parallels with events in Paris are striking. There is the same sense of a generational divide, the same brief alignment and then distancing between workers' organizations and student groups, the same solidarities with freedom fighters, and the same real, though limited, success in reforming educational structures.

The most direct link between the two movements was personal. They were bonded and indeed symbolized by the vivid personality of Daniel Cohn-Bendit, known for his hair and his politics as "Danny the Red." Born in Montauban, France, in April 1945, Cohn-Bendit attended school in Germany, and after his *Abitur* he returned to France. On a German reparations scholarship, he began his studies in sociology at the University of Paris at Nanterre. This, the tenth of Paris's university campuses, is a concrete-bloc eyesore, with few facilities for students and little contact with the working-class community of the Paris "Red Belt." If anyone sought a synonym for alienation, it was (and is) Nanterre. To be sure, bringing the University of Paris to Nanterre also symbolized a democratizing element in French higher education, but the state never provided the resources to make the site more than an architectural catastrophe.

In 1967, demonstrations against the American war effort in Vietnam led to the arrest of six students, two from Nanterre. On 22 March a mass meeting was held in Nanterre to secure their release. It turned into an occupation of the university building. A week later another mass meeting was planned, this time under threat of disruption by a right-wing organization called *Occident*. Before the meeting could take place, the rector of the university closed it down.

More student support gathered around protesting the government's plan to look into selective admission to universities, hitherto a right to all who passed the college entrance examination, the Baccalaureat. And when Rudi Dutschke was shot in Berlin, on 11 April 1968, 2,000 students demonstrated in solidarity.

The spiral of mass agitation focused for a time on Cohn-Bendit himself, one of the activists in the first stages of protest in Nanterre. On 27 April he was arrested and released. Six days later, riot police cleared the Sorbonne and arrested around 600 students. On Monday, 6 May, there was another violent confrontation between students and police in the Latin Quarter. Over 600 people were injured. More students joined in the struggle, which reached its climax on 10 May, where street battles continued through the night. Over 450 students were arrested, and 350 or so were injured.

Having made its point, the government withdrew the riot police from the university and agreed to consider the cases of those in custody. In return, the students reoccupied the university, and joined a one-day general strike with the CGT, the general confederation of labor, on 13 May. Factory occupations began in other parts of the country.[68]

By this time, Cohn-Bendit had returned to Germany, and through an order of the Conseil d'Etat (the supreme administrative court) he was deemed an undesirable alien and barred from returning to France. Here was an invitation to revive the past, since Cohn-Bendit was Jewish. No one could have missed the echoes of his case. Student banners proclaimed: "We are all German Jews," "We are all undesirables," "We are all foreigners," and within a few weeks Cohn-Bendit was back, having walked through the forests to cross the border.[69]

Although student protest continued, industrial unrest slowly subsided, and with it the potential for the transformation of popular demonstrations into a wave capable of submerging de Gaulle's administration, or indeed the whole of the French Fifth Republic. Paris '68, like Berlin '68, faded into the past as an assertion of cultural freedom rather than as a moment of institutional transformation. Still, the *'68ards* did shake the foundations both of the university world and the wider political world around it. If they did not achieve liberation, they succeeded in putting the notion of liberation of many different kinds in the minds of millions of their contemporaries. This is one way in which "minor utopias" outlast the political defeats which they suffer.

As in Berlin, one of the most powerful features of student activism was its anti-authoritarian, anti-Stalinist, strain.[70] Cohn-Bendit himself recalls walking down a street in Paris, suddenly to find a crowd of several hundred behind him. This Chaplinesque image is revealing, since it captured the spirit of transgression, of play, of mockery in Paris '68. "The question of whether revolution is still possible in the advanced capitalist countries doesn't interest me," Cohn-Bendit is reputed to have said. Festivity was the language of the young; through it, the exuberance, the transgressive rush, of collective action became the end, not the means of politics.[71] For some (though not for all) action displaced ideology, and it did so with a swagger. "Je suis Marxiste, tendance Groucho" (I am a Marxist of the Groucho persuasion), announced one graffiti artist in Paris.[72] Berlin '68 took itself much more seriously.

Another of the posters of 1968 in Paris was more specifically utopian in character. It declared, "Sous le pavé, la plage," (Under the street, the sandy beach). This double entendre had one practical meaning. Up with the paving stones; build the barricades. But it pointed to another reality, a vanished past within the socialist tradition. The echoes of 1789 and 1792 were there. Utopian socialists in the 1830s and 1840s had brought out the critical role of dreaming for those who wished to create an alternative society. Under the surface of the city, another kind of city exists. It can be glimpsed if you have the will and the force to excavate with your imagination. It is the city of utopia, just off the edges of all conventional maps.

Barricades were symbolic politics of another kind as well. They brought back images of street fighting in the liberation of Paris in 1944, as well as narratives of the Paris Commune of 1871, the first communist revolution in history. The city's streets were a palimpsest, and tearing them up was one way of disclosing the histories inscribed on the face of Paris itself.[73]

May '68 was a conscious turning away from state socialism of the Western or the Eastern varieties. Neither had the slightest intention of disturbing the post-1945 social and political order. Student revolutionaries rejected both and chose a kind of anarchistic exuberance as the only alternative to bureaucratic desiccation or co-optation within the structure of corporate capitalism. In this context, it is important to observe the ludic, childlike elements in the student movements of the period. Experimentation with drugs or in music or sexual behavior was much more important than politics to some of those caught up in these movements. The notion of a "counterculture" captured well the extent to which rebellion meant negating in public and in private the hypocritical morality of an older generation.

Cultural Revolution: Self-government and the New Social Contract

It would be profoundly wrong to see 1968 as the politics of rejection alone. Many '68ards found in the events of that year the elements of a new kind of politics, the politics of local autonomy, or *Autogestion*. It is this sense of discovery which lay behind the attempt by different groups with different visions to formulate what they saw as a new social contract.[74] Here they turned back to the French revolutionary tradition to follow the lead of Saint-Just, who had coined the term "the public moment" for that time when "the social contract is reviewed and reconstituted" through action.[75] The year 1968 was one such "public moment."

The legacy of this phase of militancy, though, was enduring. Here is the bridge between earlier visions of social transformation based on class and nation and later ones based on civil society and humanitarian action. Out of 1968 came the minor utopia of *Autogestion*, variously interpreted as local self-government, collective self-management on the local or factory level, or workers' control.[76] And from this platform emerged the social movements of the 1980s and 1990s which are surveyed in chapter 6.[77]

This set of ideas privileged action over theory, though it is evident that certain forms of theory, in particular the Marxism of the French Communist Party, were rejected root and branch by these *Autoges-tionistes*. There were multiple intellectual and political currents in this movement, represented by the ex-Dominican advocate of communitarianism and cooperation Henri Desroche,[78] by the dissident Marxist sociologist Henri Lefebvre, whose origins were also in radical Christian thinking,[79] and by the left libertarian anarchist Daniel Guérin.[80]

The set of ideas surrounding *Autogestion* were certainly not re-stricted to France. Many Europeans saw in the Israeli *kibbutzim* the germ of the central notion of autonomous production and collective life. In Belgium, liberation theologians and priests were actively drawn to the idea, and contributed to its elaboration.[81] So were trade unionists in Tito's Yugoslavia well before the events of 1968. The leaders of the military coup which seized power in Peru in 1968 also declared their commitment to installing forms of self-government of a similar kind. And in its first few years, the leadership of free Algeria proclaimed their support for decentralized institutional life; that brief period of freedom came to an abrupt end by the late 1970s.

There were, therefore, many variants to and sources of this set of ideas. Within this multinational array, three constituent elements stand out. The first is a commitment to the decentralization of political and social life, so that it is in civil society and not in parliament or in the factory per se where the search for a new order takes place. Secondly there is a demand for local autonomy in all places of work and public service. Thirdly, there is a vision of the replacement of the capitalist organization of consumption by cooperative institutions.

At the core of this program is the belief in the need to escape from the central state as the arbiter of the public good, and to substitute for its *dirigisme* more pluralistic modes of organizing the productive and creative forces of society.[82] Thus national elections were a sideshow to these militants, and so were the intricacies of trade-union politics. Instead of acting primarily to win pay raises, workers of all kinds were urged—in the words of one poster—to "demonstrate that workers' management of the firm is the power to do better for everyone what the capitalists did scandalously for a few."[83]

One key element in this movement was its dynamic quality. It worked to produce an environment in which men and women could perpetually renew their commitment to those with whom they lived. *Autogestion,* to Lefebvre, was a means and not an end, a way of doing things, not a fixed system, "a perpetual struggle, and a struggle per-petually renewed."[84]

This notion of decentralizing democratic and industrial politics was the theme of the French journal *Autogestion,* which was published from 1966 to 1986.[85] It championed workers' militancy of all forms, especially those which came from below, from the rank and file. What killed it was the conjunction of militancy of the kind evident in the workers' occupations of the Lip factories in Besançon in 1973,[86] with the economic crisis following the Arab-Israeli war of that year. A period of economic contraction is never the right time for militancy of this, or of any other, form.

These experiments in social politics of the 1960s described a conscious break with the gray austerity and coldness of the old left, in particular in its Stalinist forms.[87] In contrast, the new left wanted to bring back a sense of revolution as playfulness, as an exploration of the possibilities of delight. Lefebvre referred to 1968 as carnivalesque; it took on the character of "the eruption of play in everyday life."[88] To see it this way, Marxists like Lefebvre—a man with a surrealist past—highlighted the early Marx, on his philosophical manuscripts of 1844, and on their discussion of the phenomenon of alienation.

For Lefebvre among many others, *Autogestion* was a response to the problem of alienation.[89] But the term had another, visceral meaning, in the sense of alienation from one's own body. Personal freedom and sexual freedom were political matters in 1968. It is not at all odd that one of the flash points out of which the troubles at Nanterre emerged was the conflict over restrictions on couples visiting in university housing. What gave the university the right to enforce norms of sexual behavior?[90]

In the earlier episodes examined in this book, there was an implicit and unstated distinction between matters of public life and private life. In 1968, the line between the two was erased. The personal *was* the political; indeed, this was one of the romantic features of 1968, reflected in the excited language of the time. As Henri Lefebvre put it: "Drawn into the vacuum, spontaneity filled it up. Those days in the streets, in the amphitheaters, in the factories, the divisions evaporated between activity and passivity, between private life and social life, between the everyday and the political, between the site of carnival and the site of work, between word and text, between action and knowledge."[91] It was not necessary to be quite so exuberant to understand why in these years ideological and generational conflict was expressed in music, in dress, and in sexual comportment.[92]

Changing norms of self-presentation and shifting sexual codes succeeded fully in annoying the bourgeoisie, but there was much more at stake here than simple rebelliousness. Comportment and sexuality became fundamental themes in the critique of contemporary capitalism. Mixing the analysis of the early Marx together with elements of Freudian and aesthetic theory, former members of the Frankfurt School of Social Research, most like Herbert Marcuse in the United States, provided an intellectual lead for those at odds with the educational system. It was geared, so Marcuse wrote, to turn them all into "one dimensional" men and women, whose situation precluded an escape from their isolation. Marcuse, the author of *Eros and Civilization,* championed the student revolt, and made it a counterpoint to the ossified response of labor movements to their place within the capitalist order.[93] His emphasis on aesthetics, though, was not shared by Lefebvre, who was in 1968 a professor of sociology at Nanterre and who joined the student movement at its inception.[94] Indeed much of the upheaval of 1968 showed the limits of the very social control which Marcuse famously described.

To read the pamphlets and broadsheets of the time is to see clearly how much of Marxism, or rather variations within the Marxist tradition, were alive and well in the events of 1968. But the new left bore a relationship to the old left very similar to that occupied by liberation theology vis-à-vis the Roman Catholic Church. Both wanted to restore the original impulse behind a set of beliefs that had been corrupted over time. Both pointed to bureaucracies incapable of expressing the will and hopes of its members.

Both were attempts to construct a kind of direct democracy, where those at the bottom of the institution—priests, laymen, students, shopfloor workers—managed their own lives. In their view, representative democracy had collapsed partly through the workings of the iron law of oligarchy, and in part through the manipulation of transnational structures, be it the Catholic Church or the Comintern, in the interests of a small elite in Rome or Moscow.

The assertion of direct democracy was at the core of the new social contract. The socialist element in this vision was still there: capitalism was still the enemy, and the oppressed was still the dynamic force in opposition to the status quo. But now the focus on the notion of alienation enabled these activists to embrace many different sites of oppression, beyond the factory gates. They were active in the schools and universities, in environmental movements, and among immigrants. And they stood alongside those fighting first in the *jebels* of Algeria and later in the rice paddies of Vietnam. The revolt of 1968 had many sources, but one of them was protest over the Algerian war. The war in Vietnam was reaching its crucial turning point in 1968, following the Tet offensive, but the killing was to continue for years. Through solidarity with what Franz Fanon had called "the wretched of the earth," militancy in the 1960s developed a fundamentally transnational character.[95]

We are, therefore, at a parting of the ways in what may be termed the utopian imagination. Those fighting and dying in Algeria, in Vietnam, in Palestine, were fighting for self-determination. Many of those who supported these movements were Marxists of one kind or another, and virtually everyone used the language of class struggle to describe the problems of domestic and international life. Decolonization and class struggle went hand in hand, as the Cuban revolution and Che Guevara's futile attempt to extend revolution into Bolivia highlighted. But the nationalist element in many of these conflicts was paramount. Algerian independence took precedence over Algerian socialism. The Vietnamese communists were fighting a war of national liberation, first against the French, whom they defeated in 1954, and then against the Americans, whom they defeated in 1975. In the wake of the Israeli military occupation of 1967, Palestinians struggled to create their own nation and to lift the yoke of Israeli occupation. Here we are back at the beginning of the century, at a time when nation and social class (in that order) were at the core of visions of social transformation.

But the fertility of social thinking in the 1960s is evident in the fact that alongside these older commitments and older configurations, there emerged different vectors of social action. Women's rights became a focus of militancy just at the moment that the very first effective contraceptive appeared in the 1960s. In part as a reaction against the sexism of some militant groups, in part through a recovery of earlier political achievements, and in part through a shared sense of liberation in the struggles of 1968 itself, international feminism came out of the 1960s stronger than ever.[96] Environmental issues seized the imagination of many student activists.[97] And by the end of the decade, when the student revolt was over, and the institutions of society, though shaken, were still visibly intact, there was renewed interest in the field of human rights. The move was then from a certain vision of politics in the 1960s, partly Marxist, partly anarchist, partly libertarian, to a different vision of civil society thereafter. And that is where human rights and humanitarian action came into their own. Amnesty International was formed in London in 1961; the French organization *Médecins sans frontières* (Doctors without Borders) was formed a decade later, in 1971. The decade of their foundation was the time not only of student revolt, but also of the emergence of new forms of social action, located in civil society, and committed to the defense of human rights.

After all, 1968 was the year when René Cassin received the Nobel Peace Prize for his work in the construction of a new human rights regime. His outlook and beliefs were far from those who manned the barricades of 1968, but when the dust had settled, many of the veterans of those movements seized the legacy of ideas he and others had provided and developed them in struggles which grew in significance in the last decades of the century.

Socialism with a Human Face: the Prague Spring

The vision of an escape from the straightjacket of communism in Eastern Europe both preceded and empowered the Prague spring of

1968. The authors of that vision operated in many different spheres, but prominent among them were film, theater, and literary reviews. In these arenas, we can see many people experimenting in utopian forms—constructing an imaginary realm of pure freedom or of conjuring up its opposite—a dystopia of pure unfreedom. Both existed in the world of the arts in Central and Eastern Europe under communism after 1948, and both were corrosive of the legitimacy of the regimes constructed in the satellite states of the Soviet Union following the Second World War.

Here again we have the two central features of the utopian temperament. Imbedded in these works of art, there is first a clear indictment of the communists' betrayal of a set of propositions about equality, freedom, and progress, and secondly, there is a vision of transcendence. The playful transgression of the rules of communist life discloses a realm of truth beyond the looking glass of the lies and distortions on which the communist state rested.

There were many sources out of which emerged the challenge to communism and Soviet power which, as the following section reveals, finally brought down the Soviet empire in 1989. But not least among them were the efforts of a relatively small group of writers and artists who dreamed of the Prague spring of 1968 long before it happened.

The Theater of Václav Havel

One such writer was Václav Havel. Born in 1936 of a well-to-do family, his bourgeois origins made it difficult for him to study literature in Communist Czechoslovakia in the 1950s.[98] Instead, he became an apprentice as a chemical laboratory technician and wound up studying at the Technical University. After two years' military service, he found a way into Czech theater, first as a stagehand at the ABC theater and then at the Theater of the Balustrade.

It was in this company that Havel began composing satirical plays. The Theater of the Balustrade was one of a score of small theaters which flourished in Prague in the 1950s and 1960s. They experimented in many kinds of drama, with the sole proviso that the stage was not the place for didactic art. "We didn't try to explain the world," Havel later recalled. "We weren't interested in theses, and we had no intention of instructing anybody. It was more like a game—except the 'game' somehow mysteriously touched the deepest nerves of human existence and social life." The notion of the stage as a mirror of life was also rejected; they didn't offer portraits of identifiable characters to tell conventional stories. Instead "they posed questions or opened up themes. And—something I considered the most important thing of all—they manifested the experience of absurdity," understood as showing what the world looked like when "fundamental metaphysical certainty" was gone, when people sensed that they had "lost the ground from under [their] feet."[99]

This theatrical world was not committed to any "school," including the theater of the absurd, though it was able to catch the notion of the absurd that Havel believed was "in the air." What they and others drew upon was a set of post-1945 experiments in drama which fused a sense of the emptiness of vernacular language with a kind of gallows humor mocking the powerful while recognizing the menace they still represented. The Rumanian born playwright Ionesco was a master of this genre, as was the Irish writer Samuel Beckett. In *The Bald Soprano* and *Waiting for Godot,* these playwrights introduced millions to the vocabulary of the absurd. Language itself ceases to be a vehicle for the expression of identity or character; rather it is the reverse—the characters are there to voice words which have taken off into their own orbits of meaning. And as words fly into space, so do fixed identities. Like chameleons, characters become their opposites. Anything can happen in a world of this kind, and it usually does.[100]

Havel learned his craft in the experimental atmosphere of the Theater of the Balustrade. Beckett and Ionesco's works were performed alongside Jarry's *Ubu Roi* and a dramatization of Kafka's *The Trial.* Here Havel became a man of all the talents, from actor to set designer, and became an expert in the ways that turning reality upside down on stage could do more than make an audience laugh.[101]

Havel later described this theater as apolitical; that is to say, it did not follow a particular party line: "Absurd theater is not here to explain how things are. It does not have that kind of arrogance; it leaves the instructing to Brecht. The absurd playwright does not have the key to anything. He does not consider himself any better informed or any more aware than his audience. He sees his role in giving a form to something we all suffer from, and in reminding us, in suggestive ways, of the mystery before which we all stand equally helpless."[102]

In a way, Havel is satirizing himself. There were directly political sources of Havel's plays, and they had political ramifications. During the First World War, a group of writers and artists fashioned a movement they called "Dada," which either meant nonsense or was a reference to a child's hobby horse. Nonsense was one way of rejecting root and branch the industrialized killing just then reaching its height on the Western front. If such was reason, then Dada wanted none of it. Havel was happy to describe his sense of humor as "Dadaist"; he went further and said that his theater "threw us into the question of meaning by manifesting its absence."[103] No more Dadaistic statement could be imagined.

Similarly, Havel's work had echoes of the novels of the Czech novelist Jaroslav Hasek, whose *Good Soldier Schweik* immortalized the subversive strengths of incompetence. After the 1914–18 war, another group of artists provided a parallel strand of the rejection of murderous reason. Surrealism, a word coined by the French poet Guillaume Apollinaire, was the refuge of many writers and painters unprepared to accept Stalinism or liberalism. Many sided with Leon Trotsky and thus were at odds (or worse) with the international communist movement.

Alongside the drama of the absurd and the surreal, there were specifically Czech literary resources from which Havel drew in rich and powerful ways. The first was the work of Franz Kafka, whose dreams and nightmares of bureaucratic menace, laconically unfolded, were imbedded in much of Havel's early work. So were older legends, such as the story of the Golem of Prague, a Jewish tale describing the shaping out of clay of a figure who would protect the people and diminish the work they had to do.

The theatrical experiments Havel undertook in the early 1960s tell us much about the cultural milieu in which he operated and about the subversive mockery in which this kind of theatre reveled. In *The Garden Party* of 1963, Havel plays a series of practical jokes on bureaucrats and the people who bow and scrape before them. The Pludek family has a problem; their son Peter is too bourgeois and too intellectual to introduce to Mr. Kalabis, an official of the Liquidation Office, a good place for an up and coming young man. Liquidating what or whom is never specified. The Pludeks are delighted that this official is about to pay them the honor of a visit, since they have a second son, Hugo, who somehow does not suffer from these embarrassing bourgeois associations. Hugo is a chess fanatic, used to playing against himself. Peter is banished from the apartment, but the official never shows up, since he had a commitment to lecture on the future of mankind. So Hugo must go to Kalabis.

Hugo seeks this official out at the garden party of the Liquidation Office. He isn't there either, but Hugo is not deterred. He offers useful advice, and points out to the bureaucrats organizing the dancing that putting everyone in small dance floor C instead of in the available large dance floor A makes no sense at all. The response is emphatic:

> CLERK: You mean you'd approve if the dignified course of our garden party were disrupted by some sort of important and, as it were, functional areas as the Large Dance floor A were to opened to unbridled intellectualities. . . .
>
> SECRETARY: You mean you don't trust the resolutions of the Organizing Committee?
>
> CLERK: Composed of the leading officials of the Liquidation Office?
>
> SECRETARY: Old, experienced men who long before you were born were devotedly liquidating?

Undeterred Hugo strikes up a friendship with another bureaucratic stalwart, Mr. Maxy Falk, the organizer of the party, to whom "nothing foreign is human." This bureaucrat rises to even greater heights of the ridiculous. He tells Hugo that he is all in favor of art—"that's what I call a fighting word! I myself—sort of personally—fancy art. I think of it as the spice of life. I think our time directly calls for great dramaticals full of full-blooded heroes." He is even more passionate about technology—"that's what I call a fighting word! You know, I maintain that we're living in the century of technology—the magnet, the telephone—the magnet—not even Gill Vernon could imagine anything like this."

But Hugo can. He absorbs this nonsense like a sponge and turns it into an entire philosophy of life: "In the future art and technology will sort of harmoniously supplement each other—the lyrico-epical verses will help in the chemification of liquidation practice—the periodic table of the elements will help in the development of Impressionism—every technological product will be specially wired for the reception of aesthetic brain waves—the chimneys of the atomic power stations will be decorated by our best landscape painters—there will be public reading rooms twenty thousand leagues under the sea—differential equations will be written in verse—on the flat roofs of cyclotrons there will be small experimental theaters where differential equations will be recited in a human sort of way. Right?"

With rhetorical armor in place, Hugo confronts the director of the Liquidation Office, the liquidation of which he, Hugo, is supposed to organize. Emboldened by this triumph, he moves on to liquidate the inauguration office too, before being given the task of constructing "a great new institution, a central commission for inauguration and liquidation." Hugo's proud parents celebrate their son's achievements with the same idiocy he used to attain them.

Three years later, Havel's play *The Memorandum* was performed in Prague's Theater of the Balustrade. Here the dystopia explores a project to reform language by creating a more precise code for official communication. Gross, the director, received a memorandum announcing this project. Its aim is precision. Languages like Czech are unreliable because words have nuances and can be interchanged or charged with emotional content. To prevent this from happening, all words must "be formed by the least probable combination of letters." The result is total nonsense. Dada indeed.

The sponsors of the project really use it to depose the director. He accepts a demotion, and then uses his subordinate position to accuse the new director of incompetence, thereby getting his job back. Thus order is restored, though good sense remains elusive. Gross the hero announces to Maria, the secretary of the translation center, that "we're living in a strange, complex epoch. . . . In other words, our life has lost a sort of higher axle, and we are irresistibly falling apart, more and more profoundly alienated from the world, from others, from ourselves. Like Sisyphus, we roll the boulder of our life up the hill of its illusory meaning, only for it to roll down again into the valley of its own absurdity." Instead of counseling despair, he tells Maria to join a theater group and seek a career as an actress. The in-jokes proliferate, extending the spoof to Havel himself and his companions in the Czech version of the theater of the absurd.

In 1968 Havel produced *The Increased Difficulty of Concentration,* a spoof on immorality and social-scientific mindlessness. Here the reference to the Golem is made explicit. A group of researchers seek a way "to shape human individuality scientifically" and thereby to disclose how to control alienation. They concoct "a small automatic calculator, model CA-213," named Puzuk, whom they carry around in a suitcase. As one of the group describes him, "He's very sensitive, you know. It's always hard to make him feel acclimatized. Yet his condition is terribly important to us. When he feels right, our work literally flies along . . . He simply compares the quantum of all the possible relationships from among all the pieces of information about a particular individual which we have fed into him, or which he has acquired on his own—he compares these concurrently with the laws and norms of all the scientific disciplines previously fed into his memory. . . . Thus he gradually arrives at a certain comprehensive structure of maximally random relationships—and in fact this is already—basically—a sort of condensed model of human individuality."

After a few false starts, Puzuk finally gets going. These were some of the questions he asks: "Which is your favourite tunnel? Are you fond of musical instruments? . . . Where did you bury the dog? . . . Wherein lies the nucleus? Do you know where you're going and do you know who's going with you? Do you piss in public, or just now and then?"

All this is encapsulated in an entirely banal love triangle between the central figure, Dr, Huml, his wife, and his mistress. They exchange clichés which go on ad infinitum. Morality is either entirely foreign to this world, or it has been handed over to a machine. In either case, the farce leaves little doubt as to the rottenness of the world it satirizes.

In Praise of Folly

Is there a better one just offstage? That is the question other members of the Czech dissident community of writers and artists posed in the years leading up to 1968. Just as in the realm of theater, novelists, poets, and filmmakers shared Havel's sense of an opening. The Czech film industry, for example, had been vibrant before the war but produced very little after it. Still more and more students studied in film school, and on occasion their efforts won international recognition, something about which the regime was proud though ambivalent. Milos Forman's *Fireman's Ball* of 1968 was one such film, and its comedy helped protect it from censorship for a time. A meeting was held by the regime to gather together firemen who were supposed to be offended by the portrait of their drunkenness and petty thievery. The firemen were delighted. When Forman was asked in later years whether the film had a political point, he demurred. He just wanted to have some fun, but "somewhere back in your head you knew that you were bugging these idiots, you know, like Bilak and Jakes and Novotny and these totally corrupt people." Above all, this kind of parody helped soften the burden not of official censorship, but of self-censorship, the petty lies and compromises on which the regime rested. The audiences who laughed at Forman's films may actually have started to laugh at themselves and at those who ruled them. Forman's cunning was well known to earlier utopians. "Sometimes a fool may speak a word in season," was the way Erasmus put it to Thomas More, that master utopian, in *In Praise of Folly*, written in 1509.

Dystopias and parodies describe the world that is by constructing a distorted, exaggerated, or imaginary one. The Czech version of these literary forms have many distinguished ancestors, More's *Utopia* being the first but by no means the last of the genre. George Orwell's

1984, Aldous Huxley's *Brave New World,* and Yevgeniy Zemyatin's *We* explored this same terrain in the twentieth century. In each case a moral vision is specified, reiterated, crystallized by the unfolding of a monstrously immoral and fictional world.

In the Czech case in the 1960s, there were other routes to utopia. Many writers and artists who had made a commitment to communism felt betrayed by its deformations and its crimes. In their early years, Pavel Kohout and Milan Kundera were both fervent supporters of Czech communism. When they saw through the illusions of these beliefs, they tried to construct in their writing a set of ideas which were stripped of the crudities of communism while retaining some of the idealism which had brought them to communism in the first place.

This was the viewpoint of the Czech critic and scholar Eduard Goldstücker. He joined the Czech Communist Party in the 1930s, engaged in anti-fascist politics, and became part of the Czech government in exile in London. After the war, he was named Czech ambassador to London, Paris, and Tel Aviv but was recalled, arrested, and tried for subversive activities in the 1950s when the regime turned anti-Semitic. He was convicted, had his death sentence commuted to life imprisonment, and faced years doing hard labor in the Czech uranium mines. After Stalin's death, he was released from prison and began teaching Kafka at the Charles University in Prague. Having been "rehabilitated" himself, he decided to rehabilitate Kafka as a Czech writer, until 1967 considered unacceptable on political grounds to the regime. By then he had been elected chairman of the Czech Writers' Union and he was serving as a member of the Czech parliament. He was committed to reforming communism, to open it to free speech and free thought, but to preserve its egalitarian impulses. "Socialism with a human face" was the rallying cry of these people, alongside the ill-fated Dubcek regime which succeeded Novotny. Together with many other writers and artists, this effort infused the Prague spring with the hope that the communist experience—a betrayal of human values to be sure—could be transcended from within.[104]

On 22 August 1968, the Soviet invasion of Czechoslovakia put an end to this dream and, over time, scattered the dreamers around the world. Goldstücker sought refuge in Britain; Kundera emigrated to France, Kohout to Austria, Forman to America. Havel remained in Czechoslovakia, and together with others slowly, defiantly, and painfully prepared the ground for another leap into an alternative future.

Conclusion

Liberation theology, student revolt, Havel's theater of defiance, Dubcek's "socialism with a human face": what do these "minor utopias," these disparate movements, have in common, and why did they flourish at roughly the same time, in the late 1960s? The overall argument of this book is that the twentieth century is filled with moments of possibility, when groups of people rejected the logic of inertia and began to believe in the transformation of the world in which they lived. The fact that such moments were almost always short-lived and were followed by defeat, disillusionment, and despair did not prevent them from recurring. Visionaries returned; their impulse was irrepressible, though their immediate achievements were meager or nonexistent.

Each of the three movements described in this chapter was based on a dream. Each was profoundly moral in character; each aimed at a kind of libertarian socialism, one which sailed through the narrows separating the Scylla of Washington and the Charybdis of Moscow.[105] Liberation theologians believed that Catholicism could be restored to what they took to be its earlier mission: a shield of the poor. Student revolutionaries believed they could break through the cordon of corporate capitalism to a different, a more authentic, way of learning and living, and that they could do so without reference to the desiccated and conservative left-wing parties of their elders. Czech writers and artists believed that the communist dictatorship could be deflated by comedy, by poetry, by an appeal to the humanism so deeply ingrained within Czech culture. In each case, the dream came alive after a period of economic growth, producing both new possibilities and new problems. The space to dream was created in part by the robust development of the very forces the dreamers came to oppose. But that space closed rapidly when those in power saw the dreamers as a real threat to their positions as 1968 came to an end. The pillars were shaken but they were still visibly in place. Another 20 years would have to pass before the dreamers would return. But when they did, in 1989, they did so on the shoulders of their predecessors. No 1968, no 1989. And no movement toward global citizenship, the topic of the next chapter.

Between the 1960s and the 1990s, many of the participants of 1968 retreated into quietism. Others moved into the mainstream, as did Daniel Cohn-Bendit, adopting the European idea as a dream to realize. Others still spun off into terrorism, trying to hurry history. All they brought about was suffering, more failure, and deeper opposition to their aims. A substantial backlash against the "minor utopias" of 1968 emerged, turning the Catholic Church, for example, emphatically against liberation theology. Pope Paul VI had come to Medellín in 1968 to support the claim that the Roman Catholic Church was the church of the poor. In 2005, the Church elected a pope, Benedict XVI, whose conservatism was a direct and hostile response to the upheavals of 1968.

The year 1968 was also one of the last moments when Marxist language infused visionary projects. After the failure of the student revolt in Europe, after the Soviet invasion of Czechoslovakia, the strains within Marxism turned into fissures, which grew wider and wider as time went by. Some elements of belief persisted; Cuba was still there. Vietnam won its 40-year war of national liberation, but in the West Marxism crumbled as a way of looking at the world. Over time, the legacy of 1968 became liberation, understood not as workers' rights, nor as the right to national self-determination, but as human rights, configured in a trans-national context.

6 1992
Global Citizenship

The decade following 1989 provided dramatic images of political transformation—the collapse of the Soviet Union and the end of the Cold War in 1991; the emergence of a strengthened European Union in 1992, following the Maastricht Treaty, as a confederation of 375 million people; the release of Nelson Mandela from prison in 1991 and the final defeat of Apartheid. Thus ended by the early 1990s what Eric Hobsbawm has termed the "short twentieth century."[1]

In the same period there emerged a new kind of vision, one which echoed earlier ideas but which set them in a new framework, the framework of globalization. In a nutshell, its advocates aimed at creating a new kind of politics, which they termed the politics of "global citizenship." One of its champions, Richard Falk, sums up these vectors of creative political thinking as a process of "globalization-from-below."

Global citizens are emerging out of "an array of transnational social forces animated by environmental concerns, human rights, hostility to patriarchy, and a vision of human community based on the unity of diverse cultures seeking an end to poverty, oppression, humiliation, and collective violence." People with such beliefs changed what constituted "the real arena of politics"; no longer was the focus on oppositional activity within a particular state. Political mobilization on the local level and across borders fostered activity which aimed "to promote a certain kind of political consciousness trans-nationally that could radiate influence in a variety of directions" up and down, from the very local to the emphatically global.[2] In effect, global citizenship is a political project helping people to imagine a different kind of world. In a similar vein, Michael Peter Smith celebrates the way in which immigrants' politics describe "new forms of social and political agency that flow across national borders" just as robustly as do the people who engage in them. "Can you imagine," he asks rhetorically, that a fundamentally new kind of grassroots politics has displaced older, outmoded forms of protest and contestation.[3]

This chapter examines the claim that a new kind of citizenship— global citizenship—emerged in the 1990s, and that it is a carrier of a transformational vision, one which defines citizenship not as participation in a state-bound polity, but as participation in a trans-national set of struggles for dignity and justice. This new kind of post-national politics is rooted in identifiable *quartiers,* both in the developed "north" and in the developing "south."

First you act, and then you talk about it, says the Talmud, and, in the same spirit, the carriers of the message of global citizenship have formed theory out of practice. This chapter investigates the practice, and then examines the theory. The conclusion is that the project of global citizenship is another example of a twentieth-century emancipatory vision, a way of imagining the future which both describes and departs from political realities. It presents innovative lines of solidarity at the same time as it exaggerates the passing of the nation-state. The negotiation between these two spheres of action—national and trans-national—is a field of force, the future shape of which no one can predict.

Human Rights

In the last decades of the twentieth century, the field of trans-national politics expanded in such a way as to challenge conventional, territorially defined notions of sovereignty. This happened in the courts, on the streets, in company boardrooms, and in the efflorescence of non-governmental organizations. In many ways, these arenas of contestation left the core of state sovereignty intact. But at the margins there were highly unusual initiatives demonstrating the extent to which local politics in one context became global politics or matters of universal concern in another. I will examine this set of developments in four areas, the first of which is that of human rights.

The Pinochet Case
On 16 October 1998, General Augusto Pinochet was arrested in London at a medical clinic where he was recovering from back surgery. His arrest was ordered by a British magistrate who had received a request for Pinochet's detention from a Spanish magistrate, Baltasar Garzón, who wanted Pinochet extradited to Spain. For two years, the Spanish authorities had been investigating charges that Pinochet and other members of the junta he led since 1973 were guilty of crimes against Spanish citizens. These charges were filed by a private association of Spanish lawyers who, under Spanish law, had the right to file private criminal actions. They alleged that seven people with Spanish citizenship, two women and five men, two of whom were priests, had been murdered or had disappeared in Chile as a direct result of actions of Pinochet and his regime. Judge Garzón ordered Pinochet's arrest as a preliminary to his extradition to Spain so that he could face these charges.

The ensuing legal proceedings tell us much about one facet of the challenge to state sovereignty in the last decade of the twentieth century. Through the adherence of member states of the European Union to the Convention on Human Rights, individual states accepted that the immunity normally granted to heads of state or former heads of state from criminal prosecution would not apply when such individuals left office and were accused of crimes against humanity. In this case, the accusation was that Pinochet's regime had used torture in the course of the detention and murder of these seven Spanish citizens. Consequently, he was not immune from prosecution for these acts, because they could in no sense be described as part of the normal and legally sanctioned duties of a head of state.

The road to Pinochet's arrest is a complex one. In 1996, two Spanish magistrates were empowered to investigate accusations that Spanish nationals had been killed unlawfully in Chile and Argentina. Judge Manuel García Castillón handled the Chilean evidence, and a second magistrate, Garzón, was responsible for similar accusations of crimes against Spaniards in Argentina. Garzón found evidence that the crimes committed in Argentina were the result of orders issued by Pinochet to the secret branch of the Chilean security police, the DINA. They acted through "Operation Condor," a multi-national secret police action against "subversives" throughout the southern cone of South America. Thus the initial accusation investigated by Garzón was that Chilean agents were responsible for crimes committed against foreign nationals in Argentina. Pinochet was implicated as having authorized these crimes, and, to answer this accusation, Garzón issued his arrest warrant for the detention and subsequent extradition of Pinochet. Subsequently, the investigation of crimes against Spaniards committed in both Chile and Argentina was entrusted to him and to him alone.[4]

It was unusual to see the detention of a former head of state on a private visit to one country (Britain) on charges filed in a second country (Spain) about crimes allegedly committed in a third country (Argentina) by agents of a fourth country (Chile). But that is precisely what had happened.

In Spain, this arrest warrant was challenged by the chief public prosecutor of the Tribunal on which Garzón sat. The claim was that the Spanish court had no jurisdiction in this case; that claim was denied by Garzón and subsequently by the Appellate Criminal Chamber of the court, which ordered him to proceed in his investigation of the extraordinary charges of genocide, terrorism, and torture.

The Spanish construction of these offenses was both broader than British constructions and, to a degree, inconsistent with them. For extradition to proceed, the two countries adhering to the Extradition Treaty of 1989 had to have parallel laws making the offense actionable in both countries. That was not the case with respect to genocide, not then deemed a crime under English law. In addition, the Spanish court's construction of the meaning of genocide incorporated the killing of social groups deemed to be alien to the Chilean junta's political project. This went well beyond English constructions of the term "genocide." Secondly, the Spanish construction of terrorism as acts undermining the rule of law did not correspond directly to English statute. The only clear line of agreement was over the third charge, the accusation of torture, the Convention against which both Britain and Spain had formally signed.[5] Article 3 of the European Convention for the Protection of Human Rights and Fundamental Freedoms, initially adopted in 1950 and subsequently extended, formally outlawed torture. The European Convention for the Prevention of Torture and Inhuman or Degrading Treatment of Punishment (ETS no. 126) had entered into force on 1 February 1989, further strengthening this legal framework. Here is an instance where the framework of European integration provided the material basis for legal action to defend the rights of Europeans anywhere in the world. Whether this was the intention of the framers of these conventions is neither here nor there; the outcome was that instruments existed to internationalize the sanctions available in particularly egregious cases of the violation of human rights.

There was a convoluted period of review, including a reworking of the initial judgment on the grounds that one of the judges had worked for Amnesty International, and thereby gave the appearance of bias. Thus the first judgment, which was termed "Pinochet 1," set aside as possibly biased in "Pinochet 2," was reformulated in "Pinochet 3," the final word. Therein the Law Lords of the House of Lords concurred with the original decision of the British Home Secretary, Jack Straw, to carry forward extradition procedures enabling a Spanish court to interrogate and ultimately to try Pinochet. On 24 March 1999, by a six to one majority, the Law Lords denied a writ of habeas corpus against his arrest. They did so on complex grounds. First, a majority argued that a head of state was not necessarily liable for prosecution for acts of torture; only when countries consented could such prosecutions proceed. National ratification of the Convention on Torture by Chile, Spain, and Britain was deemed consent; furthermore, Chile's ratification had abrogated Pinochet's claim to immunity. In sum, the highest court in England had accepted that the Convention on Torture provided universal jurisdiction in national courts in cases of inhuman treatment of prisoners. However, this ruling applied only to crimes committed after the act went into effect, enabling prosecutions in the United Kingdom for torture committed elsewhere. The date when the Criminal Justice Act containing this provision became law was 8 December 1988, 15 years after the allegations initially investigated by Garzón.

There are two conservative facets of this decision which bear on the question of how large a hole in territoriality had been created by international conventions on human rights. It is evident that the claim for absolute national sovereignty in questions of human rights violations was no longer tenable. But national legal practice, and the prerogatives of nation-states, persisted. Some Chilean opinion, not at all sympathetic to Pinochet, resented the fact that a British court and not a Chilean court was the venue for such matters.[6] National prerogatives mattered to them, especially in terms of the construction of a fragile democracy.

The Lords' judgment also reinforced the national element in this supra-national incident. The legal decision had it that Britain and Chile *as nations* had to be seen to have consented to the internationalization of this set of crimes, action against which could proceed only after the date that the relevant act went into effect *in Britain*. The effect of this last restriction was to narrow the field of prosecution to cases of torture after 1988 or of conspiracies to torture, conspiracies it can be (and was) argued in the Pinochet case, that have continued from 1973 to the present day.

Whether or not such conspiracies could be proved, the outcome of this ruling was to establish that a former head of state was not immune from prosecution for crimes against humanity while he was in office. This was a massive precedent for many individuals and groups to seek redress in the courts for such violations of human rights. In the case of Pinochet himself, the proceedings never took place. Medical opinion gave the British Home Secretary the grounds—disputed by many observers—for ruling that the former Chilean head of state was unfit to stand trial. He returned to Chile, and by 2006 he had not been formally arraigned for torture or for other crimes against humanity.

It is clear that state jurisdiction in certain crimes is now complicated by international conventions on human rights abuses. But it is also clear that territoriality operates in all but exceptional cases. The claims of the nation-state are quite robust on most legal matters outside these exceptional crimes. The American refusal to countenance war crimes trials of American soldiers conducted under the aegis of the International Criminal Court is one instance of this restriction. So is the refusal of Belgian legislators to allow Belgian courts to try Israeli Prime Minister Ariel Sharon for alleged crimes against humanity in the West Bank and Gaza. Still, what is most striking about the 1990s is the extent to which sovereignty was being stretched at the margin, especially by private groups usually termed non-governmental organizations. To see how they operate, we now turn to the field of environmental politics.

Environmental Rights

Bhopal

On 2 and 3 December 1984, 40 tons of an extremely toxic gas escaped from a chemical plant in Bhopal, India. The plant was owned and run by the Union Carbide Company's Indian subsidiary (UCIL). The damage was catastrophic. Approximately 4,000 people in the vicinity were killed, and more than 50 times that number injured, a high percentage permanently incapacitated. The Indian police filed a criminal complaint against UCIL later that month, and subsequently numerous briefs were filed claiming that the parent company in the United States was liable for damages suffered in this disaster. Within India, the government moved quickly to pass legislation granting it the status of agent for the victims' legal claims.

It was therefore the government of India which sued Union Carbide in the Southern District Court of New York in April 1985. Judge John F. Keenan dismissed the case on the grounds that the proper venue was in India. He required Union Carbide to abide by the Indian decision and to use American rules of discovery in the preparation of the case.[7] On appeal, the requirement that American procedures be followed in an Indian court was set aside. The case therefore reverted to India.

In Bhopal, the case resumed as one between the government of India, acting on behalf of those injured in the disaster, and the Union Carbide Company, the American parent corporation which owned a majority interest in UCIL. Damages claimed totaled $3 billion. The plaintiff claimed that this agricultural pesticide plant used highly dangerous chemicals—especially MIC, or methyl isocyanate—the risks of which were entirely evident to the management. The company had undertaken to produce a plant which would be safe for the manufacture of these chemical products, and to train the staff in handling them. Negligence and therefore liability rested not only with the local management but with its American corporate owners.

For the purposes of my argument, what is interesting in this case is the riposte by Union Carbide. On 30 October 1986, the company argued that the concepts of "multinational corporation" and its variant "monolithic multinational," describing overall corporate control worldwide, were unknown in law. Furthermore, even if the firm were liable, so were the state and national governments of India, whose safety regulations failed in this case.

The negotiations went on for more than a year between the company and the government of India. An interim award for damages was granted, and UCIL was required to deposit a sum for distribution to the families of victims; this sum was a minute fraction of the damages initially demanded. Procedural delays extended the haggling over three years, until the Supreme Court of India settled on the sum of $425 million from Union Carbide and $45 million from UCIL. The Court also terminated all legal proceedings with respect to the Bhopal case. It claimed that compassion for the victims had to come before sorting out the legal issues of multinational corporate identity.

The court ruling was, according to some observers, a scarcely veiled government compromise, resulting in the award of a very small sum of money to individual claimants. By closing the matter, all criminal proceedings were voided, and the legal position of multi-nationals remained unfixed by law.[8]

Here we see two elements of the history of the last decades of the twentieth century in high relief. The first is that the state remained a major player, perhaps the major player, in dealing with significant incidents involving international businesses. The second is that the trans-national character of such firms presented problems which could not be handled easily by national statute or criminal codes. Globalization created conditions which went beyond them.

Environmental Movements and National Sovereignty

One effect of globalization has been to supersede the parameters within which the Bhopal case was framed. The State of India represented the victims in a class action, which was thrown out of court in the United States. In India, the Union Carbide Company denied that its multi-national operations were relevant to the workings of its Indian subsidiary. Criminal charges were dropped in the interests of "closure." All three of these elements shifted in the 1990s, such that non-governmental organizations (NGOs) came to the fore as agents in this field, business leaders came to seek clarification in international law and through international agreements in order to help their enterprises operate within a more stable framework globally, and damages awarded to victims suing large corporations have grown exponentially.

Environmental issues grew in significance in the last decade of the twentieth century, and the range of associations and individuals empowered to address them grew as well. Questions of global warming, the ozone layer, the destruction of the rain forests, the elimination of endangered species all attracted attention and mobilized many groups, which operated on a local as well as state level and in conjunction with trans-national organizations. These groups mixed the global and the local in such a way as to construct a new category of human rights discourse, the category of environmental rights.

What are environmental rights? The first element is the right to leave to one's children sufficient clean air and clean water to enable them to enjoy all the other rights at their disposal. Environmental rights are, in this sense, the right to have other rights. Here we see a key point, which follows both the 1986 Chernobyl (Ukraine) nuclear accident and the Bhopal cases. Environmental rights overlap with rights configured under conventional notions of state sovereignty. But environmental issues are sufficiently trans-national to require action both within the framework of the nation-state and beyond it. Here again we see how globalization has stretched the framework of sovereignty. The state is still at the core of the story, but there are other, newer elements at play.

Here is the key focus of innovative politics in the 1990s. It is the delegation of expertise and authority to speak on environmental issues both upward from the state to trans-national groups and movements and downward toward sub-national groups.[9] NGOs almost always operate on both levels, reflecting their origins in the peace movements of the 1960s and 1970s. These NGOs and international agencies are the arbiters of what Karen Litfin has felicitously termed "sovereignty bargains," struck by states "in order to address transboundary environmental" issues. In effect, states gain authority by losing authority to those who are able to solve environmental problems.[10] These bargains are struck by states unable to control problems of environmental pollution or degradation on their own. Their loss of autonomy can yield a gain in control, and, as importantly, a gain in legitimacy, both as defenders of the nation and as integral partners in the international community.

The variety of tactics adopted by NGOs are striking and highly controversial. Greenpeace has taken a more daring stance than other groups: blocking whaling vessels, sailing into nuclear testing areas, and circulating information in the former communist bloc of Eastern Europe as to the environmental damage done since the end of the Second World War. That this organization has earned the enmity of Norwegian, French, and East German officials is hardly surprising; what is more important is the way they shifted the agenda of political protest away from the conventional terminology of the Cold War toward what might be termed a war for the survival of the environment.

At times, these struggles have been waged alongside indigenous people, facing the transformation of their world through development. The Rainforest Action Network (RAN), founded in 1985, has stood alongside the Kayapo people to effectively stop a Brazilian project to build a dam on the Amazon which would have destroyed their habitat. RAN also organized a boycott of the fast-food chain Burger King in the United States in 1987 for importing beef from rain forest countries. After a drop in sales, the company agreed to import beef from areas where the effect of grazing would not result in deforestation.[11] Environmental politics thus spans the space between consumers and corporate sensibilities domestically, while reaching out to allies abroad.

Alongside domestic forms of appeal to consumers' consciousness and solidarity with indigenous people, NGOs have also helped transform international agreements into effective instruments to protect the environment. They have done so through monitoring compliance and fostering research into ecological issues. Thus the Vienna Convention on the Ozone Layer of 1985, which was toothless, was followed by the 1987 Montreal Protocol, itself tightened up by successive agreements in 1990, 1992, and 1994. The same has occurred with respect to acid rain, climate change, and the protection of Antarctica. International agreements provide pressure points for NGOs to investigate national facets of what are clearly transnational problems.

In this growing field of local globalism, or global localism, there have been substantial obstacles. One is the position of successive American governments of both parties to the question of the erosion of American sovereignty, for example in the Kyoto protocol on global warming. Chapter 2 noted how this question effectively shipwrecked Wilson's plan for a League of Nations in 1919. Nothing has happened since that year to diminish the commitment of American politicians to defend American "exceptionalism" and to defy international opinion and agreements on global warming, or on protecting the ozone layer. As we have seen, the government of India miscalculated when it sought much higher damages for the victims of Bhopal in an American court. The case was thrown out; had the company been European, the outcome might not have been the same, since European countries were signatories of a number of trans-national agreements through the EU, which represented a clear departure from American notions of sovereignty.

Another obstacle to the emergence of trans-national environmental politics has come from the developing world. In the Rio de Janeiro conference on environment and development of 1992, delegates from 172 countries met and agreed on a number of issues ranging from greenhouse gas emissions to the protection of endangered species. But it was evident at that meeting that the notion of environmental scrutiny of development projects in the Third World smacked of cultural imperialism. As we have seen, environmental groups worked alongside some native populations, but this was hardly welcomed by national politicians, whose own shortcomings were thereby highlighted by international publicity. The sovereignty of new and developing nations was as important to them as it was to the United States, and at times that meant opposing trans-national approaches to environmental issues.[12]

A particular group of activists has helped modulate these tensions and contribute to an ongoing erosion of conventional definitions of sovereignty with respect to environmental issues. I speak here of scientists. In 1992, Kenneth Hancock of the American National Science Foundation's chemistry division called on chemists to lead the way in redesigning industrial processes in such a way as to prevent environmental damage in the first place. They should not only help clean up the mess of environmental pollution, but also find ways of avoiding it in future. These are highly technical matters, and require major funding; but from the mid-1990s, the cash and the knowledge base were there. Small and hesitant steps were taken, and seen to be taken.[13]

Such scientific efforts were made by the private sector too, and in unusual ways. The giant pharmaceutical firm Merck struck a deal with the National Institute of Biodiversity in Costa Rica. The company would fund its conservation program in return for access to medicinal plants that are indigenous to the country.[14] In Africa, the giant producer of powdered and concentrated milk products, Nestlé, gave in to a long campaign and agreed in 1984 to adopt the World Health Organization/UNICEF International Code of Marketing of Breastmilk Substitutes. NGOs which helped change the company's mind on the need to abide by international conventions were the church-based Interfaith Center on Corporate Responsibility and Infact, a Minnesota-based group which actually ran the boycott.[15] Business sensitivity to environmental questions varied substantially, but the Union Carbide notion that multi-national corporations did not exist in law faded at precisely the time that litigation on tobacco product liability for cancer turned radically against the producers of cigarettes.

Clearly by the 1990s it paid to have a conscience, or at least it paid to be perceived by consumers as devoted to the quest for alternative ways to do business in a more environmentally conscious time. How much of this is mere window dressing and how much a real shift in corporate behavior is yet to be seen; my guess is that it is a mix of both.[16] One businessman who has dedicated himself to environmental rights is Stephan Schmidheiny. This Swiss industrialist discovered that his production line was responsible for the spread of asbestos. Taking responsibility for this lethal by-product of his firm's work, he has also been a leader in promoting environmentally sensitive business strategies. He founded the World Business Council for Sustainable Development and was principal business adviser to the Secretary General of the UN during the Earth Summit in Rio de Janeiro in 1992. He is particularly active in supporting development projects in Latin America through his Avina foundation, in which he has invested over $300 million.[17] Many of these projects reach out to indigenous people. German Politzer and his Avina-sponsored Patagonian Crusade Foundation have brought businessmen together with the Mapuche people to create a site for ecotourism. "Here you have Mapuches, landowners, industrialists ... all sectors of society seated around the same table to help create an integrated and sustainable, bicultural tourist destination, endowed with its own unique identity."[18] The firm rule of Avina is to work independently of political organizations and, with some notable exceptions in educational outreach, outside of the world of the churches. Its aim is to braid together business and what Schmidheiny terms CSOs, or civil society organizations.

The prominence of both NGOs and CSOs in these conflicts and initiatives reinforce the sense that they are the key actors in this new field of force, located on the porous boundary between state and civil society. Through its control of information and publicity, an NGO or a CSO can command the knowledge and disseminate it in such a manner as to both pressure governments and serve as interlocutors between official state agencies and international organizations. Whether or not this mediating function can actually yield a transformation in norms, in the rules that people take for granted about environmental issues, is not clear. What is apparent is that what Karen Litfin terms the "greening of sovereignty" acts alongside human rights agitation to stretch and reshape notions of politics and the sphere of popular involvement in these relatively new and increasingly urgent issues of the day.[19]

Women's Rights

The field of women's rights was a third area in which during the 1990s there was much activity and reflection about alternatives to deeply imbedded patterns of violence and deprivation. Here the obstacles were perhaps even more formidable, and the imbedded attitudes even more deeply rooted than those associated with the treatment of political prisoners or the degradation of the environment. For women's rights touch on questions of family structure and inheritance, reproductive behavior, and sexual identity, matters of profound importance inflected by religious and cultural norms evident in both the developed and the developing worlds. The core of the problem is that addressing women's rights always means addressing male identities and their construction on the premise of their gender superiority.

In the 1990s there was much work done by people committed to imagining a world in which violence against women as women was recognized as a crime against humanity. These efforts were part of a wider movement aiming at those structural inequalities, differently configured in different parts of the world, which continued to make it inevitable that from birth to death, the life chances of a female child were bound to be more restricted than the life chances of a male child.

As in all other areas of opposition and struggle in the 1990s, the gap between rhetoric and reality in the field of women's rights was huge. Statements and resolutions at international conventions rarely touched patterns of behavior. While there were some clear victories, and some concerted action to begin to dismantle facets of gender inequality, it is apparent that many material differences in life chances by sex were irreducible, at least for the foreseeable future. Furthermore, the growth in religious fundamentalism in this period has meant that the political pressure to reverse gains in women's rights over the past decades has increased. The outcome of many of the initiatives surveyed here appear limited or meager. But what is the appropriate time span to measure social progress? What matters is to recognize both the fact and the limits of such social action, which is incapable of producing new forms of gender-blind citizenship by itself. To be sure, these initiatives in feminist social action were integral to the multifaceted search for new forms of citizenship and new rules of collective behavior both within states and across their boundaries. The intersection of the discussion about women's rights with this broader movement is the subject to which we now turn.

Rape as a Crime Against Humanity

In the 1990s, advocates of women's rights increasingly located their struggle within the overall field of human rights and insisted that the term "human rights" makes no sense without a gendered dimension. The most striking incident which shows this braiding together of different strands of human rights work is the establishment in international law of the principle that rape in wartime is a crime against humanity.

In 1961 in Britain, a body which became known as Amnesty International was formed to serve as a forum for the defense of the rights of prisoners of conscience. It sought out information and disseminated it worldwide about those imprisoned for their religious or political views. By 1976, there were over 1500 branches of Amnesty all over the world, and its reports carried with them a reputation for accuracy and impartiality.[20]

It was only in the late 1980s, though, that Amnesty began to address the question of the repression of women as women. Part of the pressure to do so was applied by women's groups.[21] By the early 1990s, the civil war in Yugoslavia threw a glaring light on this particular form of human rights abuse. It became evident that Serbian forces, paramilitary groups, and their various allies were using rape as a means of ethnic cleansing. That is, the abuse of women was not only a matter of expressing ethnic hatred, but it was a way to make it clear to the target population of these crimes that they were better off living in another part of the world. At times rape was used to impregnate women with children who would be at least partly Serb, but most of the time the practice was a mixture of torture, humiliation, and political pressure on Muslims in particular to get out of Serbia or Bosnia.[22]

International judicial action for punishment of the perpetrators of these war crimes brought about the criminalization of rape as a crime against humanity. This approach was imbedded in the work of an International Criminal Tribunal for the former Yugoslavia in the Hague established under United Nations mandate in 1993 to hear evidence about war crimes committed during the civil war. Already in 1949 the fourth Geneva Convention proscribed the humiliating and degrading treatment of civilians in wartime, but it was only in the 1990s that a criminal court existed with the power to demand the seizure, trial, and, if found guilty, the imprisonment of those responsible for such acts.

In 1996, this tribunal indicted eight Serbs for crimes committed in the town of Foca between 1992 and 1993. They were charged on the basis of evidence provided by 25 Muslim women who were raped and sexually assaulted in the town. The systematic nature of these crimes was specified in the indictment read out at the trial of three of these men who had been taken into custody. In February 2001, the defendants were found guilty of violations of the laws and customs of war, and with crimes against humanity, since their crimes entailed torture and rape.[23] Three of the accused were sentenced to terms of imprisonment ranging from 12 to 28 years. The heaviest sentence was imposed on Dragoljub Kunarac, the commander of the reconnaissance unit in the Bosnian Serb Army which had occupied the town. He was found guilty both on the basis of individual and command responsibility, and as of 2003 was serving his sentence in Germany. The other two convicted men are in prison in Norway.

This verdict established the precedent in international law that rape in wartime is a crime against humanity. How strong this precedent will be in cases involving rape in peacetime is unclear. The International Criminal Court was created by the Treaty of Rome in 1998 and, having received the ratification of more than 60 nations, came into operation in July 2002. Even though the mixed group of the United States, Iraq, China, and Israel voted against the treaty, the Court now has full international jurisdiction. Its stated remit explicitly refers to the rights of women. "The ICC complements existing national judicial systems and will step in only if national courts are unwilling or unable to investigate or prosecute such crimes. The ICC will also help defend the rights of those, such as women and children, who have often had little recourse to justice."[24] It is too soon to tell if the Foca case has opened the way to future prosecutions of the crime of rape, whenever and wherever it is committed, as a crime against humanity. All we can safely say now is that in some instances men who commit crimes against women are currently liable to be prosecuted in a permanent international criminal court.

Women's Rights, Population, and Development

The international arena has provided many different venues for the development of policies aimed at eroding or eradicating the barriers women face in the full enjoyment of their lives. One such venue is the United Nations, which serves as a focal point for scores of non-governmental organizations addressing issues of women's rights. In 1979, CEDAW, or the Convention for the Elimination of All Forms of Discrimination Against Women, was ratified by the UN, but with little effect on the material foundations of gender inequality. Declarations mattered, but only when they were turned into practical policy, and that was where the struggles and the headaches started. What is evident is that women's organizations succeeded by the 1990s in placing women's issues on the agenda of international organizations and debate. By then, 50 such organizations had consultative status in the Economic and Social Council of the UN. Some were older organizations, such as the Women's International League for Peace and Freedom, active in the First World War, and the World Young Women's Christian Association. Others were relative newcomers. All helped convene major UN meetings on women's issues in Mexico City in 1975, in Copenhagen in 1980, and in 1985 in Nairobi, where 13,000 delegates addressed questions concerning women's rights, the environment, development, and peace.[25] These meetings disclosed many commonalities but also many points of friction which separated women's groups from different national or religious backgrounds. A decade later, in Beijing, a concerted effort was made to try to overcome these differences, though with uncertain effect.[26]

In 1994, the issue of women's rights was placed at the center of the World Population Conference in Cairo.[27] This was a departure from earlier world population conferences, where economists and demographers spoke of population dynamics in a positivistic language hard to square with the discourse of human rights. These "experts" on population questions were reluctant to enter into discussion of women's issues, which many believed only caused political storms and consequently made scientific debate, as they understood it, impossible. In 1974 in Bucharest and in 1984 in Mexico City, there was widespread discussion of women's rights, but at the margins of a debate by and large about numbers.

In Cairo in 1994, in contrast, women's groups seized the initiative. Women's NGOs helped prepare the documents to be examined in Cairo, and with the full support of the Clinton administration advocates of women's rights now stood center stage. Reproductive health and the empowerment of women were, not surprisingly, high up on the agenda. The program of action for the coming 20 years, adopted by 180 national delegations in Cairo, stated firmly not only that "the empowerment and autonomy of women and the improvement of their political, social, economic and health status is a highly important end in itself," but also that "improvement in the status of women . . . is essential for the long-term success of population programmes."[28] Steps to this end included

> 4.4.(d). Adopting appropriate measures to improve women's ability to earn income beyond traditional occupations, achieve economic self-reliance, and ensure women's equal access to the labour market and social security systems;
> 4.4.(g). Making it possible, through laws, regulations and other appropriate measures, for women to combine the roles of child-rearing, breast-feeding and child-rearing with participation in the workforce.[29]

The conference endorsed the campaign to end female circumcision and campaigns to defend women's right of inheritance and their access to reproductive health care. Nafis Sadik, Secretary-general of the conference and executive director of the UN Population Fund, was right to declare that the meeting represented a "quantum leap" in population politics. She told the delegates that "a woman's control over her own fertility is basic to her freedom. It is the source from which other freedoms flow."[30] Here indeed is major breakthrough in what Marilyn Danguilan called "the unbracketing of women." Even the Vatican endorsed the program of action, with some reservations over particular issues like abortion rights.[31] The momentum behind the linkage of population and women's rights was remarkably strong.

The second feature of the Cairo conference of interest in this context was its location of population policy within a wider framework of development, which included an important environmental component. Thus the broad coalition of women's groups which pushed hard for the program of action brought on board many other groups that believed in fertility decline in order to limit the pressure on resources and the disastrous effects on cities in the developing world of massive in-migration due to high fertility rates.

To be sure, the same negotiation we have seen before between national sovereignty and multi-national conventions was evident here. The 1994 Cairo conference was quick to affirm that "the implementation of the recommendations contained in the Programme of Action is the sovereign right of each country, consistent with national laws and development priorities, with full respect for the various religious and ethical values and cultural backgrounds of its people, and in conformity with universally recognized international human rights."[32] This was no more than bowing to necessity. But the thrust of the document was so forceful that it left little room for doubt that the delegates had agreed that the issue of development was indeed a matter requiring an improvement in the status of women everywhere. Restricting fertility without empowering women simply wouldn't work.

Behind this turn in both the form and content of the discussion of population questions is the work of a group of economists and philosophers who redesigned the politics of development. The most influential of these people are Amartya Sen and Martha Nussbaum. Sen, Nobel laureate in economics, developed a theory of entitlements and capabilities which provided the intellectual firepower to persuade economists and policy-makers that freedom—emphatically including women's freedoms—and development were compatible, even synergistic. Maximizing the capabilities of both men and women were at one and the same time the goal of freedom and the pathway to freedom. Once capabilities were enhanced, functionings—or the choices of how we wish to live—would become more varied and more effective, in particular in developing economies.[33] Nussbaum provided much additional support for this argument in showing that a theory of this level of generality was based on universal values consistent with respect for the particularities and dignities of non-Western cultures; no cultural imperialism here.[34] Together they affirmed a center-left project, based on a mixture of liberalism and social-democratic beliefs, wherein the achievement of women's rights is seen as part of a universal struggle for emancipation from poverty, ignorance, and human degradation.

The Local and the Global

The project sketched out by Sen and Nussbaum has powerful supporters in the World Bank. It is clear that international funding is available for projects on the local level to empower women and enhance their contributions to development as a whole. Much of this work is at the level of micro-economic activity, in the form, for example, of micro-loans to women to enable them to start businesses or manage small tracts of land in rural India.

This emphasis on work on the village level is consistent with many other facets of women's associative life in the 1990s and beyond. Some term this activism "grassroots politics." But at times the local has merged with the universal.[35] Women have been central in protesting the brutality of dictatorial regimes in ways which has arrested world attention. The role of the Mothers of the Plaza de Mayo in Argentina, insisting as mothers on an accounting from the regime of their husbands and sons who vanished under the military dictatorship of the 1970s, is a case in point. They still march every Thursday afternoon to continue their struggle; that it has taken decades to find the truth is neither here nor there. The issues are so important to them as women, as mothers, as citizens, that they refuse to go away. With the passage of time, the Grandmothers of the Plaza de Mayo have joined in the struggle. The personal is the political here in a very direct sense. The work of the Guatemalan Nobel Prize winner Rigoberta Menchu Tum is another instance of the standing in the international discourse of human rights earned by women whose lives and grievances are in their villages.

No one can deny the courage or the importance of the work accomplished by these women, alongside the other initiatives on behalf of women's rights we have surveyed in this chapter. The question remains, though, as to whether these developments constitute a form of politics of sufficient strength and appeal to do more than chip away at the gendered inequalities of both the developing and the developed world. Exemplary courage is never enough, as important as it is. The search for redress of women's grievances has raised the general level of consciousness about the impossibility of using the term "human rights" without recognizing that more than half the world's population is female. But the material achievements of general acceptance of this obvious though awkward fact are still potential rather than real. What these activists have offered is an opening, a continuing interrogation of policies and policy-makers about gender and inequality. It is unclear how stable a political platform they have achieved. All politics may be local, but not all local politics can penetrate the layers of inequality and prejudice which have truncated women's lives in the past.

Trans-National Citizenship

Human rights, environmental rights, women's rights: each of these issues marries the local and the global. None is limited by national boundaries, but all are imbedded in national institutional and legal frameworks. In the 1990s, many political movements fragmented, mutating into both sub-national and supra-national forms. Visions of alternatives to economic globalization spoke a language of community as the local, and community as the world. As such they both offered a challenge to older state-oriented politics and demonstrated the limitations of social movements which bypass the state. Above all, these trends toward new definitions of citizenship described a field of force with an uncertain future. For the state has not disappeared, and it is simply too soon to tell how its character and powers will be transformed either by global economic forces or by these oppositional movements.

Many of these localized social movements were trans-national in character, and both drew upon support from abroad. In their work, some of these activists redefined the term "citizenship" to connote the collective identities formed by people opposed to the "new world order" as it appears on both the local and the global level. "Citizenship" is thus juxtaposed to "commodity," evoking echoes of earlier appeals of 1968 and beyond. The appeal has force, because these groups work among men and women drawn to global cities, where the commodification of skilled and unskilled immigrant lives and labor is particularly evident.

What was most striking about these local/global organizations is that they worked at the margins and at times among the marginal—in global cities filled with highly mobile, multi-linguistic and multi-national populations. This marginality was both their strength and their weakness. It naturally fed into the construction of trans-national movements, drawing their support from those whose very activities in these groups help foster a sense of collective identity. At times, this kind of identity politics found echoes in the domestic political arena. But at other times, questioning the primacy of the state limited their power to influence the policies of the nations in which they lived or from which they came. This dilemma—how to target the center where power lies while working primarily on the periphery; how to challenge the state while living at a tangent to it—remains an open one.

Another source of these new political visions was disillusionment with the state as an agent of social change. All too frequently movements of national liberation, from Western imperialism to Soviet imperialism, turned conservative once power had been secured. In Algeria, in Czechoslovakia, in Cuba, in the Ukraine, self-determination had been achieved in the 1960s or the 1990s, but with mixed outcomes. Experiments in participatory democracy at the local/global level were self-conscious alternatives to a mystification of national liberation as the end of history. The problem remained though, that even if the state is not worshipped, it cannot be wished away. The new "trans-national citizenships" thus lived in vigorous incompatibility with the older territorial ones. The outcome of the encounter between them is yet to be determined.

Global Workers, Trans-National Movements

The attack on the World Trade Center on 11 September 2001 killed over 3,000 people of 90 different nationalities. It happened in the morning, when the service workers were there, cleaning the offices and catering the food for the corporate world of lower Manhattan, just a few blocks from Wall Street. The *New York Times* produced a series of biographies of these ordinary people caught up in this attack. These "portraits of grief" highlighted what is evident to any visitor to the major capitals of the world: they are both the heart of global networks and magnets to global population movements especially, but not only, of young, unskilled workers.

Who speaks for them? Who defends their interests? The reply most activists give is that they must learn to speak for themselves. Thus activism is the pathway toward constructing a collective identity captured by the term "citizenship" among newcomers to these global cities. This kind of "citizenship" is not the same as membership in a nation-state. As Yasemin Soysal has written, "Rights, participation and representation in a polity, are increasingly matters beyond the vocabulary of national citizenship."[36] Beyond older notions, yes, but that prior political grammar is there, and so are the institutions embodied by it.

To illustrate this dialectical relationship between state-bounded identities and new forms of citizenship, we may consider two different phenomena. The first is located within the European Union, and describes a multiplication of citizenships; the second is both European and extra-European, and describes the emergence of grassroots movements among immigrants, who come together to defend their rights and interests and to engage in a dialogue with the state or states in which they live. In both cases, the power of the state to describe the political realm in which this mix of the local, the national, and the global occurs, is still robustly intact. It is profoundly premature to speak of the end of territoriality.

Multiple Citizenships: Municipal, National, European

Consider the Swedish case. In 2003, roughly 5 percent of the population of nine million people living in Sweden were not Swedish nationals. A larger percentage comprised children of couples of whom at least one partner was not a citizen. In sum, one in five people living in Sweden is either a nonnational or has a parent who is not a national.

This multi-national population reflects changes in the European Community and in migratory flows. In Sweden there are three concentric circles in which individuals exercise their rights as citizens. First comes the town or municipality. On this first level, residence establishes a subset of citizenship, for example, foreigners and native-born Swedes elect the mayor of Stockholm. Around this core area of municipal citizenship is the area of national citizenship, exercised by Swedish nationals alone, who elect their Parliament. Surrounding the national area of citizenship is the European one. In European elections, all Swedes and all residents of Sweden who are citizens of a European Union member state vote for the European parliament. In the European Union, the right to vote has evolved into a three-tiered geography. From the local over the national to the European level, only the intermediate plane is restricted to nationals. Local elections are restricted to residents, and European elections include nationals from other European countries. Citizenship is not detached from nationality; rather, politics reflects different kinds of citizenship.

In January 1996, the European Union set down arrangements for the right to vote in or to stand as a candidate in municipal elections in Europe.[37] Those eligible include citizens of any member state of the European Union, and not only those born in the city or country in question. An Irish woman can, if enough voters support her, become the mayor of Athens or Rome. This right of nondiscrimination helps regularize the position of residents, who have the same bundle of rights in this respect as the national citizens of their chosen town. Here is an electoral equivalent to the single labor market, which is one of the key features of European integration.

But this measure opened the door to a further degree of separation between nationality and citizenship. On the local level, foreign nationals have the right to vote. So do foreigners living in Denmark and in Sweden. There is as yet no uniformity in this practice elsewhere in the

European community, but there are political groups, like the Green Party and the Social Democrats in Germany, dedicated to liberalizing the franchise in this way.

These instances of multiple enfranchisements—or what Rainer Baubock terms "recombinant citizenship"[38]—reflect earlier historical experience. Well before women had the vote in Britain or Canada, those with property could elect municipal officials. In 1862 unmarried Swedish women who paid taxes were given the vote on the municipal level. Women had the municipal vote in Rangoon, Burma, in 1918. It is clear that the notion of the municipality as an urban household, with services and expenditure analogous to a household, enabled women to bypass some of the prejudices preserving the franchise as a male prerogative.

Throughout Europe, there was a twofold history of migration in the period since 1945. The first period was one of positive measures taken to attract and absorb newcomers. This lasted until the 1970s. Then came the harder years, when immigrants competed for jobs and added significantly to the costs of social assistance. At the end of the twentieth century, this second phase was by no means over.

Again, the Swedish case illustrates these wider trends. After the Second World War, Swedish industry recruited workers from other parts of Scandinavia and from southern Europe. The Swedish metal industry in particular needed to attract labor, and in response it drew some 300,000 Finns, alongside around 75,000 Mediterranean workers from Yugoslavia, Greece, and Turkey. Much was accomplished to integrate these workers and their families into Swedish society. In 1966 the government deemed that these foreigners would be called "newcomers" and not "aliens." In 1969 the Swedish Immigration Board was established with authority over residence permits, citizenship, and immigrant integration.[39] State grants were made to foster bilingual education, and aid was given to immigrant associations, working with advisory councils at the local and national levels.

It is hard to image a more positive, welcoming regime for immigrants and their families. Then came the economic downturn of the 1970s, which changed the social and political environment in which immigrants were received. Immigration is usually measured in aggregates, but it always unfolds as a local phenomenon.

Local communities hard-hit by recession now saw newcomers in a very different light. This was the case in the industrial town of Söertälje, south of Stockholm. Between 1976 and 1978 13,000 Syrian Orthodox refugees from Syria, Lebanon, and southeastern Turkey came to the town. The postwar boom was a distant memory, and job competition as well as the tax burden of paying for social services for all residents, including these newcomers, increased the tension surrounding immigration. To be sure, national debates attended these issues, but it is in the neighborhoods, in the markets and in the schools that the real meaning of citizenship is negotiated and performed.

The Yugoslav war brought these issues home in powerful ways. In 1992, 85,000 asylum-seekers arrived in Sweden. Half were Bosnians and were immediately granted permanent residence. Roughly 25,000 were Kosovans, who ultimately returned home. Once again, the humanitarian impulse to help was evident, but so was anxiety over the cost. From 1983–93 approximately 300,000 people sought asylum in Sweden; this was fully one-tenth of the total for Europe as a whole. Of this population of newcomers in Sweden, 80 percent were recipients of social assistance.

In 1995, a commission on refugee policy outlined a new way of handling these problems. A new Ministry for Development Assistance and Immigration was created. The Board of Immigration was renamed the Board of Migration. Rules on asylum were tightened. But the advent of the Schengen agreement in 1990 made it unclear to Swedes as well as to other Europeans how many foreigners would enter Sweden by entering any other European country.

Sweden had done as much as any other country to dampen xenophobic responses to immigrants. Elsewhere in Europe, nativist politics resurfaced. This was especially so after 11 September 2001. The fact that much of the planning of the attack on the World Trade Center had been planned in Germany made it clear that Islamic militants were using Europe as a staging area. Older ill-informed prejudices against Islam or

Muslims were channeled by some politicians, while others tried hard to separate Islam from Fundamentalism.

This set of problems added a new dimension to the evolution of European citizenship. Fundamentalist Islam is a trans-national movement, and nation-states have mobilized their security forces against it. Immigration controls have been tightened and the surveillance of foreigners intensified. It is evident that the war on terrorism has moved the clock back to a more unitary definition of the nation. It is anybody's guess as to whether these centripetal forces, arising from security issues, will overpower the centrifugal forces underlying the decentering of citizenship.

Citizenship as Activism: From Exclusion to Inclusion
Fundamentalist Islam is a multi-national, global movement, which claims to speak for the poor and the outcast among the faithful. Among the millions of Muslims who have migrated to Europe and North America there are militants, but the overwhelming majority of immigrants are either neutral or hostile to their efforts.

Of much greater significance in the unfolding history of citizenship is the work of groups of activists who use trans-national networks within local political life. There are many examples of this kind of political work. Just two will suffice to show the parameters of the phenomenon in question.

In Portugal, as in virtually every other developed country, immigrants live in the penumbra of capital cities, frequently occupying poor or run-down housing. Some of these settlements are legal; others illegal. One such illegal community is the immigrant neighborhood of Alto da Cova da Moura, 15 kilometers from Lisbon.[40] The settlement of about 3,000 people is made up mostly of Africans, "returnees" after the collapse of Portuguese rule in Angola and Mozambique, or men and women from the Cape Verde islands. Technically, the settlement is outside the law. Migrants occupied state and private land without permission and never sought building permits for the dwellings they constructed and which constitute their permanent homes. Most of the population works in unskilled or semiskilled manual jobs or in the service trades.

The neighborhood has built its own Residents' Commission and has its own barber shops, funeral homes, and sporting clubs. The Residents' Commission negotiates with local authorities on the provisioning of basic amenities. There is as well a Cultural Association "Moino du Juventude" to provide activities for schoolchildren until their parents come home from work. It quickly became a critical counterpoint to the Residents' Commission. The Moino du Juventude championed cultural difference, offered literacy courses, ran musical groups, and operated a day care center. They also sought and received funds from both Portuguese and European Union sources to support job training schemes and other programs.

The goal of both the Residents' Commission and the Moino du Juventude was legalization. The Communist city council in the nearby town of Amadora was opposed; but when the Socialist Party came to power in 1997, after 18 years of Communist rule, the position of the two neighborhood associations was transformed. It is evident that local politics intersected with both state institutions and European ones, enabling immigrants to demand and achieve both recognition and funding for essential services.

What these people did was to construct their own political identity and then, with the help of European Union funds and with contacts in the Portuguese Socialist Party, to challenge local authorities to accept them as legal and legitimate members of their region. Nothing would have happened had they waited for charity or bureaucracy to help them. In effect, they became Portuguese by being European. Transnational entitlement yielded national standing.

The significance of local politics is evident as the locus for this form of trans-national identity politics in other countries as well. Toronto is a city with a huge immigrant population among its 2.4 million inhabitants.[41] Approximately half the population in 2003 was foreign-born. This is significantly higher than the percentage of foreign-born people in Los Angeles (27.1 percent) or New York (19.7 percent). Fully 42 percent of all immigrants to Canada since 1991 settled in the Toronto area. These newcomers concentrated not in the old city center, but in the suburban belt and towns of the metropolitan area.

There were three ways in which immigrant groups negotiated their new position within Canadian society in the 1990s. The first was to mobilize against a plan to enlarge metropolitan Toronto and thereby to diminish the significance of local authorities in key areas of urban planning. Immigrants worked to protect the smaller administrative units which were the ones dealing with their interests and aspirations. They created their own association, New Voices for a New City, and spoke up about the dangers they saw in a new megacity. This body of 63 community organizations represented Jamaican, Ethiopian, Somali, Sri Lankan, Portuguese, and Chinese populations, among others. The chair of this group, Viresh Fernando, saw its aim as "strengthening civil society" by increasing the political participation of the "socially disadvantaged." Even though the amalgamation into a new and larger conurbation took place, the new urban administrators were made aware by these activities of the need to keep alive the links between local authorities below the municipal level and immigrant populations with diverse needs and attitudes. They lost the battle but defended their interests as identifiable ethnic groups, whose ties extended back to the home country and to other ethnic populations elsewhere in Canada.

Following this amalgamation, the election for the mayor of greater Toronto turned into a contest for the immigrant vote. Candidates published in the 10 leading non-English Toronto newspapers information about the eligibility of immigrants to vote in this election, and for one candidate the mobilization paid off. Two commentators conclude that Mel Lastman won the 1997 election in part because of support from multicultural voting districts. Here is an instance where a non-French and non-Anglo politics of diversity swung the balance in Canadian politics. Immigrants from all over the world announced through the municipal ballot box that they were there and had to be considered.

This presence in the life of Toronto was performed on many occasions in these years. "Claims on public space" reinforced a sense of collective identity, in ways Dolores Hayden has shown for Los Angeles.[42] Toronto reinforces her interpretation. In 1996 there were 165 requests to the Toronto police for permission to hold a parade in public spaces.

Among these 56 were for the nonreligious celebration of ethnic identity, and 37 were religious and ethnic at the same time. Twenty-four different ethnic associations organized these parades or rituals.

Given the flow of information and individuals between and among these ethnic groups, both in Canada and in their countries of birth, there was and remains a powerful set of linkages on the urban level between North America and many parts of the world. Troubles in Sri Lanka or Ethiopia are troubles in Toronto for the members of these diasporic communities. Revenue flows are but one level of communication here; political support and solidarity of many kinds makes multi-national identities strong enough to withstand assimilationist tendencies. The place to look for these ties is at the level of the neighborhood, in the markets, in the churches and mosques, and on the streets. Once we descend below the level of the nation-state, the true complexity of trans-national citizenship unfolds.

And yet again, a caveat must be registered. This kind of identity politics was made possible by Canadian politicians like Pierre Trudeau, whose vision of Canada as an ethnic patchwork quilt was national, not global. Once again, we can see that sub-national or trans-national citizenship emerges when the state gives the green light to activists who demonstrate the compatibility of particular identities—ethnic, racial, linguistic among others—with national identity. The state is still primus inter pares.[43]

This polymorphic kind of politics is expressed well in a third example of transnational political activism. Alejandro Portes has studied Salvadoran immigrants to Los Angeles. One such local activist was asked why he stayed in Los Angeles. The answer was, "I really live in El Salvador; not in LA. When we have the regular fiestas to collect funds for La Esperanza, I am the leader and I am treated with respect. When I go home to inspect the works paid with our contributions, I am as important as the mayor."[44] Thus immigrants in the host country provide resources which are transferred to the country of origin; markets, products, cultural forms are exchanged; Brazilian groups in New York do the same.[45] "Grassroots philanthropy" operates here just as it has done for generations among Irish-Americans and Jewish-Americans.[46] So does diasporic politics. In some cases, such as that of Mexicans in the United States, the Mexican diaspora can vote in Mexican elections.

Similarly evocative of earlier generations' activism is trans-national labor militancy. Immigrants to Argentina from northern Italy brought their traditions of labor solidarity with them a century ago. At the beginning of the twenty-first century, abuses of workers' rights in Central America are exposed and combated both north and south of the American border. An American academic group, the Worker Rights Consortium, helped clothing workers in a small town in Mexico protest conditions of work in factories producing goods on license to the major American retailers Nike and Reebok.[47] The link was that these assembly factories, or *maquiladoras,* produce garments with university logos and names for the American market. As a result of this kind of pressure in the United States, factory life changed. Child labor was eliminated from the assembly line, pay rose, and the women workers in the factory gained the right to form their own union and to bypass the corrupt labor organization in place.[48] To be sure, there are thousands of sweatshops untouched by this kind of trans-national agitation. But the existence of free trade agreements creates the space in which activists in countries with stronger labor laws can insist upon improvements in the conditions of workers without such protection.

The Survival of the State

It is undoubtedly true that in the early twenty-first century, "trans-national advocacy networks" operate on the urban, national, and international level in many parts of the world.[49] There are bonds of commonality in this work, but there is also a celebration of diversity. The dignity of ethnic, racial, linguistic, or national differences is performed both in politics and in cultural life, and through such acts the collective identity of those who have rights and obligations as local inhabitants is affirmed and defended. Solidarities do exist and at times can achieve material results.[50] This area of creative political work among trans-national populations parallels the efforts of activists in the fields of human rights, women's rights, and environmental rights surveyed above.

"Think globally, act locally" is the slogan of such activists, drawn from large populations of "deterritorialized" men and women. Advocates of global citizenship believe that in a world where "old state and social structures are in the process of unravelling," trans-nationals can imagine forms of politics beyond those fashioned within nation-states.[51] This claim may be valid, but the jury is still out on how original or enduring these new forms of politics will prove to be.

The locality is the space where the "global ethnoscape," in Arjun Appadurai's arresting term, is imagined.[52] And given the trajectories of migrants, that locality is metropolitan in character. The many instances of trans-national political activism that have been studied, well beyond the few instances cited here, are not limited to urban areas, but the networks that link the old and the new worlds which migrants traverse almost always pass through cities. Migrants move viscerally between Tokyo and São Paolo more than they do between Japan and Brazil. Metropolitan identities are the ties binding members of experienced communities, people who can see the cityscape in which they and their neighbors live, even more palpably than can the citizens of the imagined communities of the nation Benedict Anderson has explored in his celebrated work.[53]

The political activity of newcomers to metropolitan centers frequently does describe a sphere of autonomy which they creatively exploit. But there are good reasons to question whether such activism constitutes a root and branch challenge to state sovereignty.[54] The unfolding of much of this activity happens at the interface between civil society and the state. The issues raised here may be universal, but redress happens when the institutions of the state accept that an overlap exists between its sovereignty and international agencies assigned to cope with trans-national problems. Pinochet was arrested because the British Home Secretary decided that it was in Britain's interest to do so, and the arrest was validated by the very British Law Lords of the House of Lords. Bhopal victims received some, admittedly inadequate, compensation when the State of India persuaded a court to find a financial settlement. The effort to secure women's rights to equal treatment follows the law, and the law is national in character.

Just as Marx underestimated the cunning of capitalism and its flexibility in coping with economic instability, so exponents of the theory of global citizenships underestimate the cunning of the state and its flexibility in coping with the volatility of political issues in an age of mass migration. To be sure, international conventions, and the nongovernmental agencies which monitor compliance with them, do circumscribe state action in many respects, and do so perhaps more vigorously than ever before. But the capacity of states to mold their procedures to take account of such pressures is still robust.[55]

It is important to recognize as well that networks of local groups link people whose concerns while similar are not identical; national contexts matter. The local is still imbricated in the national; and consequently, as Sidney Tarrow has observed, it is still the case that "most ordinary people see the state as their logical and necessary interlocutor."[56]

A second reason to doubt the claim that old state structures are "unraveling" is the atomized and exploited position of illegal immigrants. The groups whose work we have surveyed used political institutions on many levels to stretch the concept of citizenship to suit their needs and fulfill their ambitions and their desire for dignity. But what dignity attaches to those who suffer and die of asphyxiation or thirst in transports across the U.S.–Mexican border, or in containers traversing the Pacific, or atop a train passing through the Channel Tunnel? These people suffer because borders are porous and those who cross them illegally think the supposed benefits justify the risks. Many succeed but are then launched into a world of illegality, which, as Stephen Frears's recent British film *Dirty Pretty Things* shows, is a world of atomized individuals, easily exploited, people for whom trust or the simplest human bonds are luxuries they cannot afford. Politics, or citizenship of any kind, is beyond them.

Some groups make the case that illegal immigrants should be granted amnesties. These travelers certainly demonstrate a thirst for residence which most citizens lack entirely. But it is the state which decides if they can remain within its boundaries. The sovereignty of the state in questions of entry and settlement may be under siege, but it is still much stronger than the advocates of the arrival of post-national citizenship will allow.

In the context of this book, what matters is not the accuracy of the diagnosis of "trans-nationality," however defined, but rather the vitality of the social forces cohering around it and the sense of the possible, of alternative social forms the notion evokes. In the 1990s visions of trans-nationality took off from a state-circumscribed reality into another realm, just barely mapped.[57] In entering this terrain, advocates of "global citizenship" entered one of the twentieth century's most robust traditions, the visionary tradition. By constructing a "minor utopia" they term "global citizenship," they stretch our sense of the possible, of ways in which people from many parts of the world can have, in García Márquez's terms, a second chance on earth.

There is a body of literature especially concerning law that provides the common thread joining Pinochet, Bhopal, and rape as a crime against humanity. How this shared discourse about law and human rights will develop is anybody's guess. Human rights law as a minor utopia is a questionable construction. But without such a body of law, the notion of global citizenship tends to fragment into a thousand pieces.

Epilogue
An Alternative History of the Twentieth Century

Why is this century worse than those that have gone before?
In a stupor of sorrow and grief
it located the blackest wound
but somehow couldn't heal it.

The earth's sun is still shining in the West
and the roofs of towns sparkle in its rays,
while here death marks houses with crosses
and calls in the crows and the crows fly over.
—ANNA AKHMATOVA, "Why Is This Century Worse," 1919

Anna Akhmatova's poem tells us much about the twentieth century, the century of total war. Her verse announces the history of the twentieth century as the story of catastrophe after catastrophe, with death as its destination and its signature.

Most historians of the twentieth century have followed Akhmatova's lead. I am among them. For nearly four decades I have been at work trying to locate the history of the 1914–18 conflict within the contours of the twentieth century. As I noted in the introduction, in doing so, I have been aware of a kind of imbalance in the historical literature, a tendency to highlight the monstrous and the shocking, and to turn away from projects which move in other directions entirely. My studies of war have persuaded me not only that some people are capable of behavior of stupefying cruelty, but also that others, many others, manage to emerge from war with their humanity intact. I am the last to underestimate the disfiguring effects of war and collective violence, but I have become uncomfortable with the tendency among students and scholars to ignore the visions of those who passed through these events and still believed that there was another way.

To be sure, there is at work here a very fashionable tendency among students and scholars to confuse cynicism with wisdom. The notion of a different kind of international order, or an alternative vision of society, is usually treated as the stuff of children or madmen, or the irrelevant recollection of totalitarian blueprints discredited long ago.

This book has been written against the grain of these two widely shared styles of historical thinking. The first may be termed catastrophic history; the second, superior history, history written by someone self-consciously shrewder and with fewer illusions than the people under study.

The chapters in this book offer glimpses into what I have termed the visionary temperament, not to celebrate its achievements, which are few and full of incompatible and incongruent elements. It is rather to see these visions as spaces in which the contradictions of a period are embodied and performed, and new possibilities are imagined. I have not hesitated to point out the failures of these minor utopian projects, but nonetheless a world without them is a barren one.

The Universal and the Particular

In every episode recounted in this book, a group of people used universalistic language to describe a project or goal. But in each case, the use
of such language either masked or encapsulated a particular ideology,
the interests and outlook of discrete social and political formations.
Thus Albert Kahn believed firmly that his archives of the planet would
show us all what we had in common, thereby making war unthinkable; but the outlook of the imperial humanist could not achieve the
neutrality intrinsically necessary to his aim. Wilson's universalistic assertion of the right to self-determination was similarly compromised.
And the faith in science, expressed spectacularly in the Paris expo of
1937, was at the very same moment exposed as deeply flawed in the
work of Picasso.

After the Second World War, the language of universalism was
renewed once more. As I have tried to show, there was a particular
agenda behind René Cassin's declamation in Paris of the Universal
Declaration of the Rights of Man. His aim was to breathe new life into
French political culture after a period of occupation, humiliation, and
collaboration.

The universalism of the men and women of 1968 was widely evident.
The Peruvian priest Gustavo Gutierrez's liberation theology was ecumenical, to be sure, but it was also the language of social revolt, a
grammar deployed by Castro and Guevara and other revolutionaries
for particular political purposes throughout Latin America and beyond. The defeat of liberation theology and the containment of the
Cuban revolution in the decades after 1968 are well known. Both their
advocates and their enemies used universalistic language—communism versus freedom—to encapsulate a very savage and very American
political struggle for the future of the hemisphere.

After the fall of the Berlin Wall and the collapse of the Soviet empire,
the universalism of radical movements appeared again, this time in
the form of the elaboration of a new category, known in shorthand
as "global citizenship." It appealed to people who crossed borders—in
search of jobs or survival—to see their trajectories as entailing rights

and privileges defined by a new kind of citizenship. Global citizenship was everyone's right; it was not defined by birth or naturalization, but by a share in the commonality of daily life in urban centers like Toronto or São Paolo or Stockholm. This redefinition of citizenship by moving to a lower level of aggregation than that of the state enables its advocates to extend the category to everyone. Here, too, the language of universalism describes a set of strategies in the politics of immigration, which serves very particular purposes. When various forms of social activism—trade unionism, student radicalism, democratic socialism—lost their momentum, were reconfigured, or began to fade away, then it was time for the elaboration of new forms of local politics expressed in universalistic terms. The fate of these movements is anybody's guess, but the form they take—the particular clothed in the universal—is one we have seen before. And will see again.

This study of twentieth-century visions is no paean to the "party of humanity." Instead it is an attempt to treat these ideas with the critical seriousness they deserve. The language of universalism, born in the Enlightenment of the eighteenth century, is deeply problematic. Recent critics have directed our attention to many difficulties imbedded in it. How does universalism handle difference?[1] Difference can be accommodated only when groups or populations accept in some fundamental way that they are part of a collective. What happens, though, when they do not so affirm? Are they then outside the universal category—frequently termed "civilization" or "humanity"—and not to be treated in the same way as the rest of us? Are some acts, for instance terrorism or genocide, so heinous as to render their perpetrators outside the sphere of legal rights or human rights, configured as universal properties "we" all share? George W. Bush speaks of freedom as universal, and yet consigns to legal black holes those apprehended in the never-ending war on "terror." The claims of those who say they are speaking for humanity can never be taken at face value.[2] Whenever a political leader speaks of defending "humanity," it is probably wise to take cover.

The human rights discourse is also problematic. In some forms, to speak of human rights is to bypass politics entirely; it is a vague invocation of neo-liberal notions of rational individuals and rational markets. To say the least, such interpretations of human rights are stuffed with other ideological baggage.[3]

Then there is the question of the rights of minorities.[4] Between the wars, the League of Nations explicitly aimed at defending the rights of communities within nation-states. After 1948, the emphasis on individual human rights tended to eclipse the defense of collective rights. Since collectives are the targets of genocide, surely their rights as collectives need defending just as much as do their members' rights as individual human beings. The shift from social class and nation to civil society and human rights is not a change from worse to better, but from one set of historical problems to another.

Utopias, Major and Minor

The term "utopia" is one which has lost its political currency and respectability throughout the twentieth century. Nevertheless, there is no reason to avoid using the word, with caution and some qualifications, as a critical tool in a book on the twentieth century. To speak of utopia is neither to praise nor to damn the utopian; it merely calls attention to forms of transformational political thinking with long and very mixed pedigrees. This is not a book of advocacy, but of analysis.

I have insisted from the start on a distinction between major utopias—projects of state-centered social engineering which almost always turn into nightmares—and minor utopias, or projects which aim not at the total eradication of social conflict or the construction of an ideal city, but at partial transformations, steps on the way to a less violent and unjust society. The fate of these visions is very mixed, but they have not to date offered blueprints to murderers.

Minor utopias have come in many forms. Those discussed in the first part of the book aimed at the containment or outlawing of war. The solutions proposed—liberal or socialist pacifism in 1900, or self-determination in 1919, or the onward march of science in 1937—all failed. After 1945, utopians offered many different programs, from human rights to *Auto-*

gestion to global citizenship. Their fate is uncertain, but it is evident that they are neither totalitarian nor simply reformist in character. It is impossible to realize their objectives through political thuggery or political compromise.

To be sure, outlawing war, enforcing human rights, or instituting global citizenship challenges the sovereignty of the nation-state. What else is a state if not that body which has the right to go to war and the power to determine who is a citizen?[5] The question of the nature and limits of state power is at issue in all these initiatives. Major utopians "see like a state," in Jim Scott's felicitous phrase.[6] Minor utopians want to rethink what a state is, not to do away with it.

This account is in no sense the end of the story, since minor utopians are with us still. The visions of men and women who dared to think differently, to break with convention, to speculate about the unlikely in the search for a better way, are intrinsically worth recalling. But taken together, these six moments of possibility form an important and at times neglected facet of recent history. In a map of the last century, there is every reason to make room for this alternative history, inscribed against the grain of the century of total war.

Notes

Introduction

1. For a discussion of the evolution of the notion of Utopia, see George Kateb, *Utopia and its enemies.* New York, Free Press of Glencoe, 1963; George Kateb (ed.), *Utopia.* New York, Atherton Press, 1971; Krishan Kumar, *Utopianism.* Milton Keynes, Open University Press, 1991; Krishan Kumar and Stephen Bann, (eds.), *Utopias and the millennium.* London, Reaktion Books, 1993; Ruth Levitas, *The Concept of utopia.* New York, Philip Allen, 1990; Frank Manuel (ed.), *Utopias and utopian thought.* Boston, Houghton Mifflin, 1966.

2. Lyman Tower Sargeant and Roland Schaer (eds.), *Utopie. La quête de la société idéale en Occident.* Paris, Fayard, 2000.

3. The term "dystopia" was used first by John Stuart Mill in 1968. I am grateful to Ken Inglis, master of language par excellence, for drawing this usage to my attention.

4. Robert Fishman, *Urban utopias in the twentieth century, Ebenezer Howard, Frank Lloyd Wright, and Le Corbusier.* New York, Basic Books, 1977.

5. Emmanuel Sivan, "The Enclave culture," in *Fundamentalisms comprehended*, edited by Martin E. Marty and R. Scott Appleby. Chicago, University of Chicago Press, 1995, 11–70.

6. Fredric Jameson, "Of Islands and trenches, neutralization and the production of utopian discourse," in *The ideologies of theory, essays 1971–1986. Volume 2, syntax of history.* Minneapolis, University of Minnesota Press, 1988, 101.

7. Louis Marin, *Utopics, spatial play,* trans. Robert A. Vollrath. Atlantic Highlands, N.J., Humanities Press, 1984, xxii–xxiii.

8. Paul Ricoeur, *Lectures on ideology and utopia,* trans. George H. Taylor. New York, Columbia University Press, 1986, 17.

9. The horticultural metaphor was used by Zygmund Bauman in *The holocaust and modernity.* Ithaca, N.Y., Cornell University Press, 2000.

10. For the full text of the Nobel prize acceptance speech, see http://www.nobel .se/literature/laureates/1982/marquez-lecture.html.

11. Tom Stoppard, *Salvage. The coast of utopia, iii.* London, Faber and Faber, 2002, 34.

12. Reinhard Koselleck, *Futures past. On the semantics of historical time,* trans. Keith Tribe. Cambridge, MIT Press, 1985, 73ff.

13. Ricoeur, *Lectures on ideology and utopia,* 1.

14. Eric Hobsbawm, *The age of extremes, a history of the world 1914–1991.* New York, Vintage Books, 1996. Anyone interested in contemporary history must start with this extraordinary history. For an introduction to the "major utopias" omitted from this book, for example, the trajectory of the Bolshevik revolution or the fascist moment, there is no better guide.

15. Oscar Wilde, *The essays of Oscar Wilde.* New York, Cosmopolitan Book Corporation, 1916, 28.

Chapter 1. 1900: The Face of Humanity and Visions of Peace

1. Ute Frevert (ed.), *Europäische Zeitdiagnosen und Zukunftsenwürfe um 1900.* Göttingen, Vandenhoeck and Ruprecht, 2000.

2. H. G. Wells, *The war of the worlds.* London, W. Heinemann, 1898.

3. For a global sketch, see J. David Singer and Melvin Small, *The wages of war 1816–1965. A Statistical handbook.* New York, John Wiley and Son, 1972.

4. Pascal de Blignières, *Albert Kahn, les jardins d'une idée.* Paris, Editions La Bibliothèque, 1995, 12.

5. Ibid., 13–20.

6. Kahn Archive, Musée Albert Kahn, Boulogne-Billancourt. *Centenaire d'Albert Kahn (1860–1940),* reception in the departmental gardens at Boulogne, on 15 May 1960. See page 16. The Kahn archive has just been opened. I am grateful to M. Baud-Berthier, the *conservateur* of the museum, for his help in securing access to these important papers.

7. Kahn Archive, typescript, 5 May 1933, 4–6.

8. Kahn Archive, typescript, 5 May 1933, 8ff.

9. Kahn Archive, *Centenaire,* 58.

10. Archives Nationales (AN), Paris, AJ/16/7020, *Note de donateur,* n.d.

11. AJ/16/7020, letter from director of Ecole normale supérieure to Rector of University of Paris on the Kahn scholarships. The routes and costs of the four other itineraries are listed there.

12. Kahn Archive, "Albert Kahn: un homme exceptionnel," 58.

13. Marcel Thomann, "Albert Kahn de Marmoutier, financier de génie et philanthrope," *Société d'histoire d'archéologie de Saverne et environs,* Cahiers No. 30 (February 1960), 16.

14. Kahn Archive, *Société autour du monde;* Charles Ganier, "Bref histoire de la fondation," *Bulletin du Société Autour du monde,* 14 June 1931.

15. Alessandra Ponte, "Archiving the planet. Architecture and human geography," *Daidalos* 66 (1997), 121–25.

16. Mariel Jean-Brunhes Delamarre and Jeanne Beausoleil, "Deux témoins de leur temps, Albert Kahn et Jean Brunhes," in Jean Brunhes, *Autour du monde, regards d'un géographe / regards de la géographie.* Boulogne-Billancourt, Musée Albert Kahn, 1993, 91.

17. Kahn Archive, *Centenaire,* 17.

18. Philippe Soulez, *Bergson.* Paris, Flammarion, 1997, 105–29; Leszek Kolakowski, *Bergson.* Oxford, Oxford University Press, 1985, 72–87; Kahn Archives, *Centenaire,* 62.

19. Delamarre and Beausoleil, "Deux témoins," 91.

20. Ibid., 94.

21. Kahn Archive, Jean Brunhes de la Marre, in *Bulletin de la Géographie,* lxxxi (1975).

22. Marie-Claire Robic, "Administrer la preuve par l'image, géographie physique et géographie humaine," in Brunhes, *Autour du monde,* 230.

23. Kahn Archive, Brunhes-Delamarre Papers, Brunhes statement of purpose.

24. Kahn Archive, letter of Stéphane Passet, one of those who traveled with camera in hand to collect the images, to Brunhes, 18 May 1912.

25. Thomann, "Albert Kahn de Marmoutier," 16.

26. *Les boursiers de voyage de l'université de Paris.* Paris, Felix Alcan, 1904, ii; Kahn Archives, letters of Passet to Brunhes in 1913 and 1914.

27. Robic, "Administrer la preuve par l'image," 231.

28. de Blignières, *Albert Kahn,* 16; Kahn Archives, Kahn manuscript, "Décoordination," 5 May 1933.

29. See Martin Jay, "Photo-unrealism, the contribution of the camera to the crisis of ocularcentrism," in *Vision and textuality,* ed. Stephen Melville and Bill Readings. Basingstoke, Macmillan, 1995, 344–60.

30. Pascal de Blignières, *Albert Kahn, Les jardins d'une idée.* Paris, Editions de la Bibliothèque, 1995.

31. Musée Albert Kahn, *Paris sur fond de guerre: 1917–1918.* Boulogne-Billancourt, Centre départemental de documentation pédagogique, 1987.

32. Kahn Archive, "Des Droits and les devoirs du gouvernement," begun March 1917, edited June 1918, completed November 1918.

33. Jeanne Beausoleil, "Les images animées dans l'oeuvre d'Albert Kahn," *Cahiers de la Cinématèque* 75 (December 2002), 7–13.

34. Pascal Ory, "Introduction à la philosophie d'Albert Kahn," *Cahiers de la Cinématèque* 75 (December 2002), 15–18.

35. Paula Amad, "Les archives de la planète d'Albert Kahn (1908–1931): Archives ou contre-archives de l'histoire?" *Cahiers de la Cinémathèque* 74 (December 2002), 19–31.

36. Kahn Archive, "Albert Kahn. Un homme exceptionnel," 62ff.

37. Edward Steichen, *The Family of man: An exhibition of creative photography, dedicated to the dignity of man, with examples from 68 countries, conceived and executed by Edward Steichen; assisted by Wayner Miller; installation designed by Paul Rudolph; prologue by Carl Sandburg.* New York, Museum of Modern Art, 1955.

38. Richard D. Mansell, *Paris 1900, The great world's fair.* Toronto, University of Toronto Press, 1967, 65.

39. Mansell, *Paris 1900*, 64–65.

40. Paul Morand, *1900.* Paris, Editions de France, c1931, 61–62, as cited in Jeannene M. Przyblyski, "American visions at the Paris Exposition, 1900, another look at Frances Benjamin Johnston's Hampton photographs," *Art Journal* (Fall 1998), 12.

41. Jules Charles-Roux (ed.), *Le ministère des colonies à l'exposition universelle de 1900. Colonies et pays de protectorats.* Paris, Commission Exposition Universelle de 1900, 1900, 16.

42. *Colonies*, 26.

43. *Colonies*, 30–36.

44. Morand, *1900*, 114ff. See also Mansell, *Paris 1900*, 66–67. I have varied the translation from that of Mansell.

45. Edward Said, *Orientalism.* New York, Random House, 1980.

46. *Colonies*, 661.

47. Ibid.

48. On this theme in general, see Max Jones, *The last great quest, Captain Scott's Antarctic sacrifice.* Oxford, Oxford University Press, 2003.

49. A. Abramson, *The history of television, 1880 to 1941.* New York, MacFarland, Jefferson, 1987, 23.

50. Brigitte Schroder-Gudehus and Anne Rasmussen, *Les faces du progrès. Le guide des expositions universelles 1851–1992.* Paris, Flammarion, 1992, 132–39.

51. Rosalind H. Williams, *Dream worlds, mass consumption in late nineteenth-century France.* Berkeley, University of California Press, 1982, 66.

52. Maurice Talmeyr, "L'école de Trocadéro," *Revue des Deux Mondes* (1899–1900), from a series of 13 articles, as cited in Williams, *Dream worlds*, 62–63.

53. Paul Greenhalgh, *Ephemeral vistas, The expositions universelles, great exhibitions and world fairs, 1851–1939.* Manchester, Manchester University Press, 1988, ch. 3.

54. Joseph Conrad, *Heart of darkness.* Oxford, Oxford University Press, 2002, 55, 87.

55. Robert W. Rydell, "Gateway to the 'American century': The American representation at the Paris universal exposition of 1900," in *Paris 1900. The "American school" at the universal exposition,* ed. Diana P. Fisher. New Brunswick, N.J., Rutgers University Press, 1999, 141.

56. Shawn Michelle Smith, *American archives: Gender, race and class in visual culture.* Princeton, Princeton University Press, 1999, 161. See also Przyblyski, "American Visions."

57. David Levering Lewis and Deborah Willis, *A Small nation of people. W. E. B. Du Bois and African-American portraits of progress.* New York, Amistad, 2003, 10.

58. W. E. B. Du Bois, *The Souls of black folk.* New York, New American Library, 1969, 1.

59. Steichen, *The Family of man.*

60. Rydell, "Gateway," 133.

61. Robert Rosenblum, Maryanne Stevens, and Ann Dumas, *1900. Art at the crossroads.* New York, Harry N. Abrams, 2000, 59.

62. Diana P. Fischer (ed.), *Paris 1900. The "American school" at the universal exposition.* New Brunswick, N.J., Rutgers University Press, 1999, 119.

63. On his views on the matter, see Walter Benjamin, *The Arcades project.* Cambridge, Mass., Harvard University Press, 2001.

64. Walter Benjamin, "Paris, the capital of the nineteenth century," in *Charles Baudelaire. A lyric poet in the era of high capitalism.* London, Verso, 1980, 155–76.

65. Michel Launay, *Jaurès orateur ou l'oiseau rare.* Paris, Jean-Paul Rocher, 2000.

66. Jean Sagnes, *Jean Jaurès et le Languedoc viticole.* Montpellier, Presses du Languedoc, 1988.

67. Harvey Goldberg, *The life of Jean Jaurès, 1859–1914.* Madison, University of Wisconsin Press, 1962, 78.

68. On this phase of his life, see George Tétard, *Essais sur Jean Jaurès suivis d'une bibliographie méthodique et critique.* Colombes, Centre d'apprentissage d'imprimerie, 1959, which is a compendium of articles on Jaurès and a useful bibliography of his writings and of writings on him before the appearance of Goldberg's definitive biography, which now, 40 years later, is still the place to start for anyone interested in this period and in Jaurès himself.

69. On this set of issues, see Marcelle Auclair, *La vie de Jean Jaurès, ou, La France d'avant 1914.* Paris, Editions du Seuil, 1954.

70. Goldberg, *Jaurès,* 70.

71. Gilles Candar, *Jean Jaurès, 1859–1914: "l'intolérable,"* 36. Paris, Editions Ouvrières, 1984.

72. Candar, *Jean Jaurès,* 37. See also Vincent Peillon, *Jean Jaurès et la religion du socialisme.* Paris, Bernard Grasset, 2000.

73. James Joll, *The Second International, 1889–1914*. New York, Harper and Row, 1966, 40.

74. Georges Haupt, *Bureau socialiste international. Comptes rendus des réunions manifestes et circulaires*. Paris, Mouton, 1969, meeting of 1900, 16.

75. Meeting of 1900, 700.

76. Meeting of 1900, 705.

77. Georges Haupt, *Aspects of international socialism, 1871–1914, essays*, trans. Peter Fawcett. Cambridge, Cambridge University Press, 1986, 70–72; *Bulletin Périodique*, 15/1/1910.

78. Haupt, *International socialism*, 475.

79. Pierre Muller, *Jaurès, vocabulaire et rhetorique*. Paris, Klincksieck, 1994, 290ff; Launay, *Jaurès orateur*, 157ff.

80. *Bulletin Périodique du Bureau Socialiste International*, no. 10, Compte rendu analytique du Congrès Socialiste International extraordinaire tenu à Bâle les 24 et 25 novembre 1912, 30–36.

81. Again, see Launay, *Jaurès orateur*, and Muller, *Jaurès, vocabulaire et rhetorique*.

82. For that story, see Marcel Le Clère, *L'assassinat de Jean Jaurès*. Tours, Mame, 1969.

83. Jean Jaurès, *Patriotisme et internationalisme*. Paris, Au Bureau du Socialiste, 1895.

84. Jean Jaurès, *La nouvelle armée*. Paris, Rouff, 1911.

Chapter 2. 1919: Perpetual War/Perpetual Peace

1. Erez Manela, *The Wilsonian moment: Self-determination and the international origins of anti-colonial nationalism*. New York, Oxford University Press, 2006.

2. Arno J. Mayer, *Political origins of the new diplomacy, 1917–1918*. New Haven, Yale University Press, 1959; Arno J. Mayer, *Politics and diplomacy of peacemaking, containment and counterrevolution at Versailles, 1918–1919*. New York, Knopf, 1967.

3. Paul Valéry, "La crise de l'esprit," *La nouvelle revue française* xiii, 1 (August 1919), 321.

4. For a recent survey, see Thomas J. Knock, *To end all wars: Woodrow Wilson and the quest for a new world order*. New York, Oxford University Press, 1992. The best single volume on Wilson still remains John Morton Blum, *Woodrow Wilson and the politics of morality*. Boston, Little, Brown, 1956.

5. On the vast literature centering on these questions, see the judicious summary of Michla Pomerance, "The United States and self-determination: Perspectives on the Wilsonian conception," *American Journal of International Law* lxx, 1 (January 1976), 16ff.

6. As cited in Lawrence E. Gelfand, *The Inquiry. American preparations for peace, 1917–1919*. New Haven, Yale University Press, 1963, 347.

7. On whom, see Yale University Library, Sidney E. Mezes papers.

8. Neil Smith, *American empire: Roosevelt's geographer and the prelude to globalization.* Berkeley, University of California Press, c2003.

9. Harold Josephson, *James T. Shotwell and the rise of internationalism in America.* Rutherford, N.J., Fairleigh Dickinson University Press, 1974; Antoine Prost and Jay Winter, *Penser la grande guerre.* Paris, Le Seuil, 2004, ch. 5.

10. On Lippmann, see Annette Messemer, *Walter Lippmann und die Mächte: eine ideengeschichtliche Studie zu Entwicklung, Positionen und Konzepten eines amerikanischen Denkers der internationalen Beziehungen.* Bonn, Rheinische Friedrich-Wilhelms-Universität zu Bonn, 1995, and Stephen D. Blum, *Walter Lippmann, cosmopolitanism in the century of total war.* Ithaca, Cornell University Press, 1984.

11. Lippmann to Executive Committee, 7 December 1917, Shotwell papers, Columbia University.

12. Inquiry document No. 882, Foreign relations of the United States 1919. The Paris Peace Conference. I., 82–83.

13. A word or two is needed about the danger of equating Wilson's views with those of his advisers in the Inquiry. This body was an adjunct of his executive agent, Colonel House. It worked outside and at odds with the State Department, which viewed its operations as unprofessional at best and as undermining its authority and compromising American national interests at worst. Wilson certainly respected the advice of men like himself—academics who believed in the application of reason to the affairs of state. Like them, he considered it essential to strengthen a case for justice by detailed knowledge of the terrain under scrutiny. But his use of the Inquiry's expertise, like his relationship with the Inquiry's godfather, Colonel House, was neither stable nor direct. As the peace conference unfolded, Wilson's long friendship with House fell apart. And only some members of the Inquiry of 1917–19 accompanied the president to Europe on the *George Washington.* The interest of their work is in the affinity of their ideas with Wilson's rather than in any direct correspondence between what they said and what he did. They formed part of a discursive field of liberal and internationalist opinion, from which Wilson drew in his formulation of peace terms at the end of the war.

14. James Joll, *1914: The unspoken assumptions.* London, Weidenfeld and Nicolson, 1968.

15. Henry R. Winkler, *The League of Nations movement in Great Britain, 1914–1919.* New Brunswick, Rutgers University Press, 1952; Roland N. Stromberg, "Uncertainties and obscurities about the League of Nations," *Journal of Contemporary History* xxxi, 1 (January 1972), 139–54.

16. W. E. Dodd, "The present state of the Monroe Doctrine," 14. Yale University Library, Inquiry Papers (hereafter cited as IP), 8/III Box 16, Folder 233.

17. As cited in Margaret Macmillan, *Paris 1919. Six months that changed the world.* New York, Random House, 2002, 96.

18. George Curry, "Woodrow Wilson, Jan Smuts and the Versailles settlement," *American Historical Review* lxiv, 4 (July 1961), 968–86.

19. J. C. Smuts, "East Africa," *Geographical Journal* li, 3 (March 1918), 129–45, esp. 145.

20. G. L. Beer, "The German colonies in Africa," 28 February 1918, 77, IP, 8/III Box 8, Folder 6.

21. "Suggested statement of peace terms," written by Mezes, Lippmann, and Miller, with Miller dissenting, IP, 8/III Box 16, Folder 245, 69.

22. Ray Stannard Baker and William E. Dodd (eds.), *The public papers of Woodrow Wilson, war and peace.* New York, Harper and Brothers, 1925–27, I, 180.

23. O. J. Campbell, "Palestine," 23 August 1918, 8/III Box 16, Folder 241 and Folder 242: "Zionism: A summary."

24. R. J. Kerner, "The German and Austrian solution of the near eastern question," 17, IP, 8/III Box 7, Folder 67.

25. Edward Said, *Orientalism.* New York, Vintage, 1978.

26. J. K. Birge, "Ottoman Turks in Asia Minor," IP, 8/III, Box 24, Folder 362.

27. Jay Winter (ed.), *America and the Armenian genocide.* Cambridge, Cambridge University Press, 2003.

28. "Suggested statement of peace terms," February 1918, 65, IP, 8/III, Box 16, Folder 252.

29. As cited in Imanuel Geiss, *The Pan-African movement. A history of Pan-Africanism in America, Europe and Africa,* trans. Ann Keep. New York, Holmes and Meier, 1974, 185.

30. W. E. B. Du Bois, *An ABC of color.* New York, International Publishers, 1969, 20.

31. W. E. Burghardt Du Bois, *The African roots of war.* New York, National Association for the Advancement of Colored People, 1915.

32. As cited in Clarence G. Contee, "Du Bois, the NAACP, and the Pan-African Congress of 1919," *Journal of Negro History* lvii, 1 (1972), 16.

33. Ibid., 14.

34. On Diagne, see: Amady Aly Dieng, *Blaise Diagne, député noir de l'Afrique.* Paris, Editions Chaka, 1990; and Obeye Diop (ed.), *Blaise Diagne. Sa vie, son oeuvre.* Dakar, Nouvelles Editions Africaines, n.d., 38ff.

35. Contee, "Du Bois, the NAACP, and the Pan-African Congress of 1919," 23.

36. Ibid., 22.

37. Geiss, *The Pan-African movement,* 237.

38. "Pan-African Congress," *The Crisis* xvii, 6 (April 1919), 271–74.

39. Alexandre Mboukou, "The Pan-African movement 1900–1945: A study in leadership conflicts among the disciples of Pan-Africanism," *Journal of Black Studies* xiii, 3 (March 1983), 275–87.

40. At times Du Bois used the term "semi-civilized peoples" when describing parts of Africa. See "The future of Africa," *The Crisis* xvii, 3 (January 1919), 119.

41. "My mission," *The Crisis* xviii, 1 (May 1919), 9.

42. W. W. Willoughby and C. G. Fenwick, "States that are less than sovereign," IP, 8/III, Box 21, Folder 318.

43. Thomas Edward La Fargue, *China and the world war.* Stanford, Stanford University Press, 1937.

44. Chinese memorandum, 23 April 1919, as cited in Xu Guoqi, *The First World War and China's quest for national identity.* Cambridge, Cambridge University Press, 2004, 337.

45. Columbia University Library, Wellington Koo papers. Permission to consult these papers included a restriction on any direct citations.

46. Harold Nicolson, *Peacemaking 1919.* London, Allen and Unwin, 1933, 146.

47. Wen-ssu Chin, *China at the Paris peace conference.* Jamaica, N.Y., St. John's University Press, 1961, 26.

48. Yale University Library, House Papers, House diary, 4 February 1919.

49. As cited in Macmillan, *Paris 1919,* 319.

50. Yale University Library, Auchincloss papers, Auchincloss diary, 10 and 12 April 1919.

51. Manela, *The Wilsonian moment.*

52. For an edition prepared with the League of Nations in mind, see Immanuel Kant, *Perpetual peace,* Los Angeles, Calif., U.S. library association, inc., 1932. See also James Bohman and Matthias Lutz-Bachmann (eds.), *Perpetual peace: Essays on Kant's cosmopolitan ideal.* Cambridge, Mass., MIT Press, 1997.

53. For a caustic statement of this point, see Sir Ivor Jennings, *The Approach to self-government.* Cambridge, Cambridge University Press, 1956, 55–56.

54. Salvador de Madariaga, *The World's design.* London, Allen and Unwin, 1938, 32.

55. Antoine Prost, *Les anciens combattants et la société française 1914–1939.* Paris, Fondation nationale des sciences politiques, 1977; Martin Ceadel, *Pacifism in Britain, 1914–1945: The defining of a faith.* Oxford, Clarendon Press, 1980.

Chapter 3. 1937: Illuminations

1. Louis Marin, "A signification for social space," in *On representation,* trans. Catherine Porter. Stanford, Stanford University Press, 2001, 47.

2. Bernard Barraqué, "La lumière à l'exposition," in *Paris 1937: Cinquantenaire. De l'Exposition internationale des arts et des techniques dans la vie moderne.* Paris, Institut Français de l'Architecture/Paris Musées, 1987, 404–9.

3. Archives Nationales, Paris (hereafter cited as AN), F/12/12118.

4. AN, F/12/118.

5. AN, F/12/945, Commission supérieure de l'exposition internationale, 18 November 1936.

6. *Exposition internationale. Arts and crafts in modern life* (English edition). Paris, Editions de la société pour le développement du tourisme, 1937, 75–76.

7. AN, F/12/12143 on Palais de la découverte.

8. Mary Jo Nye, "Science and socialism: The case of Jean Perrin in the Third Republic," *French Historical Studies* ix, 1 (1975), 141–69.

9. Gilles Plum, "Aéronautique" and "Chemins de fer," in *Paris 1937,* 206–8, 218–21.

10. Bernard Dorival, *La belle histoire de la Fée Electricité.* Paris, La Palme, 1953, 8.

11. Bertrand Lemoine and Philippe Rivoirard, "Electricité et lumière," in *Paris 1937,* 222.

12. Dorival, *La belle histoire,* 20.

13. As cited in Jacques Lassaigne, *Dufy,* trans. J. Emmons. New York, Skira, 1959, 75.

14. James E. Brittain, "The International diffusion of electrical power technology, 1870–1920," *Journal of Economic History* xxxiv, 1 (1974), 108–21.

15. "Danger lurks in Dufy masterpiece," CNN, 26 July 2001, europe.cnn.com/2001/WORLD/europe/07/26/paris.painting/.

16. Daniel Kevles, *The Physicists: The history of a scientific community in modern America.* New York, Knopf, 1977.

17. AN, F/12/12544, Spanish Pavilion, and Catherine Blanton Freedberg, *The Spanish pavilion at the Paris world's fair.* New York, Garland Publishing, 1986, 602.

18. As cited in Freedberg, *The Spanish pavilion,* 604.

19. Meyer Shapiro, *The Unity of Picasso's Art.* New York, George Braziller, 2000, 174ff.

20. AN, F/12/12115.

21. AN, F/12/12143. Clipping from *Le Matin,* 11 May 1935.

22. AN, F/60/955, compte rendu de la Commission permanente.

23. AN, F/12/12143.

24. AN, F/60/971, papers of Prime Minister, discussion of Pavillon de la Paix, 1937; Letter of 12 March 1937 from Rassemblement Universel pour la Paix. The French committee was composed of: René Cassin, Henri Pichot, S. Grumbach, E. Herriot, L. Jouyaux, Paul Reynaud, Col. Picot, Victor Basch, Marcel Cachin, Prof. Rivet, and Prof. Langevin.

25. See Antoine Prost, "The French contempt for politics among veterans of the Great War," in his collection of essays, *Representations of France in war and peace.* Oxford, Berg, 2002, 202–40.

26. AN, F/12/12143. Clipping from *Le Petit Journal,* 8 July 1937.

27. AN, F/12/12143, Clipping from *L'Humanité,* 10 September 1937.

28. AN, F/12/12143.

29. AN, F/12/12143.

30. AN, F/12/12114.

31. Marko Daniel, "Spain: Culture at war," in Dawn Ades et al., *Art and power: Europe under the dictators 1930–45.* London, Thames and Hudson, 1995, 64.

32. *Exposition internationale des arts et des techniques dans la vie moderne. Paris 1937. Tome II. Catalogue officiel. Catalogue des Pavilions,* 178.

33. AN, F/12/12562 Palestine.

34. The literature on Speer is enormous; see Léon Krier, "Une architecture du désir," in *Albert Speer. Architecture 1932–1942.* Brussels, Aux archives d'architecture moderne, 1958, 13ff.; and Barbara Lane Miller, "Architects in power: Power and ideology in Ernst May and Albert Speer," *Journal of Interdisciplinary History,* xvii (1986), 283–310.

35. Karen A. Fiss, "Deutschland in Paris. The 1937 German Pavilion and Franco-German cultural relations," Ph.D. diss., Yale University, 1995, 49.

36. AN, F/12/12143.

37. Fiss, "Deutschland in Paris," ch. 4 and figs. 54–55.

38. Ibid., 8.

39. Ibid., 30.

40. Ibid., 34.

41. Jeffrey Herf, *Reactionary modernism: Technology, culture, and politics in Weimar and the Third Reich.* Cambridge, Cambridge University Press, 1986.

42. Fiss, "Deutschland in Paris," 60.

43. Karen A. Fiss, "The German Pavilion," in Ades et al., *Art and power,* 108–10.

44. Dawn Ades, "Paris 1937: Art and the power of nations," in Ades et al., *Art and Power,* 60. Fiss is skeptical of this explanation; see Fiss, "Deutschland in Paris," 43.

45. See Gayatri Spivak, *A critique of postcolonial reason: Toward a history of the vanishing present.* Cambridge, Mass., Harvard University Press, 1999.

46. AN, F/12/12373.

47. AN, F/1/12373.

48. Daniel Williams, "Homecoming of relic taken by Mussolini's forces would end long dispute," *Washington Post,* July 20, 2002, A15.

49. Alice L. Conklin, "Colonialism and human rights, a contradiction in terms? The case of France and West Africa, 1895–1914," *American Historical Review* ciii, 2 (1998), 419–42.

50. Catherine Hodeir, "La France d'outre mer," in *Paris 1937,* 288.

51. James D. Herbert, *Paris 1937. Worlds on exhibition.* Ithaca, Cornell University Press, 1998, ch. 1.

52. AN, F/12/544, Letter of Joseph Arisi, Administrator of Spanish pavilion to E. Labbé, 17 July 1939.

53. See Walter Benjamin, *The Arcades Project.* Cambridge, Mass., Harvard University Press, 2001.

54. Walter Benjamin, *Illuminations,* trans. H. Zorn. London, Fontana, 1971, 258. Herewith the original German citation: Walter Benjamin, "Es ist niemals ein Dokument der Kultur, ohne zugleich ein solches der Barbarei zu sein" (VII in Ueber den Begriff der Geschichte), in *Gesammelte Schriften,* ed. Rolf Tiedemann and Hermann Schweppenhaeuser, vol. 1–2, 696.

55. Walter Benjamin, *Illuminations,* trans. Harry Zorn. London, Fontana, 1977, 258.

Chapter 4. 1948: Human Rights

1. See the introduction, x.

2. Paris, Archives Nationales, 382AP/1, "Souvenirs de la campagne 1914–1915." These memoirs were composed about a year after the outbreak of the war. Cassin wrote that they constituted a "Temoignage vécu, à l'histoire d'une campagne d'un regiment de ligne au cours de la guerre franco-allemande."

3. AN 382AP/1, Guerre 14–18, "Souvenirs de la campagne 1914–1915."

4. AN 382 AP/10, "Anciens combattants."

5. Marc Agi, "De l'idée d'universalité comme fondatrice du concept des droits de l'homme d'après la vie et l'oeuvre de René Cassin," thèse pour le doctorat d'Etat, Université de Nice, 10 December 1979. Antibes, Editions Alp'azur, 1980.

6. See Antoine Prost, "Veterans and politicians," in *Representing the Republic.* Oxford, Berg, 2002.

7. AN 382AP/10, Cassin's report on the Commission de la Paix sur la CIAMAC.

8. AN 382AP/14, "League of Nations. Speech on disarmament to League of Nations," September 1929.

9. Marc Agi, *René Cassin, 1887–1976. Prix Nobel de la paix.* Paris, Perrin, 1998, 54, 57.

10. AN AP382/14, "League of Nations, René Cassin, La xè assemblée vue par un ancien combattant, *Le Journal,* 13 Oct 1929."

11. AN AP382/14, "League of Nations, Speech on disarmament, September 1929."

12. René Cassin, "La nouvelle conception du domicile dans le règlement des conflits de lois," in *Académie de droit international, the Hague. Receuil des cours* (1930), 658–809.

13. Cassin, "La nouvelle conception," 771.

14. Cassin directly cites this declaration in "La nouvelle conception," 770, 801.

15. I am grateful for the suggestion of the anonymous referee for Yale University Press, who drew this point to my attention. See Jean Lacouture, *De Gaulle,* trans. Patrick O'Brian. New York, Norton, 1990, 2 vols.

16. René Cassin, *Les hommes partis de rien.* Paris, Plon, 1974, 273.

17. Ibid., 404.

18. AN 382AP/128, "La France d'aujourd'hui et les droits de l'homme."

19. AN 382AP/128, "Draft statement on Conseil d'Etat under Vichy."

20. See René Cassin, *La pensée et l'action.* Paris, F. Lalou, 1972, 63–79.

21. Cassin, *La pensée,* 8.

22. Mary Ann Glendon, *A world made new: Eleanor Roosevelt and the Universal Declaration of Human Rights.* New York, Random House, 2001.

23. René Cassin, "La déclaration universelle et la mise en oeuvre des droits de l'homme," *Académie de droit international, the Hague. Receuil des Cours* (1950), 241–367.

24. AN 382AP/128, speech of 9 December 1948.

25. See the comments of Ferydon Hoveyda, the last living signatory of the Universal Declaration, in "Human rights at fifty," a broadcast of Common Ground Radio, 8 December 1998, http://ww.commongroundradio.org/transcpt/98/9849.html.

26. AN 382AP/128.

27. Martti Koskenniemi, *The gentle civilizer of nations: The rise and fall of international law 1870–1960.* Cambridge, Cambridge University Press, 2001.

Chapter 5. 1968: Liberation

1. For a sense of the variety of liberation theologies in the Latin American context, see Rosino Givellini (ed.), *Frontiers of liberation theology in Latin America,* trans. by John Drury. Maryknoll, N.Y., Orbis Books, 1983.

2. Michael Löwy, *The war of gods: Religion and politics in Latin America London.* Verso, 1996, 43.

3. Christian Smith, *The emergence of liberation theology: Radical religion and social movement theory.* Chicago, University of Chicago Press, 1991, 104. Emilion A. Núñez, *Liberation theology,* trans. Paul E. Sywulka. Chicago, Moody Press, 1985; Enrique Dussel, *A history of the church in Latin America: Colonialism to liberation (1492–1979),* trans. Alec Neeley. Grand Rapids, Mich., Eerdmans, 1971. In Dussel's words, Latin American theology took this turn in part because of "the study in Europe by many Latin American seminary professors and theological teachers" (p. 32).

4. Rosino Gibellini (ed.), *Frontiers of theology in Latin America.* Maryknoll, N.Y., Orbis Books, 1983, 240–59; Alfred T. Hennelly, *Liberation theologies. The global pursuit of justice.* Mystic, Conn., Twenty Third Publications, 1997, 26–48.

5. See Ernesto Cardenal, *The gospel in Solentiname,* trans. Donald D. Walsh. Maryknoll, N.Y., Orbis Books, c1976–c1982, 3 vols.

6. Jose Miguez Bonino, *Concilio abierto: una interpretacion protestante del Concilio Vaticano II.* Buenos Aires, Editorial La Aurora, 1967. See also Jose Miguez Bonino, *Doing theology in a revolutionary situation.* Philadelphia, Fortress Press, 1988.

7. Phillip Berryman, *Liberation theology. The essential facts about the revolutionary movement in Latin America and beyond.* New York, Pantheon Books, 1987.

8. Enrique Dussel (ed.), *The church in Latin America 1492–1992.* Maryknoll, N.Y., Orbis Books, 1992, ch. 9.

9. Roger Beaunez et al., *Jocistes dans la tourmente: Histoire des jocistes (JOC-JOCF) de la région parisienne, 1937–1947.* Paris, Editions du temoignage chrétien, 1989; Edmund Arbuthnott, *Joseph Cardijn: Priest and founder of the Y.C.W.* London, Darton, Longman, Todd, 1966.

10. A sympathetic introduction to Gutiérrez's work is Robert McAffee Brown, *Gustavo Gutiérrez. Makers of contemporary theology.* Atlanta, John Knox Press, 1980.

11. Curt Cadorette, "Peru and the mystery of liberation: The nexus and logic of Gustavo Gutiérrez's theology," in *The future of liberation theology. Essays in honor of Gustavo Gutiérrez,* ed. Marc H. Ellis and Otto Maduro. Maryknoll, N.Y., Orbis Books, 1989, 38–48.

12. Curt Cadorette, *From the heart of the people. The theology of Gustavo Gutiérrez.* Oak Park, Ill., Meyer-Stone Books, 1988, 69–77.

13. Brown, *Gustavo Gutiérrez,* 25.

14. Gustavo Gutiérrez, "Towards a theology of liberation," *Theological Studies,* xxxi (1970), 243–61.

15. Gustavo Gutiérrez, *A Theology of Liberation,* trans. Caridad Inda and John Eagleson. Maryknoll, N.Y., Orbis Books, 1988, xviii.

16. In later years, the Nobel Prize–winning economist Amartya Sen provided a secular version of this position in his book *Development as Freedom;* Gutiérrez offered a Catholic form of the same argument 30 years before. See Amartya Sen, *Development as freedom.* New York, Knopf, 1999.

17. Gustavo Gutiérrez, *Essential writings,* ed. James B. Nickoloff. Maryknoll, N.Y., Orbis Books, 2002, 25–27.

18. Alfred T. Hennelly (ed.), *Liberation theology: A documentary history.* Maryknoll, N.Y., Orbis Books, 1990, 68–69.

19. Ibid., 70.

20. Ibid., 72.

21. Ibid., 74–75.

22. Michael Löwy, *The War of Gods: Religion and politics in Latin America.* London, Verso, 1996, 81–93; Rosino Gibellini (ed.), *Frontiers of theology in Latin America.* Maryknoll, N.Y., Orbis Books, 1983, 58–78; see also Hugo Assmann, *Practical theology of liberation,* trans. Paul Burns. London, Search Press, 1975.

23. Gustavo Gutiérrez, *The density of the present. Selected writings.* Maryknoll, N.Y., Orbis Books, 1999, ch. 3.

24. Brown, *Gutiérrez,* 16–17.

25. Hennelly (ed.), *Liberation theology,* 111. The internal quote is from the Pope's encyclical, *Populorum progressio.*

26. For Gutiérrez's thoughts on Medellín, written in 1989, see his collection of essays *The Density of the present. Selected Writings.* Maryknoll, N.Y., Orbis Books, 1999, 59–101.

27. James B. Nickoloff (ed.), *Gustavo Gutiérrez. Essential Writings.* Maryknoll, N.Y., Orbis Books, 2002, 4.

28. Hennelly (ed.), *Liberation theology,* 115, 117, 118.

29. Gustavo Gutiérrez, "Notes for a theology of liberation," *Theological Studies,* xxxi (1970), 250–52.

30. Gutiérrez, "Notes," 249–50.

31. Gutiérrez, *A Theology of Liberation,* 24.

32. Camilo Torres, *Revolutionary writings,* trans. Robert Olsen and Linda Day. New York, Herder and Herder, 1969.

33. Gutiérrez, *A Theology of Liberation,* 24.

34. Cardenal, *The Gospel in Solentiname;* the book first appeared in Spanish in 1977.

35. Cardenal, *Solentiname,* vol. 3, 3.

36. Ibid., 50–51.

37. Ibid., 132–33.

38. Ibid., 192.

39. Andrew Dawson, "The origin and character of the base ecclesial community: A Brazilian perspective," in *The Cambridge Companion to Liberation Theology,* ed. Christopher Rowland. Cambridge, Cambridge University Press, 1999, 109–28.

40. Andrew Dawson, *The birth and impact of the base ecclesial community and liberative theological discourse in Brazil.* San Francisco, Catholic Scholars Press, 1999, chs. 4–5.

41. This discussion is drawn largely from Dawson's treatment of this theme. See above citation and, among other works, Leonardo Boff, *Ecclesiogenesis: The base communities reinvent the church,* trans. R. R. Barr. London, Collins, 1986; Dominique Barbé, *Grace and power: Base communities and non-violence in Brazil,* trans. J. P. Brown. Maryknoll, N.Y., Orbis Books, 1986; and John R. Pottenger, *The political theory of liberation theology. Toward a reconvergence of social values and social science.* Albany, State University of New York Press, 1989, 138–43.

42. See Peter Hebblethwaite, "Liberation theology and the Roman Catholic Church," in *The Cambridge companion to liberation theology,* ed. Christopher Rowland. Cambridge, Cambridge University Press, 1999, 179–98.

43. Gutiérrez was deeply influenced by Bonhoeffer's writing. See his *The power of the poor in history: Selected work,* trans. Robert R. Barr. Maryknoll, N.Y., Orbis Books, 1983, 203.

44. As cited in Curt Cadorete, *The Theology of Gustavo Gutiérrez. From the heart of the people.* Oak Park, Ill., Meyer Stone Books, 1988, 1.

45. G. Clarke Chapman, Jr, "Bonhoeffer and liberation theology," 147–95, and John D. Godsey, "Bonhoeffer and the third world: West Africa, Cuba, Korea," 257, both in *Ethical responsibility: Bonhoeffer's legacy to the churches,* ed. John B. Godsey and Geffrey B. Kelly. Toronto Studies in Theology vol. 6. New York, Edwin Mellen Press, 1981.

46. Christine-Ruth Müller, *Dietrich Bonhoeffers Kampf gegen die nationalsozialistische Verfolgung und Vernichtung der Juden: Bonhoeffers Haltung zur Judenfrage im Vergleich mit Stellungnahmen aus der evangelischen Kirche und Kreisen des deutschen Widerstandes.* Munich, Kaiser, c1990.

47. Dietrich Bonhoeffer, *No rusty swords. Letters, lectures and notes 1928–1936,* ed. and trans. Edwin H. Robertson and John Bowden. London, Collins, 1965, 225–26.

48. As cited in Bethge, "Dietrich Bonhoeffer and the Jews," in Godsey and Kelly (eds.), *Ethical responsibility,* 71.

49. Jürgen Schmidt, *Martin Niemöller im Kirchenkampf.* Hamburg, Leibniz-Verlag, 1971; and James Bentley, *Martin Niemöller, 1892–1984.* New York, Free Press, c1984.

50. Raymond Mengus, "Dietrich Bonhoeffer and the decision to resist," *Journal of Modern History,* lxiv (1992), supplement, 134–46.

51. As cited in Bethge, "Dietrich Bonhoeffer and the Jews," 80, 76.

52. Eberhard Bethke, *Dietrich Bonhoeffer. Theologian, Christian, contemporary.* London, Collins, 1970, 559ff.

53. Bethge, "Dietrich Bonhoeffer and the Jews," 89.

54. Barbara and John Ehrenreich, *Long march, short spring. The student uprising at home and abroad.* London, Monthly Review Press, 1969, 28–29.

55. See Dagmar Herzog, *Sex after fascism: Memory and morality in twentieth-century Germany.* Princeton, Princeton University Press, 2005. See also Robert G. Moeller, *Protecting motherhood: Women and the family in the politics of postwar West Germany.* Berkeley, University of California Press, 1993.

56. As cited in Mengus, "Dietrich Bonhoeffer," 135.

57. Cornelia Brink, "Auschwitz in der Paulskirche," in *Erinnerungspolitik in Fotoausstellungen der sechziger Jahre.* Marburg, Jonas-Verlag, 2000.

58. Miriam Hansen and Michael Geyer, "German-Jewish memory and national consciousness," in *Holocaust remembrance: The shapes of memory,* ed. Geoffrey Hartmann. Oxford, Oxford University Press, 1994, 175. See also Harold Marcuse, "The Revival of Holocaust awareness in West Germany, Israel and the United States," in *1968: The world transformed,* ed. Carol Fink, Philip Gassert, and Detlef Junker. Cambridge, Cambridge University Press, 1998, 424.

59. John P. Teschke, *"Hitler's legacy": West Germany confronts the aftermath of the Third Reich.* New York, P. Lang, c1999.

60. On this problem, and the rhetoric of comparative victimhood, see Robert G. Moeller, *War stories: The search for a usable past in the Federal Republic of Germany.* Berkeley, University of California Press, 2001.

61. Dörte von Westernhagen, *Die Kinder der Täter: das Dritte Reich und die Generation danach.* Munich, Kösel, c1988. Sabine von Dirke, *"All power to the imagination!" The West German counterculture from the student movement to the Greens.* Lincoln, Neb., University of Nebraska Press, 1997; and Christian Geissler, *The sins of the fathers,* trans. James Kirkup. New York, Random House, 1962.

62. T. W. Adorno et al., *The authoritarian personality.* New York, Harper, 1950. See also Dagmar Herzog, *Sex after fascism,* for the domestic echoes of this theme.

63. Heinz Bude, "The German *Kriegskinder:* Origins and impact of the generation of 1968," in *Generations in conflict. Youth revolt and generation formation in Germany 1770–1968,* ed. Mark Roseman. Cambridge, Cambridge University Press, 1995, 290–305.

64. Andrei S. Markovits and Philip S. Gorski, *The German left. Red, green and beyond.* Cambridge, Polity Press, 1993, 47.

65. Annemarie Tröger, "Les enfants du tertiaire: Le mouvement étudiant en RFA de 1961 à 1969," *Mouvement social,* 143 (April–June 1988), 13–38.

66. Ronald Fraser et al., *1968. A student generation in revolt.* London, Chatto and Windus, 1988, 235.

67. Horst Mewes, "The German new left," *New German Critique,* 1 (1973), 22–41.

68. John Gretton, *Students and workers. An analytical account of dissent in France May–June 1968.* London, MacDonald, 1969, 207ff.

69. Andrew Freedberg and Jim Freedman, *When poetry ruled the streets. The French May events of 1968.* Albany, State University of New York Press, 2001, 50–53.

70. Daniel Cohn-Bendit and Gabriel Cohn-Bendit, *Obsolete communism. The left-wing alternative,* trans. Arnold Pomerans. New York, McGraw-Hill, 1968, 58.

71. Paul Berman, *A tale of two utopias. The political journey of the generation of 1968.* New York, W. W. Norton, 1996, 61.

72. Ehrenreich and Ehrenreich, *Long march,* 73.

73. Ronald Fraser et al., *1968,* 185; Ingrid Gilcher-Holtey, "May 1968 in France: The rise and fall of a new social movement," in Fink et al., *1968,* 261.

74. For a later configuration of this point, see Henri Lefebvre, *Du contrat de citoyenneté.* Paris, Editions Périscope, 1990, 37.

75. Louis Antoine de Saint-Just, *L'esprit de la révolution.* Paris, UGE, 1963, 20, as cited in Feenberg and Freedman, *When poetry ruled the streets,* 151.

76. Frank Georgi (ed.), *Autogestion. La dernière utopie?* Paris, Publications de la Sorbonne, 2003, 8ff; Pierre Rosanvallon, *L'âge de l'autogestion.* Paris, Le Seuil, 1976.

77. Lefebvre, *Du contrat de citoyenneté,* passim.

78. Henri Desroche, *Les dieux rêvés; théisme et athéisme en Utopie.* Paris, Desclée, 1972.

79. Rémi Hess, *Henri Lefebvre et l'aventure du siècle.* Paris, A. M. Métailié, 1988.

80. Daniel Guérin, *Le feu du sang: Autobiographie politique et charnelle.* Paris, B. Grasset, 1977.

81. Georgi (ed.), *Autogestion,* 13, 143–56.

82. Alain Schnapp and Pierre Vidal-Naquet, *Journal de la commune étudiante, textes et documents, novembre 1967–juin 1968.* Paris, Editions du Seuil, 1969.

83. "We are continuing the struggle—May 28," as cited in Feenberg and Freedman, *When poetry ruled the streets,* 165.

84. Michel Trebitsch, "Henri Lefebvre et l'autogestion," in Georgi (ed.), 74; Georgi (ed.), *Autogestion,* 24.

85. Claudie Weill, "La revue *Autogestion,*" in Georgi (ed.), *Autogestion,* 55–62.

86. Joëlle Beurrier, "La mémoire Lip ou la fin du mythe autogestionnaire?" in Georgi (ed.), *Autogestion,* 451–66.

87. Andrew Feenberg, "Remembering the May events," *Theory and Society,* vi, 1 (1978), 29–53.

88. Patricia Latour and Francis Combes, *Conversation avec Henri Lefebvre.* Paris, Messidor, 1991, 71.

89. Georgi (ed.), *Autogestion,* 13–14.

90. I am grateful to Jean-Louis Robert for bringing this point to my attention.

91. Hess, *Henri Lefebvre,* 251.

92. Jean-Pierre Le Goff, *Mai 68, l'héritage impossible.* Paris, Editions la Découverte, 1998, 267ff.

93. For his own retrospective view, see Herbert Marcuse and Biddy Martin, "The failure of the new left?" *New German Critique,* 18 (1979), 3–11. On Marcuse, see Douglas Kellner, *Herbert Marcuse and the crisis of Marxism.* London, Macmillan, 1984; and John Bokina and Timothy J. Lukes (eds.), *Marcuse. From the new left to the next left.* Lawrence, Kans., University of Kansas Press, 1994; Robert Pippin, Andrew Feenberg, and Charles P. Webel (eds.), *Marcuse. Critical theory and the promise of utopia.* London, Macmillan, 1988.

94. Hess, *Henri Lefebvre,* 245.

95. Franz Fanon, *Les damnés de la terre.* Paris, François Maspero, 1961.

96. Luisa Passerini, "Peut-on donner de 1968 une histoire à la première personne?" *Mouvement Social,* 143 (April–June 1988), 3–11; and Luisa Passerini, "Le mouvement de 1968 comme prise de parole et comme explosion de la subjectivité: Le cas de Turin," *Mouvement social,* 143 (April–June 1988), 70–74.

97. Le Goff, *Mai 68,* 279, 390.

98. See Havel's own comments on this matter in Antonin J. Liehm, *The politics of culture,* trans. Peter Kussi. New York, Grove Press, 1968, 378ff; "Second wind," in Václav Havel, *Open letters. Selected prose 1965–1990.* London, Faber and Faber, 1991, 4–9; and Eda Kriseová, *Václav Havel. The authorized biography,* trans. Caleb Crain. New York, St. Martin's Press, 1993, 35ff.

99. Václav Havel, *Disturbing the peace. A conversation with Karel Hvížďala,* trans. Paul Wilson. New York, Alfred Knopf, 1990, 52–53.

100. Paul I. Trentsky, "Václav Havel and the language of the absurd," *Slavic and East European Journal,* xiii, 1 (1969), 44.

101. Havel, *Disturbing the peace,* 54.

102. Ibid.

103. Ibid.

104. Eduard Goldstücker et al., *Zwanzig Jahre nach dem Prager Frühling: Protokoll eines Seminars, veranstaltet vom Österreichischen CSSR-Solidaritätskomitee.* Wien, Österreichisches CSSR-Solidaritätskomitee, c1989.

105. Berman, *A tale of two utopias,* 63.

Chapter 6. 1992: Global Citizenship

1. Eric Hobsbawn, *The age of extremes. A history of the world 1914–1991.* New York, Vintage Books, 1994.

2. Richard Falk, "The making of global citizenship," in *Global visions. Beyond the new world order,* ed. Jeremy Brecher, John Brown Childs, and Jill Cutler. Boston, South End Press, 1993, 39, 47.

3. Michael Peter Smith, "Can you imagine? Transnational migration and the globalization of grassroots politics," *Social text,* 39 (Summer 1999), 16.

4. Richard J. Wilson, "The Spanish proceedings," in *The Pinochet papers. The case of Augusto Pinochet in Spain and Britain,* ed. Reed Broady and Michael Ratner. The Hague, Kluwer Law International, 2000, 23ff.

5. Article 3 of the European Convention for the Protection of Human Rights and Fundamental Freedoms, initially adopted in 1950 and subsequently extended, formally outlawed torture. The European Convention for the Prevention of Torture and Inhuman or Degrading Treatment of Punishment (ETS no. 126) had entered into force on 1 February 1989, further strengthening this legal framework.

6. Roger Burback, *The Pinochet affair: State terrorism and global justice.* London, Zed Books, 2003.

7. Monroe Leigh, "In re Union Carbide Corp. Gas plant disaster at Bhopal, India in December 1984, 634 F. Supp. 842," *American Journal of International Law* 80, 4 (October 1986), 964–67.

8. Kailash Thakur, *Environmental protection law and policy in India.* New Delhi, Deep and Deep Publications, 1997, 340–55.

9. Kau Raustiala, "States, NGOs, and international environmental institutions," *International Studies Quarterly* 41, 4 (December 1997), 719–40.

10. Karen T. Litfin, "Sovereignty in world ecopolitics," *Mershon International Studies Review,* 41 (1997), 171ff.

11. For references, see: http://www.ran.org/about_ran/mission.html

12. "The earth summit on population," *Population and Development Review* 18, 3 (September 1992), 571–82.

13. Ivan Amato, "The slow birth of green chemistry," *Science* 259, 5101 (12 March 1993), 1538–41.

14. Litfin, "Sovereignty," 189.

15. Kathryn Sikkink, "Codes of conduct for transnational corporations: The case of the WHO/UNICEF code," *International Organization* 40, 4 (Autumn 1986), 815–40.

16. John S. Dryzek et al., *Green states and social movements. Environmentalism in the United States, United Kingdom, Germany, and Norway.* Oxford, Oxford University Press, 2003, 189.

17. Charles O. Holliday, Stephan Schmidheiny, and Philip Watts, *Walking the talk: The business case for sustainable development.* Sheffield, Greenleaf, 2002. I am grateful to Alicia Delapianne for drawing this work to my attention. Her own project "Aletheia," dedicated to introducing the teaching of solidarity into school curricula in several countries, is another example of imaginative politics on the local and global level.

18. For details, see the Avina Web site at: http://www.avina.net/web/
avinawebfinal3.nsf/LK_GCMask2/3~4~8~1?Open&LANG=Eng.

19. Karen Litfin, "Sovereignty in world ecopolitics," 194.

20. Amnesty International, *1961–1976. A chronology.* London, Amnesty International, 1976.

21. Elisabeth Friedman, "Women's human rights: The emergence of a movement,"
in *Women's rights, human rights: International feminist perspectives,* ed. Julie Peters
and Andrea Wolper. New York, Routledge, 1995, 25–27.

22. Teitelbaum and Winter, *A question of numbers,* 78ff.

23. For full documentation, see the ICTY Web site: http://www.un.org/icty/
glance/index.htm.

24. See the documentation on the Human Rights Watch Web site: http://www
.hrw.org/campaigns/icc/.

25. Carolyn M. Stephenson, "Women's international nongovernmental organizations at the United Nations," in *Women, politics, and the United Nations,* ed. Anne
Winslow. Westport, Conn., Greenwood Press, 1995, 147ff.

26. Tessa Kaplan, "Women's rights as human rights: Grassroots women redefine
citizenship in a global context," in *Women's rights and human rights. International
historical perspectives,* ed. Patricia Grimshaw, Katie Holmes, and Marilyn Lake.
Basingstoke, Palgrave, 2001, 290–308.

27. Nadine Taub, *International conference on population and development.*
American Society of International Law Issue Papers on World Conferences, no. 1.
Washington, American Society of International Law, 1994.

28. For relevant documents, and a general discussion, see Robert Cliquet and
Kristiaan Thienpont, *Population and development. A message from the Cairo conference.* Dordrecht, Kluwer Academic Publishers, 1995, 98.

29. C. Alison McIntosh and Jason L. Finkle, "The Cairo conference on population
and development: A new paradigm?" *Population and development review* 21, 2 (June
1995), 224.

30. As cited in Stanley Johnson, *The Politics of population. The international conference on population and development.* London, Earthscan Publications, 1995, 133.

31. Marilyn J. Danguilan, *Women in brackets: A chronicle of Vatican power and
control.* Manila, Philippine Center for Investigative Journalism, 1997, 113.

32. Cliquet and Thienpont, *Population and development,* 95.

33. Amartya Sen, *Development as freedom.* New York, Knopf, 1999.

34. Martha Nussbaum and Jonathan Glover (eds.), *Women, culture, and development: A study of human capabilities.* Oxford, Clarenden Press, 1995.

35. For a broad discussion, see Sonia E. Alvarez, Evelina Dagnino, and Arturo
Escobar (eds.), *Culture of politics, politics of cultures. Re-visioning Latin American
social movements.* Boulder, Westview Press, 1998, esp. ch. 12.

36. Yasemin Soysal, *Limits of citizenship: Migrants and postnational membership
in Europe.* Chicago, University of Chicago Press, 1994, 165.

37. Article 19 (8b) and 189–91 (137–38a) of the European Community Treaty, 1 January 1996.

38. Rainer Baubock, *Recombinant citizenship*. Political Science Series no. 67. Vienna, Institute for Advanced Studies, 1999.

39. Jonas Widgren, "Sweden and immigration—an exceptional or a standard western European case?" typescript, n.d.

40. This discussion is derived from the research of Anna Paula Beja Horta, "Transnational networks and the local politics of migrant grassroots organizing in post-colonial Portugal."

41. The following discussion draws directly from Myer Siemiatycki and Engin Isin, "Immigration, diversity, and urban citizenship in Toronto," *Canadian Journal of Regional Science* 21, 2 (Spring 1997), 73–102.

42. Dolores Hayden, *The Power of place: Urban landscapes as public history*. Cambridge, MIT Press, 1996.

43. I am grateful to Nomi Lazar for her perceptive critique of these, and other points.

44. As cited in Sidney Tarrow, "Anti-globalizers and rooted cosmopolitans," Conference on "Reshaping Globalization," Central European University, Budapest, 17 October 2001. See also Cecilia Menjivar, *Fragmented ties. Salvadoran immigrants in the United States*. Berkeley, University of California Press, 2001.

45. See the work of Leona Forman, supported by the Avina foundation. For details, see: http://www.avina.net/web/avinawebfinal3.nsf/LK_GCMask2/3~4~10 ~1?Open&LANG=Eng.

46. The term is used in a report on the Comparative Immigrant Entrepreneurship Project of the Center for Migration and Development at Princeton. For its work, see http://cmd.princeton.edu/ciep.shtml.

47. On the Worker Rights consortium, see: http://www.workersrights.org/.

48. Ginger Thompson, "Mexican labor protest gets results," *New York Times*, 3 October 2001.

49. Margaret E. Keck and Kathryn Sikkink (eds.), *Activists beyond borders. Advocacy networks in international politics*. Ithaca, Cornell University Press, 1998.

50. J. A. Scholte, "The geography of collective identities in a globalizing world," *Review of International Political Economy*, 3–4 (1996), 565–608.

51. Michael Peter Smith, "Can you imagine? Transnational migration and the globalization of grassroots politics," *Social Text*, 39 (Summer 199), 16.

52. Arjun Appadurai, *Modernity at large: Cultural dimensions of globalization*. Minneapolis, University of Minnesota Press, 1996, 23.

53. See Jay Winter and Jean-Louis Robert, *Capital cities at war: Paris, London, Berlin 1914–1919*. Cambridge, Cambridge University Press, 1997, ch. 1.

54. For a similar argument on the state-bounded character of economic globalization, see Saskia Sassen, *Globalization and its discontents*. New York, The New Press, 1998, ch. 10.

55. For a stimulating presentation of these issues, see Seyla Benhabib, *Transformations of citizenship. Dilemmas of the nation state in the era of globalization.* Amsterdam, Koninklijke van Gorcum, 2001.

56. Tarrow, "Anti-globalizers and rooted cosmopolitans," 3.

57. For one of the better maps, see David Jacobson, *Rights across borders. Immigration and the decline of citizenship.* Baltimore, Johns Hopkins University Press, 1996.

Epilogue

Epigraph: Anna Akhmatova, *Selected poems,* trans. Richard McKane. London, Bloodaxe Books, 1989, 96.

1. For instance, Dipesh Chakrabarty, *Provincializing Europe: Postcolonial thought and historical difference.* Princeton, Princeton University Press, 2000; and Gayatri Chakravorty Spivak, *A critique of postcolonial reason: Toward a history of the vanishing present.* Cambridge, Mass., Harvard University Press, 1999.

2. Wilhelm Rasch, "Human rights as geopolitics," *Cultural critique,* 54 (2003), 19–38.

3. See Makau Mutua, *Human rights: A political and cultural critique.* Philadelphia, Pa., University of Pennsylvania Press, 2002.

4. See Mark Mazower, "The strange triumph of human rights, 1933–50," *Historical Journal,* xlvii (2004), 379–98.

5. See Antoine Prost and Jay Winter, *Penser la grande guerre.* Paris, Le Seuil, 2004, 23.

6. James C. Scott, *Seeing like a state: How certain schemes to improve the human condition have failed.* New Haven, Yale University Press, 1998.

Bibliography

Archives

London
National Archives (Public Record Office)
    Foreign Office papers, 1900, 1918–19, and 1937
    Cabinet papers, 1918–19
New Haven, Connecticut
Yale University, Department of Manuscripts and Archives
    Auchincloss Papers
    House Papers
    Inquiry Papers
    Lippmann Papers
    Sidney E. Mezes Papers
New York
Columbia University
    Shotwell Papers
    Wellington Koo Papers

United Nations
    Papers and documents on the Universal Declaration of Human Rights
Paris
Archives Nationales
    392/AP (Fonds Cassin)
    AJ/16
    F/12
    F/1
    F/60
    F/23
Institut d'histoire du vingtième siècle, University of Paris—I
    Papers on 1968
Musée Albert Kahn, Boulogne-Billancourt
    Kahn collection
    Brunhes—Delamarre papers

Books and Articles

Abramson, A., *The history of television, 1880 to 1941*. (New York, MacFarland, Jefferson, 1987).

Ades, Dawn, et al. *Art and power: Europe under the dictators 1930–45*. (London, Thames and Hudson, 1995).

Adorno, T. W., et al., *The authoritarian personality*. (New York, Harper, 1950).

Agi, Marc, *De l'idée d'universalité comme fondatrice du concept des droits de l'homme d'après la vie et l'oeuvre de René Cassin*. Thèse pour le doctorat d'état, Université de Nice, 10 December 1979. (Antibes, Editions Alp'azur, 1980).

———, *René Cassin, 1887–1976. Prix Nobel de la paix*. (Paris, Perrin, 1998).

Akhmatova, Anna, *Selected poems*, trans. Richard McKane. (London, Bloodaxe Books, 1989).

Albert Speer. Architecture 1932–1942. (Brussels, Aux archives d'architecture moderne, 1958).

Alexander, P. (ed.). *Utopias*. (London, Duckworth, 1984).

Alvarez, Sonia E., Evelina Dagnino, and Arturo Escobar (eds.). *Culture of politics, politics of cultures. Re-visioning Latin American social movements*. (Boulder, Westview Press, 1998).

Amato, Ivan, "The slow birth of green chemistry," *Science* 259, 5101 (12 March 1993), 1538–41.

Amnesty International, 1961–1976. A chronology. (London, Amnesty International, 1976).

Appadurai, Arjun, *Modernity at large: Cultural dimensions of globalization*. (Minneapolis, University of Minnesota Press, 1996).

Arbuthnott, Edmund, *Joseph Cardijn: Priest and founder of the Y.C.W.* (London, Darton, Longman, Todd, 1966).

Arrighi, G., "Marxist century, American century," in R. Blackburn (ed.), *After the fall: The failure of communism and the future of socialism*. (London, Verso, 1991), 126–65.

Auclair, Marcelle, *La vie de Jean Jaurès, ou, La France d'avant 1914*. (Paris, Editions du Seuil, 1954).

Avenel, Jean-David, *Interventions alliées pendant la guerre civile russe, 1918–1920*. (Paris, Economica, c2001).

Baczko, B., *Utopian lights: The evolution of the idea of social progress*. (New York, Paragon House, 1989).

Baker, Ray Stannard and William E. Dodd (eds.), *The public papers of Woodrow Wilson, war and peace*. (New York, Harper and Brothers, 1925–27).

Barbé, Dominique, *Grace and power: Base communities and non-violence in Brazil*, trans. J. P. Brown. (Maryknoll, N.Y., Orbis Books, 1986).

Barraqué, Bernard, "La lumière à l'exposition," in *Paris 1937: Cinquantenaire. De l'exposition internationale des arts et des techniques dans la vie moderne*. (Paris, Institut Français de l'Architecture/Paris Musées, 1987), 404–9.

Baubock, Rainer, *Recombinant citizenship*. Political Science Series no. 67. (Vienna, Institute for Advanced Studies, 1999).

Bauman, Zygmunt, *Modernity and the Holocaust*. (Ithaca, N.Y., Cornell University Press, 1989).

———, *Socialism: The active utopia*. (New York, Holmes and Meier, 1976).

Beaunez, Roger, et al., *Jocistes dans la tourmente: histoire des jocistes (JOC-JOCF) de la région parisienne, 1937–1947*. (Paris, Editions du temoignage chrétien, 1989).

Beer, George Louis, *African questions at the Paris peace conference*. (New York, Macmillan, 1923).

Beilharz, P., *Labour's utopias: Bolshevism, fabianism, social democracy*. (London, Routledge, 1992).

Bellamy, E., *Looking backward, 2000–1887*. (Cambridge, Mass., Belknap Press of Harvard University Press, 1967 edition).

Benhabib, Seyla, *Transformations of citizenship. Dilemmas of the nation state in the era of globalization*. (Amsterdam, Koninklijke van Gorcum, 2001).

Benjamin, Walter, *The arcades project*. (Cambridge, Mass., Harvard University Press, 2001).

———, *Illuminations*, trans. H. Zorn. (London, Fontana, 1971).

Bentley, James, *Martin Niemöller, 1892–1984*. (New York, Free Press, c1984).

Berman, Paul, *A tale of two utopias. The political journey of the generation of 1968*. (New York, W. W. Norton, 1996).

Berneri, M. L., *Journey through utopia*. (Boston, The Beacon Press, 1967).

Berryman, Phillip, *Liberation theology. The essential facts about the revolutionary movement in Latin America and beyond*. (New York, Pantheon Books, 1987).

Bethke, Eberhard, *Dietrich Bonhoeffer. Theologian, Christian, contemporary*. (London, Collins, 1970).

———, "Dietrich Bonhoeffer and the Jews," in John B. Godsey and Geffrey B. Kelly (eds.), *Ethical responsibility: Bonhoeffer's legacy to the churches*. Toronto Studies in Theology vol. 6. (New York, Edwin Mellen Press, 1981), 119–50.

Blackburn, R. (ed.), *After the fall: The failure of communism and the future of socialism*. (London, Verso, 1991).

Blignières, Pascal de, *Albert Kahn, les jardins d'une idée*. (Paris, Editions La Bibliothèque, 1995).

Bloch, E., *The utopian function of art and literature: Selected essays*. (Cambridge, Mass., MIT Press, 1988).

Blum, John Morton, *Woodrow Wilson and the politics of morality*. (Boston, Little, Brown, 1956).

Blum, Stephen D., *Walter Lippmann, cosmopolitanism in the century of total war*. (Ithaca, Cornell University Press, 1984).

Bobbio, N., "The upturned utopia," in R. Blackburn (ed.), *After the fall: The failure of communism and the future of socialism*. (London, Verso, 1991), 1–10.

Boff, Leonardo, *Ecclesiogenesis: The base communities reinvent the church*, trans. R. R. Barr. (London, Collins, 1986).

Bohman, James and Matthias Lutz-Bachmann (eds.), *Perpetual peace: Essays on Kant's cosmopolitan ideal*. (Cambridge, Mass., MIT Press, 1997).

Bokina, John and Timothy J. Lukes (eds.), *Marcuse. From the new left to the next left*. (Lawrence, Kansas, University of Kansas Press, 1994).

Bonhoeffer, Dietrich, *No rusty swords. Letters, lectures and notes 1928–1936*, ed. and trans. Edwin H. Robertson and John Bowden. (London, Collins, 1965).

Bonino, Miguez, *Doing theology in a revolutionary situation*. (Philadelphia, Fortress Press, 1988).

Boscus, Alain and Rémy Cazals, (eds.), *Sur les pas de Jaurès*. (Toulouse, Privat, 2004).

Les boursiers de voyage de l'université de Paris. (Paris, Felix Alcan, 1904).

Brecher, Jeremy, John Brown Childs, and Jill Cutler (eds.), *Global visions. Beyond the new world order*. (Boston, South End Press, 1993).

Brink, Cornelia, *"Auschwitz in der Paulskirche." Erinnerungspolitik in Fotoausstellungen der sechziger Jahre*. (Marburg, Jonas-Verlag 2000).

Brittain, James E., "The international diffusion of electrical power technology, 1870–1920," *Journal of Economic History* xxxiv, 1 (1974), 108–21.

Broady, Reed and Michael Ratner (eds.), *The Pinochet papers. The case of Augusto Pinochet in Spain and Britain*. (The Hague, Kluwer Law International, 2000).

Brown, Robert McAffee, *Gustavo Gutiérrez. Makers of contemporary theology*. (Atlanta, John Knox Press, 1980).

Brunhes, Jean, *Autour du monde: Regards d'un géographe/Regards de la géographie*. (Boulogne-Billancourt, Musée Albert Kahn, 1993).

Buber, Martin, *Paths in utopia*. (London, Routledge, 1949).

Bude, Heinz, "The German Kriegskinder: Origins and impact of the generation of 1968," in Mark Roseman (ed.), *Generations in conflict. Youth revolt and generation formation in Germany 1770–1968*. (Cambridge, Cambridge University Press, 1995), 290–305.

Bulletin périodique du Bureau Socialiste International 1900.

Burback, Roger, *The Pinochet affair: State terrorism and global justice*. (London, Zed Books, 2003).

Cadorette, Curt, *From the heart of the people. The theology of Gustavo Gutiérrez*. (Oak Park, Ill., Meyer-Stone Books, 1988).

———, "Peru and the mystery of liberation: The nexus and logic of Gustavo Gutiérrez's theology," in Marc H. Ellis and Otto Maduro (eds.), *The future of liberation theology. Essays in honor of Gustavo Gutiérrez.* (Maryknoll, N.Y., Orbis Books, 1989), 38–48.

———, *The Theology of Gustavo Gutierrez. From the heart of the people.* (Oak Park, Ill., Meyer Stone Books, 1988).

Capek, K., *R.U.R. (Rossum's universal robots): A fantastic melodrama.* (Garden City, Doubleday, Page and Co., 1923).

———, *War with the Newts.* (New York, G. P. Putnam's Sons, 1937).

Cardenal, Ernesto, *The Gospel in Solentiname,* trans. Donald D. Walsh. (Maryknoll, N.Y., Orbis Books, 3 vols., c1976–c1982).

Cassin, René, "La déclaration universelle et la mise en oeuvre des droits de l'homme," in *Académie de droit international, the Hague. Recueil des cours* (1950), 241–367.

———, *Les hommes partis de rien.* (Paris, Plon, 1974).

———, "La nouvelle conception du domicile dans le règlement des conflits de lois," in *Académie de droit international, the Hague. Receuil des cours* (1930), 658–809.

———, *La pensée et l'action.* (Paris, F. Lalou, 1972).

Ceadel, Martin, *Pacifism in Britain, 1914–1945: The defining of a faith.* (Oxford, Clarendon Press, 1980).

Chakrabarty, Dipesh, *Provincializing Europe: Postcolonial thought and historical difference.* (Princeton, Princeton University Press, 2000).

Chapman, G. Clarke Jr., "Bonhoeffer and liberation theology," in John B. Godsey and Geffrey B. Kelly (eds.), *Ethical responsibility: Bonhoeffer's legacy to the churches.* Toronto Studies in Theology vol. 6. (New York, Edwin Mellen Press, 1981), 147–95.

Charles-Roux, J. (ed.), *Colonies et pays de protectorats.* (Paris, Exposition universelle, 1900).

Chin, Wen-ssu, *China at the Paris Peace conference.* (Jamaica, N.Y., St. John's University Press, 1961).

Clark, Donald and Robert Williamson (eds.), *Self-determination: International perspectives.* (Basingstoke, Macmillan, 1996).

Cliquet, Robert and Kristiaan Thienpont, *Population and development. A message from the Cairo conference.* (Dordrecht, Kluwer Academic Publishes, 1995).

Cohn-Bendit, Daniel and Gabriel Cohn-Bendit, *Obsolete communism. The left-wing alternative,* trans. Arnold Pomerans. (New York, McGraw-Hill, 1968).

Compte rendu analytique du Congrès Socialiste International extraordinaire tenu à Bâle les 24 et 25 novembre 1912. (Basle, n.p., 1913).

Conklin, Alice L., "Colonialism and human rights, a contradiction in terms? The case of France and West Africa, 1895–1914," *American Historical Review* ciii, 2 (1998), 419–42.

Contee, Clarence G., "Du Bois, the NAACP, and the Pan-African Congress of 1919," *Journal of Negro History* lvii, 1 (1972), 1–16.

———, "W. E. B. Du Bois and African nationalism: 1914–1945." Ph.D. diss., American University, 1969.

Cooper, John Milton, *Breaking the heart of the world. Woodrow Wilson and the fight for the League of Nations.* (Cambridge, Cambridge University Press, 2001).

Curry, George, "Woodrow Wilson, Jan Smuts and the Versailles settlement," *American Historical Review* lxiv, 4 (July 1961), 968–86.

"Danger lurks in Dufy masterpiece," CNN, 26 July 2001. http:\\www.Europe.cnn .com/2001/WORLD/europe/07/26/paris.painting/.

Danguilan, Marilyn J., *Women in brackets: A chronicle of Vatican power and control.* (Manila, Philippine Center for Investigative Journalism, 1997).

Daniel, Marko, "Spain: Culture at war," in Dawn Ades et al., *Art and power: Europe under the dictators 1930–45.* (London, Thames and Hudson, 1995), 64.

Danspeckgruber, Wolfgang (ed.), *The Self-determination of peoples. Community, nation, and state in an interdependent world.* (London, Lynne Rienner, 2002).

Dawson, Andrew, *The birth and impact of the base ecclesial community and liberative theological discourse in Brazil.* (San Francisco, Catholic Scholars Press, 1999).

———, "The origin and character of the base ecclesial community: A Brazilian perspective," in Christopher Rowland (ed.), *The Cambridge companion to liberation theology.* (Cambridge, Cambridge University Press, 1999), 109–28.

Delamarre, Mariel, Jean-Brunhes, and Jeanne Beausoleil, "Deux témoins de leur temps: Albert Kahn et Jean Brunhes," in Jean Brunhes, *Autour du monde: Regards d'un géographe/Regards de la géographie.* (Boulogne-Billancourt, Musée Albert Kahn, 1993).

Desroche, Henri, *Les dieux rêves; théisme et athéisme en Utopie.* (Paris, Desclée, 1972).

Dieng, Amady Aly, *Blaise Diagne, député noir de l'Afrique.* (Paris, Editions Chaka, 1990).

Diop, Obeye (ed.), *Blaise Diagne. Sa vie, son oeuvre.* (Dakar, Nouvelles Editions Africaines, n.d.).

Dorival, Bernard, *La belle histoire de la fée electricité* (Paris, La Palme, 1953).

Dryzek, John S., et al., *Green states and social movements. Environmentalism in the United States, United Kingdom, Germany, and Norway.* (Oxford, Oxford University Press, 2003).

Du Bois, W. E. B., *An ABC of color.* (New York, International Publishers, 1969).

———, *The African roots of war.* (New York, National Association for the Advancement of Colored People, 1915).

———, *The Autobiography of W. E. B. Du Bois; a soliloquy on viewing my life from the last decade of its first century.* (New York, International publishers, 1968).

———, "The future of Africa," *The Crisis* xvii, 3 (January 1919), 119.

———, "My mission," *The Crisis* xviii, 1 (May 1919), 9.

———, "Pan-African congress," *The Crisis* xvii, 6 (April 1919), 271–74.

———, *The world and Africa: An inquiry into the part which Africa has played in world history.* (New York, Viking Press, 1947).

Dussel, Enrique, *A history of the church in Latin America: Colonialism to liberation (1492–1979),* trans. Alec Neeley. (Grand Rapids, Michigan, Eerdmans, 1971).

——— (ed.), *The church in Latin America 1492–1992.* (Maryknoll, N.Y., Orbis Books, 1992).

"The earth summit on population," *Population and Development Review* xviii, 3 (September 1992), 571–82.

Edkins, Jenny, Nalini Perstram, and Vèronique Pin-Fat (eds.), *Sovereignty and subjectivity.* (London, Lynne Rienner, 1999).

Ehrenreich, Barbara and John Ehrenreich, *Long march, short spring. The student uprising at home and abroad.* (London, Monthly Review Press, 1969).

Ellis, Marc H. and Otto Maduro (eds.), *The future of liberation theology. Essays in honor of Gustavo Gutiérrez.* (Maryknoll, N.Y., Orbis Books, 1989).

Enzensberger, H. M., "Ways of walking: A postscript to utopia," in R. Blackburn (ed.), *After the fall: The failure of communism and the future of socialism.* (London, Verso, 1991), 18–24.

Exposition internationale. Arts and crafts in modern life. English edition. Paris 1937. Official guide. (Paris, Editions de la société pour le développement du tourisme, 1937).

Exposition internationale des arts et des techniques dans la vie moderne. Paris 1937. Tome II. Catalogue officiel. Catalogue des pavilions. (Paris, Editions de la société pour le développement du tourisme, 1937).

Falk, Richard, "The making of global citizenship," in Jeremy Brecher, John Brown Childs, and Jill Cutler (eds.), *Global visions. Beyond the new world order.* (Boston, South End Press, 1993), 39–48.

Fanon, Franz, *Les damnés de la terre.* (Paris, François Maspero, 1961).

Feenberg, Andrew, "Remembering the May events," *Theory and Society* vi, 1 (1978), 29–53.

Feenberg, Andrew and Jim Freedman, *When poetry ruled the streets. The French May events of 1968.* (Albany, State University of New York Press, 2001).

Fink, Carol, Philip Gassert, and Detlef Junker (eds.), *1968: The world transformed.* (Cambridge, Cambridge University Press, 1998).

Fisher, Diana P. (ed.), *Paris 1900. The "American school" at the universal exposition.* (New Brunswick, N.J., Rutgers University Press, 1999).

Fishman, R., *Urban utopias in the twentieth century: Ebenezer Howard, Frank Lloyd Wright, and Le Corbusier.* (New York, Basic Books, 1977).

Fiss, Karen A., "Deutschland in Paris. The 1937 German pavilion and Franco-German cultural relations," Ph.D. diss., Yale University, 1995.

———, "The German Pavilion," in Dawn Ades et al., *Art and power: Europe under the dictators 1930–45.* (London, Thames and Hudson, 1995).

Fraser, Ronald, et al., *1968. A student generation in revolt.* (London, Chatto and Windus, 1988).

Freedberg, Catherine Blanton, *The Spanish pavilion at the Paris World's Fair.* (New York, Garland, 1986).

Friedman, Elisabeth, "Women's human rights: The emergence of a movement," in Julie Peters and Andrea Wolper (eds.), *Women's rights, human rights: International feminist perspectives.* (New York, Routledge, 1995), 20–37.

Gay, Peter, *The party of humanity: Essays in the French enlightenment.* (New York, Knopf, 1964).

Geiss, Imanuel, *The Pan-African movement. A history of Pan-Africanism in America, Europe and Africa,* trans. Ann Keep. (New York, Holmes and Meier, 1974).

Geissler, Christian, *The sins of the fathers,* trans. James Kirkup. (New York, Random House, 1962).

Gelfand, Lawrence E., *The inquiry. American preparations for peace, 1917–1919.* (New Haven, Yale University Press, 1963).

George, Alexandre L. and Juliette L., *Woodrow Wilson and Colonel House. A personality study.* (New York, The John Day Company, 1956).

Georgi, Frank (ed.), *Autogestion. La dernière utopie?* (Paris, Publications de la Sorbonne, 2003).

Gibellini, Rosino (ed.), *Frontiers of liberation theology in Latin America,* trans. John Drury. (Maryknoll, N.Y., Orbis Books, 1983).

Gilcher-Holtey, Ingrid, "May 1968 in France: The rise and fall of a new social movement," in Carol Fink, Philip Gassert, and Detlef Junker (eds.), *1968: The world transformed.* (Cambridge, Cambridge University Press, 1998), 261–80.

Glendon, Mary Ann, *A world made new: Eleanor Roosevelt and the universal declaration of human rights.* (New York, Random House, 2001).

Godsey, John D., "Bonhoeffer and the third world: West Africa, Cuba, Korea," in John B. Godsey and Geffrey B. Kelly (eds.), *Ethical responsibility: Bonhoeffer's legacy to the churches.* Toronto Studies in Theology vol. 6. (New York, Edwin Mellen Press 1981), 250–67.

Godsey, John B. and Geffrey B. Kelly (eds.), *Ethical responsibility: Bonhoeffer's legacy to the churches.* Toronto Studies in Theology vol. 6. (New York, Edwin Mellen Press 1981).

Goldberg, Harvey, *The life of Jean Jaurès, 1859–1914.* (Madison, University of Wisconsin Press, 1962).

Goldstücker, Eduard, et al., *Zwanzig Jahre nach dem Prager Frühling: Protokoll eines Seminars, veranstaltet vom Österreichischen CSSR-Solidaritätskomitee.* (Wien, Österreichisches CSSR-Solidaritätskomitee, c1989).

Greenhalgh, Paul, *Ephemeral vistas: The expositions universelles, great exhibitions and world fairs, 1851–1939.* (Manchester, Manchester University Press, 1988).

Gretton, John, *Students and workers. An analytical account of dissent in France May–June 1968.* (London, MacDonald, 1969).

Grimshaw, Patricia, Katie Holmes, and Marilyn Lake (eds.), *Women's rights and human rights. International historical perspectives.* (Basingstoke, Palgrave, 2001).

Guérin, Daniel, *Le feu du sang: Autobiographie politique et charnelle.* (Paris, B. Grasset, 1977).

Gutiérrez, Gustavo, *The density of the present. Selected writings.* (Maryknoll, N.Y., Orbis Books, 1999).

——, *Essential writings,* ed. James B. Nickoloff, (Maryknoll, N.Y., Orbis Books, 2002).

——, *The power of the poor in history: Selected work,* trans. Robert R. Barr. (Maryknoll, N.Y., Orbis Books, 1983).

——, *A theology of liberation,* trans. Caridad Inda and John Eagleson. (Maryknoll, N.Y., Orbis Books, 1988).

——, "Towards a theology of liberation," *Theological Studies,* xxxi (1970), 243–61.

Halévy, D., *Essai sur l'accélération de l'histoire.* (Paris, Les Îles d'or, 1948).

——, *Histoire de quatre ans 1997–2001.* (Paris, Editions Kimé, 1997 ed.).

Hansen, Miriam and Michael Geyer, "German-Jewish memory and national consciousness," in Geoffrey Hartmann (ed.), *Holocaust remembrance: The shapes of memory.* (Oxford, Oxford University Press, 1994), 56–80.

Hardach, Gerd, *The First World War 1914–1918.* (London, Penguin 1980).

Hartmann, Geoffrey (ed.), *Holocaust remembrance: The shapes of memory.* (Oxford, Oxford University Press, 1994).

Haschak, P. G., *Utopian/dystopian literature: A bibliography of literary criticism.* (Metuchen, N.J., Scarecrow Press, 1994).

Haupt, Georges, *Aspects of international socialism, 1871–1914: Essays,* trans. Peter Fawcett. (Cambridge, Cambridge University Press, 1986).

Havel, Václav, *Disturbing the peace. A conversation with Karel Huižďala,* trans. Paul Wilson. (New York, Alfred Knopf, 1990).

——, *Open letters. Selected prose 1965–1990.* (London, Faber and Faber, 1991).

Hayden, Dolores, *The power of place: Urban landscapes as public history.* (Cambridge, MIT Press, 1996).

Hebblethwaite, Peter, "Liberation theology and the Roman Catholic Church," in Christopher Rowland (ed.), *The Cambridge companion to liberation theology.* (Cambridge, Cambridge University Press, 1999), 179–98.

Helmreich, Paul C., *From Paris to Sèvres. The partition of the Ottoman empire at the peace conference of 1919–20.* (Columbus, Ohio State University Press, 1974).

Hennelly, Alfred T., *Liberation theologies. The global pursuit of justice.* (Mystic, Conn., Twenty Third Publications, 1997).

——, (ed.), *Liberation theology: A documentary history.* (Maryknoll, N.Y., Orbis Books, 1990).

Herbert, James D., *Paris 1937. Worlds on exhibition.* (Ithaca, N.Y., Cornell University Press, 1998).

Herf, Jeffrey, *Reactionary modernism: Technology, culture, and politics in Weimar and the third reich.* (Cambridge, Cambridge University Press, 1986).

Herzog, Dagmar, *Sex after fascism: Memory and morality in twentieth-century Germany.* (Princeton, Princeton University Press, 2005).

Hess, Rémi, *Henri Lefebvre et l'aventure du siècle.* (Paris, A. M. Métailié, 1988).

Hobsbawm, E. J., *The age of extremes. A history of the world, 1914–1991.* (New York, Vintage Books, 1996).

——, "Goodbye to all that," in R. Blackburn (ed.), *After the fall: The failure of communism and the future of socialism.* (London, Verso, 1991), 115–25.

Hodeir, Catherine, "La France d'outre mer," in *Paris 1937: Cinquantenaire. De l'exposition internationale des arts et des techniques dans la vie moderne.* (Paris, Institut Français de l'Architecture/Paris Musées, 1987), 288.

Holliday, Charles O., Stephan Schmidheiny, Philip Watts, *Walking the talk: The business case for sustainable development.* (Sheffield, Greenleaf, 2002).

House, Edward Mandell and Charles Seymour, *What really happened at Paris. The story of the peace conference, 1918–1919.* (New York, Charles Scribner's Sons, 1921).

"Human rights at fifty," a broadcast of Common Ground Radio, 8 December 1998, http://ww.commongroundradio.org/transcpt/98/9849.html.

Huttenbach, Henry and Francesco Privitera (eds.), *Self-determination. From Versailles to Dayton. Its historical legacy.* (Ravenna, Longo editore, 1999).

Huyssen, Andreas. "Memories of utopia," in his *Twilight memories: Marking time in a culture of amnesia.* (London, Routledge, 1995), 85–101.

Jacobson, David, *Rights across borders. Immigration and the decline of citizenship.* (Baltimore, Johns Hopkins University Press, 1996).

Jameson, Fredric, "Conversations on the new world order," in R. Blackburn (ed.), *After the fall; The failure of communism and the future of socialism.* (London, Verso, 1991), 255–68.

——, "Of islands and trenches: Neutralization and the production of utopian discourse," in *The ideologies of theory: Essays 1971–1986. Volume 2: Syntax of history.* (Minneapolis, University of Minnesota Press, 1988).

Jaurès, Jean, *La nouvelle armée.* (Paris, Rouff, 1911).

——, *Patriotisme et internationalisme.* (Paris, Au bureau du *Socialiste*, 1895).

Jay, Martin, "Photo-unrealism: The contribution of the camera to the crisis of ocular-centrism," in Stephen Melville and Bill Readings (eds.), *Vision and textuality.* (Basingstoke, Macmillan, 1995), 344–60.

Jennings, Ivor, *The approach to self-government.* (Cambridge, Cambridge University Press, 1956).

Johnson, Harold S., *Self-determination within the community of nations.* (Leyden, A. W. Sijthoff, 1967).

Johnson, Stanley, *The politics of population. The international conference on population and development.* (London, Earthscan Publications, 1995).

Joll, James, *1914: The unspoken assumptions.* (London, Weidenfeld and Nicolson, 1968).

——, *The second international, 1889–1914.* (New York, Harper and Row, 1966).

Josephson, Harold, *James T. Shotwell and the rise of internationalism in America.* (Rutherford, N.J., Fairleigh Dickinson University Press, 1974).

Kamenka, E., (ed.), *Utopias: Papers presented to the 15th annual symposium of the Australian academy of the humanities, 1984.* (Canberra, Oxford University Press, 1987).

Kant, Immanuel, *Perpetual peace,* preface by Nicholas Murray Butler. (Los Angeles, Calif., U.S. library association, Inc., 1932).

Kaplan, L., (ed.), *Fundamentalism in comparative perspective.* (Amherst, Mass., The University of Massachusetts Press, 1992).

Kaplan, Tessa, "Women's rights as human rights: Grassroots women redefine citizenship in a global context," in Patricia Grimshaw, Katie Holmes, and Marilyn Lake (eds.), *Women's rights and human rights. International historical perspectives.* (Basingstoke, Palgrave, 2001), 290–308.

Kateb, G., *Utopia and its enemies.* (New York, Free Press of Glencoe, 1963).

——, (ed.), *Utopia.* (New York, Atherton Press, 1971).

Keck, Margaret E. and Kathryn Sikkink (eds.), *Activists beyond borders. Advocacy networks in international politics.* (Ithaca, N.Y., Cornell University Press, 1998).

Kellner, Douglas, *Herbert Marcuse and the crisis of Marxism.* (London, Macmillan, 1984).

Kevles, Daniel, *The physicists: The history of a scientific community in modern America.* (New York, Knopf, 1977).

Knock, Thomas J., *To end all wars: Woodrow Wilson and the quest for a new world order.* (New York, Oxford University Press, 1992).

Kolakowski, Leszek, "Amidst moving ruins," *Daedalus* (1992), 43–56.

——, *Bergson.* (Oxford, Oxford University Press, 1985).

——, "The death of utopia reconsidered," in S. M. McMurrin (ed.), *The Tanner lectures on human values*. (Cambridge, Cambridge University Press, 1983), 228–47.

Koselleck, Reinhard, *Critique and crisis: Enlightenment and the pathogenesis of modern society*. (Cambridge, Mass., The MIT Press, 1988).

——, *Futures past. On the semantics of historical time,* trans. Keith Tribe. (Cambridge, MIT Press, 1985).

Koskenniemi, Martti, *The gentle civilizer of nations: The rise and fall of international law 1870–1960*. (Cambridge, Cambridge University Press, 2001).

Krier, Léon, "Une architecture du désir," in *Albert Speer. Architecture 1932–1942*. (Brussels, Aux archives d'architecture moderne, 1958).

Kriseová, Eda, *Václav Havel. The authorized biography,* trans. Caleb Crain. (New York, St. Martin's Press, 1993).

Krumeich, Gerd (ed.), *Versailles 1919. Ziele-Wirkung-Wahrnehmun.* (Essen, Klartext Verlag, 2001).

Kumar, K., *Utopianism.* (Milton Keynes, Open University Press, 1991).

Kumar, Krishan and Stephen Bann, (eds.), *Utopias and the millennium.* (London, Reaktion Books, 1993).

Lacouture, Jean, *De Gaulle,* trans. Patrick O'Brian. (New York, Norton, 1990, 2 vols.).

La Fargue, Thomas Edward, *China and the world war.* (Stanford, Stanford University Press, 1937).

Lassaigne, Jacques, *Dufy,* trans. J. Emmons. (New York, Skira, 1959).

Latour, Patricia and Francis Combes, *Conversation avec Henri Lefebvre.* (Paris, Messidor, 1991).

Launay, Michel, *Jaurès orateur ou l'oiseau rare.* (Paris, Jean-Paul Rocher, 2000).

Le Clère, Marcel, *L'assassinat de Jean Jaurès.* (Tours, Mame, 1969).

Lefebvre, Henri, *Du contrat de citoyenneté.* (Paris, Editions Périscope, 1990).

Le Goff, Pierre, *Mai 68, l'héritage impossible.* (Paris, Editions la Découverte, 1998).

Leigh, Monroe, "In re Union Carbide Corp. gas plant disaster at Bhopal, India in December 1984, 634 F. Supp. 842," *American Journal of International Law* lxxx, 4 (October 1986), 964–67.

Lemoine, Bertrand and Philippe Rivoirard, "Electricité et lumière," in *Paris 1937: Cinquantenaire. De l'exposition internationale des arts et des techniques dans la vie moderne.* (Paris, Institut Français de l'Architecture/Paris Musées, 1987), 222.

Levitas, Ruth. *The concept of utopia.* (New York, Philip Allen, 1990).

Lewis, David Levering and Deborah Willis, *A small nation of people. W. E. B. Du Bois and African-American portraits of progress.* (New York, Amistad, 2003).

Liehm, Antonin J., *The politics of culture,* trans. Peter Kussi. (New York, Grove Press, 1968).

Lippmann, Walter, *The political scene. An essay on the victory of 1918.* (New York, Henry Holt, 1919).

Litfin, Karen T., "Sovereignty in world ecopolitics," *Mershon International Studies Review,* 41 (1997), 171–89.

Löwy, Michael, *The war of gods: Religion and politics in Latin America.* (London, Verso, 1996).

Mabire, Jean-Christophe (ed.), *L'exposition universelle de 1900.* (Paris, L'Harmattan, 2000).

Macmillan, Margaret, *Paris 1919. Six months that changed the world.* (New York, Random House, 2002).

Madariaga, Salvador de, *The world's design.* (London, Allen and Unwin, 1938).

Manela, Erez, *The Wilsonian moment: Self-determination and the international origins of anti-colonial nationalism.* (New York, Oxford University Press, 2004).

Mansell, Richard D., *Paris 1900: The great world's fair.* (Toronto, University of Toronto Press, 1967).

Manuel, Frank Edward, (ed.) *Utopias and utopian thought.* (Boston, Houghton Mifflin, 1966).

Marcuse, Harold, "The revival of Holocaust awareness in West Germany, Israel and the United States," in Carol Fink, Philip Gassert, and Detlef Junker (eds.), *1968: The world transformed.* Cambridge, Cambridge University Press, 1998, 268–92.

Marcuse, Herbert and Biddy Martin, "The Failure of the New Left?" *New German Critique,* 18 (1979).

Marin, Louis, *On representation,* trans. Catherine Porter. (Stanford, Stanford University Press, 2001).

———, *Utopics: Spatial play,* trans. Robert A. Vollrath. (Atlantic Highlands, N.J., Humanities Press, 1984).

Markovits, Andrei S. and Philip S. Gorski, *The German left. Red, green and beyond.* (Cambridge, Polity Press, 1993).

Márquez, Gabriel García, "The solitude of Latin America," Nobel Prize Lecture, 8 December 1982.

Marsden, G. M., *Fundamentalism and American culture: The shaping of twentieth-century evangelicalism: 1870–1925.* (Oxford, Oxford University Press, 1980).

Mayer, Arno J., *Political origins of the new diplomacy, 1917–1918.* (New Haven, Yale University Press, 1959).

———, *Politics and diplomacy of peacemaking, containment and counterrevolution at Versailles, 1918–1919.* (New York, Knopf, 1967).

Mazower, Mark, "The strange triumph of human rights, 1933–50," *Historical Journal,* xlvii (2004), 379–98.

Mboukou, Alexandre, "The Pan-African movement 1900–1945: A study in leadership conflicts among the disciples of Pan-Africanism," *Journal of Black Studies* xiii, 3 (March 1983), 275–87.

McIntosh, C. Alison and Jason L. Finkle, "The Cairo conference on population and development: A new paradigm?" *Population and Development Review* xxi, 2 (June 1995), 220–24.

McMurrin, S. M. (ed.), *The Tanner lectures on human values.* (Cambridge, Cambridge University Press, vol. iv, 1983).

Melville, Stephen and Bill Readings (eds.), *Vision and textuality.* (Basingstoke, Macmillan, 1995).

Mengus, Raymond, "Dietrich Bonhoeffer and the decision to resist," *Journal of Modern History,* lxiv (1992), supplement, 134–46.

Menjivar, Cecilia, *Fragmented ties. Salvadoran immigrants in the United States.* (Berkeley, University of California Press, 2001).

Messemer, Annette, *Walter Lippmann und die Mächte: eine ideengeschichtliche Studie zu Entwicklung, Positionen und Konzepten eines amerikanischen Denkers der internationalen Beziehungen.* (Bonn, Rheinische Friedrich-Wilhelms-Universität zu Bonn, 1995).

Mewes, Horst, "The German new left," *New German Critique,* 1 (1973), 22–41.

Miller, Barbara Lane, "Architects in power: Power and ideology in Ernst May and Albert Speer," *Journal of Interdisciplinary History,* xvii (1986), 283–310.

Milza, Pierre and Raymond Poidevin (eds.), *La puissance française à la belle époque. Mythe ou réalité?* (Paris, Editions Complexe, 1992).

Mitchell, Thomas, "The world as exhibition," *Comparative Studies in Society and History* xxxi, 2 (April 1989), 217–36.

Moeller, Robert G., *Protecting motherhood: Women and the family in the politics of postwar West Germany.* (Berkeley, University of California Press, 1993).

———, *War stories: The search for a usable past in the federal republic of Germany.* (Berkeley, University of California Press, 2001).

Moore, Sara, *Peace without victory for the allies 1918–1932.* (Oxford, Berg, 1994).

Morand, Paul, *1900.* (Paris, Editions de France, c1931).

Morris, W., *News from nowhere; or, an epoch of rest: Being some chapters from a utopian romance.* (London, Longmans, Green and Co., 1906).

Müller, Christine-Ruth, *Dietrich Bonhoeffers Kampf gegen die nationalsozialistische Verfolgung und Vernichtung der Juden: Bonhoeffers Haltung zur Judenfrage im Vergleich mit Stellungnahmen aus der evangelischen Kirche und Kreisen des deutschen Widerstandes.* (Munich, Kaiser, c1990).

Muller, Pierre, *Jaurès, vocabulaire et rhetorique.* (Paris, Klincksieck, 1994).

Mutua, Makau, *Human rights: A political and cultural critique.* (Philadelphia, University of Pennsylvania Press, 2002).

Negley, G. R., *Utopian literature: A bibliography with a supplementary listing of works influential in utopian thought.* (Lawrence, Kans., Regents Press of Kansas, 1977).

Nelson, W. (ed.), *Twentieth century interpretations of utopia: A collection of critical essays.* (Englewood Cliffs, N.J., Prentice-Hall, 1968).

Nicolson, Harold, *Peacemaking 1919.* (London, Allen and Unwin, 1933).

Núñez, Emilion A., *Liberation theology,* trans. Paul E. Sywulka. (Chicago, Moody Press, 1985).

Nussbaum, Martha and Jonathan Glover (eds.), *Women, culture, and development: A study of human capabilities.* (Oxford, Clarenden Press, 1995).

Nye, Mary Jo, "Science and socialism: The case of Jean Perrin in the third republic," *French Historical Studies* ix, 1 (1975), 141–69.

Paris 1937: Cinquantenaire. De l'exposition internationale des arts et des techniques dans la vie moderne. (Paris, Institut Français de l'Architecture/Paris Musées, 1987).

Passerini, Luisa, "Le mouvement de 1968 comme prise de parole et comme explosion de la subjectivité: Le cas de Turin," *Mouvement Social,* 143 (April–June 1988), 70–74.

———, "Peut-on donner de 1968 une histoire à la première personne?" *Mouvement Social,* 143 (April–June 1988), 3–11.

Peillon, Vincent, *Jean Jaurès et la religion du socialisme.* (Paris, Bernard Grasset, 2000).

Peters, Julie and Andrea Wolper (eds.), *Women's rights, human rights: International feminist perspectives*. (New York, Routledge, 1995).

Pippin, Robert, Andrew Feenberg, and Charles P. Webel (eds.), *Marcuse. Critical theory and the promise of utopia*. (London, Macmillan, 1988).

Plum, Gilles, "Aéronautique" and "Chemins de fer," both in *Paris 1937: Cinquantenaire. De l'exposition internationale des arts et des techniques dans la vie moderne*. (Paris, Institut Français de l'Architecture/Paris Musées, 1987), 206–8, 218–21.

Pomerance, Michla, "The United States and self-determination: Perspectives on the Wilsonian conception," *American Journal of International Law* lxx, 1 (January 1976), 1–40.

Ponte, Alessandra, "Archiving the planet. Architecture and human geography," *Daidalos*, 66 (1997), 121–25.

Pottenger, John R., *The political theory of liberation theology, toward a reconvergence of social values and social science*. (Albany, State University of New York Press, 1989).

Prochasson, Christophe, *Paris 1900. Essai d'histoire culturelle*. (Paris, Calmann Lévy, 1999).

Prost, Antoine, *Les anciens combattants et la société française 1914–1939*. (Paris, Fondation nationale des sciences politiques, 3 vols., 1977).

———, "The French contempt for politics among veterans of the Great War," in *Republican identities in war and peace. Representations of France in the 19th and 20th centuries*. (Oxford, Berg, 2002), 202–40.

———, *Republican identities in war and peace. Representations of France in the 19th and 20th centuries*. (Oxford, Berg, 2002).

Prost, Antoine and Jay Winter, *Penser la grande guerre*. (Paris, Le Seuil, 2004).

Przyblyski, Jeannene M., "American visions at the Paris exposition, 1900: Another look at Frances Benjamin Johnston's Hampton photographs," *Art Journal* (Fall 1998), 12–38.

Rasch, Wilhelm, "Human rights as geopolitics," *Cultural Critique*, 54 (2003), 19–38.

Raustiala, Kau, "States, NGOs, and international environmental institutions," *International Studies Quarterly* xli, 4 (December 1997), 719–40.

Richter, P. E. (ed.), *Utopia/dystopia?* (Cambridge, Mass., Schenkman, 1968).

Ricoeur, P., *Lectures on ideology and utopia*, trans. George H. Taylor. (New York, Columbia University Press, 1986).

Robic, Marie-Claire, "Administrer la preuve par l'image: Géographie physique et géographie humaine," in Jean Brunhes, *Autour du monde: Regards d'un géographe/regards de la géographie*. (Boulogne-Billancourt, Musée Albert Kahn, 1993), 230.

Roseman, Mark (ed.), *Generations in conflict. Youth revolt and generation formation in Germany 1770–1968*. (Cambridge, Cambridge University Press, 1995).

Rosenbaum, Robert, Maryanne Stevens, and Ann Dumas, *1900. Art at the crossroads*. (New York, Harry N. Abrams, 2000).

Rowland, Christopher (ed.), *The Cambridge companion to liberation theology*. (Cambridge, Cambridge University Press, 1999).

Sagnes, Jean, *Jean Jaurès et le Languedoc viticole*. (Montpellier, Presses du Languedoc, 1988).

Said, Edward, *Orientalism*. (New York, Vintage, 1978).

Sargeant, Lyman Tower and Roland Schaer (eds.), *Utopie. La quête de la société idéale en Occident.* (Paris, Fayard, 2000).

Sassen, Saskia, *Globalization and its discontents.* (New York, The New Press, 1998).

Schmidt, Jürgen, *Martin Niemöller im Kirchenkampf.* (Hamburg, Leibniz-Verlag, 1971).

Schnapp, Alain and Pierre Vidal-Naquet, *Journal de la commune étudiante, textes et documents, novembre 1967–juin 1968.* (Paris, Editions du Seuil, 1969).

Scholte, J. A., "The geography of collective identities in a globalizing world," *Review of International Political Economy,* 3–4 (1996), 565–608.

Schroder-Gudehus, Brigitte and Anne Rasmussen, *Les faces du progrès. Le guide des expositions universelles 1851–1992.* (Paris, Flammarion, 1992).

Scott, James C., *Seeing like a state: How certain schemes to improve the human condition have failed.* (New Haven, Yale University Press, 1998).

Seligman, A. B. (ed.), *Order and transcendence: The role of utopias and the dynamics of civilizations.* (Leiden, E. J. Brill, 1989).

Sen, Amartya, *Development as freedom.* (New York, Knopf, 1999).

Seymour, Charles, *The intimate papers of Colonel House.* (Boston, Houghton Mifflin, 1928, 4 vols.).

———, *Letters from the Paris peace conference,* ed. Harold B. Whiteman. (New Haven, Yale University Press, 1965).

Shapiro, Meyer, *The unity of Picasso's art.* (New York, George Braziller, 2000).

Shklar, J. N., *After utopia: The decline of political faith.* (Princeton, Princeton University Press, 1957).

Shotwell, James T., *The autobiography of James T. Shotwell.* (Indianapolis, Bobbs Merrill, 1961).

———, *At the Paris peace conference.* (New York, Macmillan, 1937).

Siebers, T. (ed.), *Heterotopia: Postmodern utopia and the body politic.* (Ann Arbor, University of Michigan Press, 1994).

Siemiatycki, Myer and Engin Isin, "Immigration, diversity, and urban citizenship in Toronto," *Canadian Journal of Regional Science,* xxi, 2 (Spring 1997), 73–102.

Sikkink, Kathryn, "Codes of conduct for transnational corporations: The case of the WHO/UNICEF code," *International Organization* xl, 4 (Autumn 1986), 815–40.

Sivan, Emmanuel, "The enclave culture," in Martin E. Marty and R. Scott Appleby (eds.), *Fundamentalisms comprehended.* (Chicago, University of Chicago Press, 1995), 11–70.

Slusser, G., Paul Alkon, Roger Gaillard, and Daniele Chatelain (eds.), *Transformations of utopia: Changing views of the perfect society.* (New York, AMS Press, 1999).

Smith, Christian, *The emergence of liberation theology: Radical religion and social movement theory.* (Chicago, University of Chicago Press, 1991).

Smith, Michael Peter, "Can you imagine? Transnational migration and the globalization of grassroots politics," *Social Text,* 39 (Summer 1999), 1–16.

Smith, Neil, *American empire: Roosevelt's geographer and the prelude to globalization.* (Berkeley, University of California Press, c2003).

Smuts, J. C., "East Africa," *Geographical Journal* li, 3 (March 1918), 129–45.

Soulez, Philippe, *Bergson.* (Paris, Flammarion, 1997).

Soysal, Yasemin, *Limits of citizenship: Migrants and postnational membership in Europe.* (Chicago, University of Chicago Press, 1994).

Spivak, Gayatri, *A critique of postcolonial reason: Toward a history of the vanishing present.* (Cambridge, Mass., Harvard University Press, 1999).

Stephenson, Carolyn M., "Women's international nongovernmental organizations at the United Nations," in Anne Winslow (ed.), *Women, politics, and the United Nations.* (Westport, Conn., Greenwood Press, 1995), 130–47.

Stites, Richard, *Revolutionary dreams: Utopian visions and experimental life in the Russian revolution.* (New York, Oxford University Press, 1989).

Stoppard, Tom, *Salvage. The coast of utopia, iii.* (London, Faber and Faber, 2002).

Stromberg, Roland N., "Uncertainties and obscurities about the league of nations," *Journal of Contemporary History* xxxi, 1 (January 1972), 139–54.

Talmeyr, Maurice, "L'école de trocadéro," *Revue des deux mondes* (1899–1900).

Tarrow, Sidney, "Anti-globalizers and rooted cosmopolitans," Conference on "Reshaping Globalization," Central European University, Budapest, 17 October 2001.

Taub, Nadine (ed.), *International conference on population and development. American society of international law issue papers on world conferences, no. 1.* (Washington, American Society of International Law, 1994).

Teitelbaum, Michael S. and Jay Winter, *A question of numbers: Low fertility, high migration, and the politics of national identity since the 1960s.* (New York, Hill and Wang, 1998).

Teschke, John P., *"Hitler's legacy": West Germany confronts the aftermath of the Third Reich.* (New York, P. Lang, c1999).

Tétard, George, *Essais sur Jean Jaurès suivis d'une biblographie méthodique et critique.* (Colombes, Centre d'Apprentissage d'Imprimerie, 1959).

Thakur, Kailash, *Environmental protection law and policy in India.* (New Delhi, Deep and Deep, 1997).

Thomann, Marcel, "Albert Kahn de Marmoutier: financier de genie et philanthrope," *Société d'Histoire d'Archéologie de Saverne et Environs,* no. 30 (February 1960), 16.

Thompson, Ginger, "Mexican labor protest gets results," *New York Times,* 3 October 2001.

Tillman, Seth P., *Anglo-American relations at the Paris peace conference.* (Princeton, Princeton University Press, 1961).

Todorov, T., *The morals of history.* (Minneapolis, University of Minnesota Press, 1995).

Torres, Camilo, *Revolutionary writings,* trans. Robert Olsen and Linda Day. (New York, Herder and Herder, 1969).

Trentsky, Paul I., "Vaclav Havel and the language of the absurd," *Slavic and East European Journal* xiii, 1 (1969), 30–44.

Valéry, Paul, "La crise de l'esprit," *La Nouvelle Revue Française* xiii, 1 (August 1919), 321–40.

von Dirke, Sabine, *"All power to the imagination!" The West German counterculture from the student movement to the greens.* (Lincoln, Nebraska, University of Nebraska Press, 1997).

von Westernhagen, Dörte, *Die Kinder der Täter: das Dritte Reich und die Generation danach.* (Munich, Kösel, c1988).

Walworth, Arthur, *Wilson and his peacemakers. American diplomacy at the Paris peace conference, 1919.* (New York, W. W. Norton, 1986).

Wells, H. G., *A modern utopia*. (London, Collins, 1906).

Widgren, Jonas, "Sweden and immigration—an exceptional or a standard western European case?" International Center for Migration Policy Development papers (1998).

Wilde, Oscar, *The soul of man under socialism. The essays of Oscar Wilde*. (New York, Cosmopolitan Book Corporation, 1916).

Williams, Daniel, "Homecoming of relic taken by Mussolini's forces would end long dispute," *Washington Post*, July 20, 2002, A15.

Williams, Rosalind H., *Dream worlds: Mass consumption in late nineteenth-century France*. (Berkeley, University of California Press, 1982).

Wilson, Richard J., "The Spanish proceedings," in Reed Broady and Michael Ratner (eds.), *The Pinochet papers. The case of Augusto Pinochet in Spain and Britain*. (The Hague, Kluwer Law International, 2000), 20–40.

Winkler, Henry R., *The League of Nations movement in Great Britain, 1914–1919*. (New Brunswick, Rutgers University Press, 1952).

Winslow, Anne (ed.), *Women, politics, and the United Nations*. (Westport, Conn., Greenwood Press, 1995).

Winter, Jay (ed.), *America and the Armenian genocide*. (Cambridge, Cambridge University Press, 2003).

Winter, Jay and Jean-Louis Robert, *Capital cities at war: Paris, London, Berlin 1914–1919*. (Cambridge, Cambridge University Press, 1997).

Wittman, Rebecca, *Beyond justice: The Auschwitz trial*. (Cambridge, Mass., Harvard University Press, 2005).

Wright, Quincy, *Mandates under the League of Nations*. (Chicago, University of Chicago Press, 1930).

Xu, Guoqi, *China and the Great War: China's pursuit of a new national identity and internationalization*. (Cambridge, Cambridge University Press, 2005).

Zamiatin, E., *We*. (New York, Penguin Books, 1993 edition).

Index